"I have always found Peter's writing to be extremely insightful."

- **Lucien Gauthier, Esq., LL.M., CPA, President of the Boston Tax Institute Inc.**

"Over the years, Peter Reilly's ***Your Tax Matters Partner*** blog has been one of my go-to sources for current tax developments and incisive commentary."

- **Paul Streckfus, Editor, *EO Tax Journal***

"Peter Reilly, CPA, is a well-respected Forbes blogger with a balanced viewpoint and a practical approach. Well worth reading."

- **Lewis Taishoff, USTCP and fellow blogger**

"I have enjoyed Peter's blogs and email correspondence over the years. What I appreciate most is Peter's interest in the stories of people involved in significant tax developments, usually cases involving some types of punishments, civil or criminal. Peter finds and reports the backstory, trying to understand why the people acted as they did to draw IRS or DOJ scrutiny. Peter tells their stories with empathy."

- **Jack Townsend, tax lawyer, former adjunct professor of law, author, and blogger**

THE PRIME DIRECTIVE:

If You Don't Have Documentation, At Least Have A Plausible Story.

As a tax planner, Peter made a few mistakes and saw others make many. As a blogger at *YourTaxMattersPartner.com* and a columnist for Forbes and *Think Outside the Tax Box*, Peter comments on the opinions on tax matters that the courts issue at the federal and state level. He distills lessons with clarity and a touch of humor that make them easy for tax planners to apply to their clients' situations.

Reilly's Laws of Tax Planning grew organically with consistent themes and lessons emerging with each tax case Peter reviewed. The laws started out as jokes in his posts. He numbered them inconsistently, but commenters alerted Peter to when he mixed up the fifth and sixth laws and wondered how many laws there were. Peter recalls, "So as my sainted mother used to say, 'I got organized.'"

Reilly's Laws of Tax Planning now number 18 and include:

- It is what it is. Deal with it.
- Any clever idea that pops into your head probably has (or will have) a corresponding rule that will make it not work.
- Joint filing is an election. It is not a marital vow.
- Tell the preparer what the plan is.

Tax planning wisdom made real.

- Reilly uses a story to introduce and illustrate each law. He follows up with the implications of each law beyond tax planning.

Learn the legal ways to cut tax bills by taking proactive measures. Perfect for:

- Tax professionals
- Financial advisors
- Small business owners

ABOUT THE AUTHOR

Peter J. Reilly

Drawing on over 40 years of tax experience, Peter Reilly is a co-founder of CCR LLP, which grew to be one of the largest regional CPA firms in New England. He started blogging on what became *Your Tax Matters Partner*, and eventually he was asked to contribute to Forbes in 2011. Peter always brings the perspective of a practical large local/regional CPA who provides sound advice to clients that are not that patient.

ABOUT THE PUBLISHER

ThinkOutsideTheTaxBox.com

Think Outside the Tax Box provides tax reduction strategies with implementation advice that helps tax planning professionals help their clients reduce their federal tax payments. Peter Reilly is a regular contributor to the site.

DEDICATION

For my parents.

Muriel Lyons Reilly (1917-1993) was once a bookkeeper, who made the best oatmeal chocolate chip cookies in the history of the world. She was dubious about her son becoming an accountant but let me do her return anyway.

Jerome Reilly (1912-1965) who set an example of scrupulous honesty and told me Wall Street jokes that I didn't get until long after he died.

Reilly's LAWS of Tax Planning (*& Life!*)

Peter J. Reilly, CPA

Published by Think Outside the Tax Box, Inc.

www.ThinkOutsideTheTaxBox.com

Published by Think Outside the Tax Box, Inc., San Diego, CA

THINK OUTSIDE THE TAX BOX

Think Outside the Tax Box, Inc. is a registered trademark

Printed in the United States of America.

ISBN: 978-1-961038-00-4

This publication is designed to provide accurate and authoritative information with regard to the subject matter covered. It is sold with the understanding that the publisher is not engaged in rendering legal, accounting, or other professional advice. If legal advice or other expert assistance is required, the services of a competent professional should be sought. The opinions expressed by the author in this book are not endorsed by Think Outside the Tax Box, Inc. and are the sole responsibility of the author rendering the opinion.

This title is available at special quantity discounts for bulk purchases for sales promotions, premiums, fundraising, and educational use. Special versions or book excerpts can also be created to fit specific needs.

For more information, please write:

Think Outside the Tax Box, Inc., 8885 Rio San Diego Drive Ste 237 San Diego, CA 92108

or email admin@thinkoutsidethetaxbox.com

Visit us online at www.ThinkOutsideTheTaxBox.com.

Table of Contents

Foreword

MICHAEL NOVOGRADAC, CPA
Managing Partner of Novogradac & Company LLP

Peter J. Reilly is one of those professionals I have worked with throughout my decades as a certified professional accountant who seems like he's always been there. He's the person you have known for so long that you don't know how long you have known them. Our professional paths have crossed at so many points over the years.

Maybe that's because the course of Peter's 40-plus-year career is similar to my own. Both of our careers were shaped drastically by the Tax Reform Act of 1986, which brought lasting and monumental change to America's affordable housing landscape. With the inception of the low-income housing tax credit in 1986, both Peter and I, he on the east coast, me on the west, began advising clients as to how to use this incentive to help build and renovate affordable housing throughout the country. While the firm I founded in 1989 that bears my name has worked for more than three decades to provide tax and audit services, consulting, and more to clients across the nation across a periodically expanding slate of tax incentives, Peter's career took a detour. Through the 1990s to the early 2010s, Peter expanded his horizons as a partner with firms where he deepened his knowledge of federal, state, income, and gift taxes, with a specialty in partnership taxation. Ultimately, Peter ceased practicing as a CPA to dedicate himself to writing about the fuller tax landscape.

While our professional relationship stretches across several decades, only more recently have I become familiar with Peter's talent for writing about the intricacies of taxes and tax planning in a fun and engaging way. The world has had a chance to see that since he began writing his blog, *Passive Activities and Other Oxymorons*, which he launched in 2009 and continued when he joined Forbes.com in 2011. Combined, the blog and column have amassed more than 2,000 entries. Not only does Peter highlight fascinating tax-related topics, he does so with a wry style that makes his excitement and enthusiasm for finance come through the screen. The blog's name is a good example of this. Even when I don't agree with his column—which I admit happens sometimes—I always find his work amusing and insightful.

You'll find that wisdom, voice, and style continue in these pages. Through his work for Forbes came the foundation for this book. The laws seemed to begin in that signature humorous tone, a mythical list of concepts that everyone knows and references innately, but evolved later into a tangible, numbered list.

Many of his readers will be familiar with his laws as he refers to them periodically in his column. It's a service to all taxpayers that he's providing more detail through the pages of this book. While several of Peter's laws may seem like practical wisdom, all of them can be better illuminated with a fuller explanation of their importance and significance. In the chapters of this book, Peter aims to give readers that detail through examples that better illustrate the origins behind his laws. I think readers will benefit greatly from the fact he more fully explains in detail each of the laws, pulling that practical wisdom into a useable application.

Taxes and tax credits can be complicated, and Peter's laws help provide perspective. I've always valued his maxims, and now he's added what I would consider regulations behind the laws. Some of them make so much sense, such as Rule No. 16, which is that being right without substantiation can be as bad as being wrong. I know from my own experience the truth of Rule No. 3, which is that any clever idea I've had often has a corresponding rule that makes it not work. I have often cited Rule No. 2: "Sometimes, it's better to just pay the taxes."

You would be surprised how practical advice like that can be. To those who would point to the possibly humorous origins of Peter's laws—that sense that they are innate, recognizable, or self-evident—I think of the words of Stephen Covey, author of *The 7 Habits of Highly Effective People.* In an afterword to newer editions of the book, Covey said the habits "are common sense, but what is common sense is not always common practice." That same plainness and truth in Peter's laws will resonate with readers of this book. Peter's laws are a valuable roadmap to any accountant or taxpayer navigating the world of tax planning. They're valuable thoughts to keep in mind, and the depth you will gain from reading this book will pay dividends for years to come.

Peter has often told me he admires my foresight to build a practice around the low-income housing tax credit and other tax incentives. What he attributes to foresight, I would attribute to hard work and notable luck. Regardless, he's hinted that some day he would like to write more about Novogradac & Company LLP and our history. If he does, I welcome it. I know he would bring the same curious, inviting style that he has to his other writings about finance. Much like my professional relationship with Peter, I know our story would be familiar to him—it seems like he's always been there.

While it's true taxes, tax credits and tax planning can be intricate, I might be biased, but they can also be fascinating. Peter and his rules provide a valuable map for navigating that terrain. The laws are a must-read for tax professionals as well as anyone who pays taxes, which is to say that they're essential for everybody. I hope you find them as valuable as I do.

DISCLAIMER

Reilly's Laws (of Tax Planning & Life!) does not provide tax, legal or accounting advice. The materials provided have been prepared for informational purposes only, and are not intended to provide tax, legal or accounting advice. The materials may or may not reflect the most current legislative or regulatory requirements or the requirements of specific industries or of states. These materials are not tax advice and are not intended or written to be used, and cannot be used, for purposes of avoiding tax penalties that may be imposed on any taxpayer. Readers should consult their own tax, legal and accounting advisors before applying the laws to their particular situations or engaging in any transaction.

Introduction

The tax planning lessons I have learned from my own experience were hard, but there were, fortunately, not that many of them. Mostly, I learned from other people's experiences. For many years, I read a very large proportion of opinions on tax matters that federal courts issued and a fair sampling of state decisions. Originally, that was part of my job as one of the available resources of a regional accounting firm. It became the foundation of my writing career, as I found that besides the valuable insights, I sometimes discovered that opinions contained great stories.

Originally, I defined what I wrote about as stuff I found interesting. Over time I found that three themes emerged: practical utility, humor, and the intersection of tax with larger issues, such as the separation of church and state and gender equity. Much as I relish the dream of becoming a humorist or a public intellectual, that first principle of practical utility still grabs me. I love it when I highlight something that people can use or a trap they need to avoid.

It was largely out of practical utility that my laws of tax planning emerged. They started as a sort of joke in my posts, and I was inconsistent about how I numbered them and the like, but then commenters alerted me that I had mixed up the third and fourth law and they wanted to know how many there were. So as my sainted mother used to say, "I got organized."

Reilly's Laws of Tax Planning now number 18—more than the Ten Commandments or Wilson's Fourteen Points but nowhere near the Ferengi (of Star Trek fame) Rules of Acquisition, which are, in fact, a great store of business wisdom. As noted by Rule 284, Deep down everyone's a Ferengi.

I have selected one or more stories to illustrate each law. I will introduce the stories with an explanation of each law. And I will follow up with some thoughts about how the law has implications beyond tax planning. I just need to scratch that itch to be a public intellectual.

I don't know what you will do with my laws. I hope you will become informed and amused, but as Georges Clemenceau said of the Fourteen Points, "God gave us the Ten Commandments, and we broke them. Wilson gives us the Fourteen Points. We shall see." (They failed.)

FIRST LAW OF TAX PLANNING

It Is What It Is. Deal With It.

This first law I developed from practice. At Joseph B Cohan and Associates, a large local firm in Worcester, Massachusetts, there was a certain resistance to looking things up. There was a tendency to "follow last year" and, when push came to shove, to "ask Jim Carney," who did look things up. My odd entry into the accounting profession as a dropout from graduate work in history inclined me to become the second JBC person who looked things up, which probably had something to do with my becoming a partner a couple of years after Jim Carney made partner.

At any rate, after, to the best of my ability, I explained some rules to a staffer more junior than myself, they would often say "Oh. That makes sense." I was always quick to correct them by saying, "That is not a requirement." All tax provisions made sense to somebody at some point, but that does not mean they will ever make sense to you. And it doesn't matter. Getting straight into what the rules are is challenging enough.

Frank and Fanny left Georgia in 2010 due to Frank's foreign service job moving them to the U.K. They had no intention of ever returning to Georgia, but since the U.K. assignment was temporary, Georgia remained their domicile. Domicile blindsides many taxpayers.

The Stickiness of Domicile
Hard to Leave State Income Tax Behind

Moving to Florida before you shove off on your foreign adventures is probably the moral of a decision of the Georgia Tax Tribunal[1]. The taxpayers involved are referred to as Petitioner F-1 and F-2. So, I will call them Frank and Fanny. The court sealed their identities due to Frank's position as a U.S. attaché. Given the amount of detail in the case, I suspect even my meager investigative skills could uncover their identities, but there is no point in that. Georgia Department of Revenue wants them to pay Georgia income tax on their U.S. Government salaries for 2011. Frank and Fanny left Georgia in 2010, having lived there with their children since 2006. They have not decided where they will go once Frank's tour as an attaché ends.

The Basics

Frank and Fanny would have sold their Georgia home when they shoved off for the U.K., but the tough real estate market discouraged that. That meant they had to rent the home out requiring them to file a Georgia non-resident return. The domicile issue would have been there regardless, but the return makes it a lot easier for Georgia to pick it up. They had Georgia driver's licenses and voted in the 2012 presidential election, although no state elections. Their ballots in the Presidential election had a box checked indicating they were U.S. citizens living abroad, whose return was uncertain.

The driver's license and voting can weigh very heavily in a typical domicile case, but not for someone who is living abroad. Expatriates are still United States citizens, but driver's licenses and voter registration tie into the states. A while ago I wrote about the convoluted case of someone, I called Lois Lane. She lived in Japan but kept her Rhode Island driver's license and voter registration. Rhode Island was OK with that, but when she went to New York to study, intending to return to Japan, Rhode Island tried to tax her.

The Stickiness of Domicile

What Frank and Fanny ran afoul of is what I call the "stickiness of domicile."[2] Of course, they might call it the "ickiness of domicile." The principles, which are what they are even though they don't reflect the reality of some mobile lifestyles, are that everybody has a domicile and that once a domicile is established, it does not change until it is abandoned and a new domicile is established.[3]

Frank and Fanny live in housing provided by the State Department to U.S. Embassy employees in London. Their children attend the American School in London[4], presumably to assure them of the opportunity to enter debt bondage by attending an American college. The rub is that they live in the U.K. under diplomatic residence permits, which expire 90 days after their jobs end. The court made much of the fact that they do not pay U.K. income taxes. Regardless, even though they plan to have lived in the U.K. longer than they lived in Georgia, they have not established a U.K. domicile, since they are not set up to live in the U.K. indefinitely. That means they continue to have Georgia domicile even if they have no intent to return to Georgia.

If Frank and Fanny were working for a Big Four accounting firm on a long foreign assignment, the sticky Georgia domicile might not be such a hardship, since most, if not all, of their work income would be covered by the foreign earned income exclusion. The income exclusion does not apply to federal government employees, so it does not help these taxpayers. The court expressed a bit of sympathy, which it then back-pedaled on:

> The result in this case, although arguably harsh, should not come as a surprise. It is well-known in the diplomatic community that a diplomat must continue to pay income taxes to that person's state of legal residence.

Sylvia Dion Weighs In

This case was interesting enough to reach out to my brain trust. I did not give much notice, but I was pleased that SALT (state and local tax) expert Sylvia Dion[5] got back to me. Her response is consistent with

Reilly's First Law of Tax Planning—*It is what it is. Deal with it.*

While I'd love to find grounds on which to side with the petitioners, in this situation I do think the Georgia Tax Tribunal was correct to side with the Georgia Commissioner of Revenue. The nature of the petitioner's assignment with the U.S. Embassy in London was clearly to be temporary (for a two-to-five-year period)—thus, the petitioners did not relocate to London with the intent of establishing permanent residency in London. ◊

This is one of those stories where the story behind the story is inherently more interesting.

No Foreign Income Tax Exclusion for Army Civilians in Afghanistan

"You have been in Afghanistan I perceive" is one of my favorite lines in literature, so I just cannot pass up a Tax Court decision that concerns service in Afghanistan. And then there is the taxpayer's name, Samuel Striker. Something in my mind associated that with the trope of the ethnically, if not racially, diverse WWII infantry squad—Murphy, Kowalski, Cohen, Running Deer—led by a generic American sergeant like Sergeant Fury or Sergeant Rock or Sergeant Saunders. Then, it dawned on me. The one time that John Wayne in all his martial glory deigned to portray an enlisted man, it had been Sergeant Stryker in *The Sands of Iwo Jima.*

Not A Sergeant

As it happens Samuel Striker was not a sergeant. It is Doctor Striker, although I don't know if he goes by that in the field. In this profile of him by Western Michigan University they call him Sam Striker. (That's what I would use in the movie, so the young soldiers could call him Uncle Sam.)

Striker is a social scientist in intelligence field operations. He is attached to various U.S. and NATO combat forces, and his work is about the subtle ways the military can become an enabling force rather than an occupying force.

"We're not fighting armies in uniform," he says. "To be effective, the military has to understand the population on a socio-demographic level.

"My role is to get into villages, talk to people, and find out what the needs and wants of the village are—things like farming equipment, water resources, safety, and security. During the process, I sometimes also uncover actionable security issues."

The Tax Issue

As with many of my blog posts (https://yourtaxmatterspartner.com/), the story behind the story is more intrinsically interesting than the issues the Tax Court was dealing with. The stakes were high, with just over $50,000 in tax for the years 2010 and 2011.

The issue was the foreign earned income exclusion.

Petitioner attached to his returns Form 2555, Foreign Earned Income, on which he claimed under section 911 exclusions of $91,500 and $92,900 for 2010 and 2011, respectively. (His actual wages for performing services in Afghanistan were higher; the exclusions he claimed represented the maximum amounts allowed for each year.) On the Forms 2555 petitioner listed his occupation as "defense contractor"; listed his employer as "Defense Finance & Accounting Services"; stated that his employer was a "U.S. company"; listed his employer's U.S. address as a location in Cleveland, Ohio; and listed his employer's foreign address as a location in Kabul, Afghanistan.

What Was He Doing in Afghanistan Anyway?

> Petitioner's mission as a social science expert was to function as a liaison between the NATO command and the local people of Kandahar and its surrounding area. He sought to help military officers gain a better cultural understanding of this population. He also gathered and analyzed information concerning local commerce (including illicit commerce) to help NATO create a successful local security apparatus. Petitioners regularly participated in NATO-sponsored training and workshops, some of which were mandatory.

Whom Was He Working For?—That is the Question

U.S. government employees assigned overseas do not qualify for the foreign-earned income exclusion. Why is that? I'm going to invoke **Reilly's First Law of Tax Planning**—***"It is what it is. Deal with it."***

Mr. Striker, reasonably, took the position that he was working for NATO. Unfortunately, the IRS had a different view and some facts to back up that position.

> The record includes a DCIPS evaluation of the petitioner for his second deployment. It is 12 pages long and rates his overall performance as "outstanding." The rating official who signed this evaluation was a colonel in the U.S. Army. The reviewing official who reviewed this evaluation was likewise a U.S. Army officer and was part of TRADOC, the same "organizational element" to which the petitioner belonged.
>
> The Army paid the petitioner on the basis of standard U.S. Government pay scales. He had a GS-13 grade during his first deployment and a GS-14 grade during his second. The Army provided him with standard DoD fringe benefits, including health and retirement benefits.

Tax Court Has Dealt with This Before

The Tax Court had sorted this out whether somebody was working for NATO and qualifying for the exclusion or working for the Army and not qualifying. In Samuel Striker's case, the weight fell on him being still in the Army, even though he was not exactly in the Army.

The Other Exclusion

It is worth noting that if Striker had been in the Army, Section 112—Certain combat zone compensation of members of the Armed Forces—would have excluded much of his pay. There has been a bit of litigation on that issue[6], but no taxpayers have ever gotten anywhere with it. That is noted on the Enterprise Access Management Service – Army, which outlines rules concerning civilians whom the Army sends into harm's way.

> All salary earned during a deployment is subject to income tax. There have been several attempts to have legislation passed on this matter, but to date, no attempt has succeeded. ◊

Just because you are not in the United States does not mean you are in a foreign country.

Tax Court Rules International Waters Not Foreign Country but Misses That Mariners Are Not Marines

If you got yourself a job sweeping out the Halls of Montezuma or sailing along the shores of Tripoli and otherwise qualify, you can exclude what you earn from your taxable income thanks to the foreign earned income exclusion.[7] If your work is "on the sea," though, maybe not so much. That is the holding in the recent Tax Court decision in the case of Wendell

Wilson[8]. Mr. Wilson is a U.S. citizen, a resident of Mexico, and a ship's engineer in the Merchant Marine.

What's in a Name?

And here we need to clear something up. Judge Gerber wrote:

> The Marine Engineers Benefits Association (MEBA) posts jobs, and **merchant marines** are able to bid on them. Petitioner would bid on jobs through MEBA and, ultimately, would sign a contract with a ship's captain for a specific voyage. Petitioner worked on five voyages during 2009 and five during 2010. Each of the contracts the petitioner entered into specified an itinerary that included time in foreign ports. All 10 of the voyages began and ended in California. He did not work or earn income in Mexico during 2009 and 2010 but would generally leave his home in Mexico and travel to California where he would board a ship for a voyage to foreign ports. (Emphasis added.)

According to a U.S. Coast Guard FAQ[9]:

> What do you call people who are in the Merchant Marine? Mariners. Seamen. Seafarers. Sailors. Never marines! Mariners is the preferred designation, just like the Seattle professional baseball team. **The term Merchant Marines is incorrect. (Emphasis added.)**

Foreign Earned Income Exclusion

Back to the tax issues. In 2009, Mr. Wilson was on voyages for 175 days and earned $76,055.45. In 2010 he earned $113,086.15 for 146 days. That seems neat. In 2009, he spent 41 days in foreign ports and the territorial waters of foreign countries, and 22 such days in 2010. The rest of his voyage days were in international waters.

Wilson was subjected to an audit for the years 2005 to 2008. He had excluded all his voyage income in those years and there were no adjustments for those years. As we used to say at Joseph Cohan and Associates, "Better to be lucky than good."

Wilson had less luck with his 2009 and 2010 audits. To qualify for the foreign earned income credit, a "qualified individual" must earn the income. That was not an issue. The income must be "foreign earned income." "Foreign earned income" is income "from sources within a foreign country or countries." International waters are not foreign countries.

This rule has tripped scientists working in Antarctica and at least one international flight attendant in the last couple of years. It strikes me as unfair, but that is **Reilly's First Law of Tax Planning.** ◊

Read on for tax lessons from presidential tax shenanigans.

Trump Foundation Imbroglio With New York AG Serves as a Lesson for Small Foundations

So recently, I wrote that I think the New York Attorney General's complaint[10] against The Donald J. Trump Foundation and the frenzied response to it is way out of proportion. Naturally, that got my Facebook buds a bit upset with me. One of them directed me to the front page of the New York Times. I love the New York Times, but when it comes to its tax coverage, don't get me started. Surprisingly, though, there was a piece by somebody who knows what he is talking about. Philip T. Hackney wrote an opinion piece titled *"Why the IRS Should Go After Trump."*[10]

> As a former attorney for the chief counsel of the IRS who specialized in nonprofit organizations, I believe Mr. Trump is also criminally liable for his actions. If I were still at the IRS, based on the lawsuit, I would make a criminal referral, on charges of tax evasion or false statements on a tax return, or both.

This is not a sudden flash of insight on the part of Professor Hackney. Back in October 2016, before Donald Trump was even President-elect, he wrote for The Surly Subgroup *"Trump's Abuse of Trump Foundation—Criminal Tax Implications."*[11]

> I think there is enough evidence to open a criminal investigation into his activities. Nevertheless, criminal prosecution is highly unlikely for both political reasons and issues of proof (ignorance of the law is a defense). Still, I think the IRS must open an investigation under the egregious set of facts I lay out.

I decided to give Professor Hackney a call. Since he answered with "Hi, this is Phil," I'm going to go with that. Phil and I had a nice chat. We are both hardcore tax geeks. He, of course, is elite. IRS Chief Counsel's office and now a law school professor. I, on the other hand, spent my career in large local and then regional public accounting. I did have the distinction of being one of the guys who looked things up, which is what sparked my writing career.

That difference in background accounts for a difference in perspective, even though we understand each other's perspective. As we discussed the issue, Phil kept hammering on what it means for money to be in a foundation. I am going to tell you a story that I think illustrates the difference dramatically, although I can't rule out that you will find it fairly dumb or not get it. It is about my seminary days.

It's Just Bread

From September 1975 to June 1976, I lived in a seminary. I was not studying for the priesthood. The Chicago Theological Seminary for reasons I was not privy to, had a lot of extra dormitory space. The University of Chicago used it to house graduate students. Quite a few were divinity schools, but the balance was a random mix of graduate students. I was the only budding historian. (I was nipped in the bud.) It was the most fascinating group of people I ever hung out with—or close to[12]. Somehow one of the seminarians got me going to University Church[13]. It was the first time I had attended a church that was not Roman Catholic. And after a couple of weeks, I got an incredible shock.

They didn't have communion all that often, maybe once a month. At St. John's in Fairview, New Jersey, it was twice a day, except Sunday when it was six times. Well, that was not shocking. And it was regular bread rather than this special wafer that monks baked or something, and was unleavened—whatever that meant. That was not shocking, either. Here is the shocker. After the service, there was a coffee hour with snacks. And there on the snack table was the leftover bread from the communion service.

If you can't see why that is shocking, you probably can't reel off *Ad Deum qui laetificat, juventutem meam*[14] like an altar boy in 1962 could. The consecrated hosts were secure in a tabernacle on the altar. An altar rail separated people from those hosts. They would kneel at the altar rail and have the host placed on their tongue by the priest who could handle it. Then we, as altar boys, would stand there holding this gold-coated thing under our tongues, or maybe chins, in case a crumb dropped (the priests told us to be careful not to whack them in the throat). There was more to it. If you want to get into the theology of it, Google transubstantiation.

Here is the thing. In the legal view that Phil was putting out, putting money into your private foundation is an act of transubstantiation. It is now holy money to be used for holy purposes.[15] Doing anything else with it is as bad as breaking into the church at night to go into the tabernacle to get hosts to use in a black mass. Think of the Attorney General as being the bishop or even the Inquisition, although nobody expects that anymore. And you can't just say, "Oh, I didn't know that was the communion bread. I'll go get another loaf for you." There need to be consequences—dire consequences.

Cash Is Fungible

In the real estate world, it is generally not like that. For much of my career, I did audit and tax work for low-income housing projects. It would be an exaggeration to say that it was fiendishly complicated, but it was complicated enough that many of the people involved did not understand or care about the structure. The financing agencies, HUD or MHFA, considered the project to be an entity apart from its owner. The owner was a limited partnership. In our case, the limited partners were mostly dentists. The general partner was a corporation without much substance. Its sole purpose was to be the general partner of that partnership. A community development corporation (a special type of not-for-profit) was the general partner. There were cash inflows and outflows related to syndication, construction financing, permanent financing, and operations.

Our task was to sort all that stuff out and create the required reports, including tax returns. The other people involved had a housing project to build and run and had to make a living themselves. There were bills piling up. Often, more bills than money to pay them or bills that had a higher priority and were due before the pot of money designated to pay them. In the end, it would often get sorted out on green analysis paper with a lot of journal entries referring to "Due from sponsor" or "Due to general partner."

As I was coping with all of this, I received some insight from people who had been in the business a long time. Once, I was asking a controller for a developer where the records for the development fee, the general partner guaranty fee, and the asset management fee were. He sat me down and said, "You know, those are just names for the money that they get to take out of the deal."

A guy who ran a management company once said to me wistfully "It was a lot better in the old days, before there were all these audits. The strong projects could help out the weaker ones." Those projects might have had the same sponsor who owned each of the general partners, but they likely had different sets of limited partners. Of course, they might not care since what they were interested in was tax savings, but that is another story.

The Most Scandalous Trump Foundation Transactions

Phil directed me to coverage of Trump's charitable giving by David A. Fahrenthold, which I had missed because up till now I have been too cheap to subscribe to the Washington Post. I ended up springing for his book, *Uncovering Trump—The Truth Behind Donald Trump's Charitable Giving.*[16]

The really nasty older transactions that people think Trump should get in a lot of trouble for are a political contribution, lawsuit settlements, and two paintings that ran through the foundation.

> In most cases, political contributions were paid out of Trump's own account. But, in this case, that didn't happen. In March, Trump's chief financial officer [Allen Weisselberg] told the Post that a mistake occurred when an accounting clerk, following office protocol, looked in a book that contained a list of all official charities. The clerk's standing order from Trump was that, if the payee was listed in this book of charities, the check should be paid from the Trump Foundation, not from Trump's own account.

That is really horrible not-for-profit governance, but it is hardly shocking and no indication of a criminal mastermind at work. It shows a Donald Trump not trying to get away with something but being kind of sloppy.

The painting and the lawsuit settlements look a lot similar, only they are even dumber. If I were doing the tax planning for those transactions, I would have wanted the business entities that were involved in the settlements to make the payments to get an ordinary business deduction. There was nothing gained by using dollars that had cycled through the foundation. And it is hard to see what changed by shifting income to the foundation rather than recognizing it and donating it.

Finally, the paintings and the lawsuits and the political donation stack up to less than $500,000. If you want to see how a New York billionaire does tax scamming on a grand scale, take a look at Stephen Ross[17] who tried to get a $30 million deduction for going about $3 million out of pocket to the University of Michigan. Or maybe dig into Donald Trump's conservation easement deductions. There is some real money there, $60 million as noted by Fahrenthold (and me too, by the way).[18]

The paintings, lawsuits, and political contributions can be horrible, only because of the "foundation money is holy" belief. And admittedly that is the law. Remember **Reilly's First Law of Tax Planning—*"It is what it is. Deal with it."***

All Pledge, No Check

Fahrenthold does an excellent job of highlighting Trump's aggrandizing of himself, but in some ways that is a little like shooting fish in the barrel. Like the "all hat, no cattle" expression that Chuck Schumer mangled recently, Farenthold shows us the "All pledge, no check" theme of Trump philanthropy. If you look, though, you will see this is consistent with what Trump says about himself in the greatest business handbook since *Extraordinary Popular Delusions and the Madness of Crowds*[19]—*The Art of the Deal*[20]

> The final key to the way I promote is bravado. I play to people's fantasies. People may not always think big themselves, but they can still get excited by those who do. That's why a little hyperbole never hurts. People want to believe that something is the biggest and the greatest and the most spectacular. I call it truthful hyperbole. It is an innocent form of exaggeration—and a very effective form of promotion.

Mixing the Campaign with the Foundation

The way the campaign interacted with the foundation in raising money for veterans is the more current issue. It is hard to see how that is going to go anywhere given the way the IRS has been driven from dealing with the interaction of not-for-profits and politics. That is what is at the heart of the interminable IRS scandal, which has effectively neutered the agency. It would be really tough to make a case for putting resources into untangling that given that it is a fairly unique occurrence. Also, as with the lawsuits and the paintings, it is hard to see what Trump gained by involving the foundation. The IRS needs to leverage its meager enforcement resources to discourage people from doing things that harm tax collection. I really do not think you have to worry about a repetition of this travesty. Paul Streckfus of *EO Tax Journal* wrote me:

> As I've indicated the IRS will not want to touch this case, but it sets a horrible example that others can use as an excuse for their

> actions. Because there is little or no IRS enforcement of the more sophisticated tax dodges in the EO area, the standards of practice keep going down. I keep hearing stories of lawyers losing clients because they find someone who will approve pretty much anything they want to do. As Trump might say, "Sad."

The Lesson

The heart of the AG complaint is not the specific actions, but the poor governance of the Donald J. Trump Foundation.

> The foundation's directors failed to meet basic fiduciary duties and abdicated all responsibility for ensuring that the foundation's assets were following the law.
>
> The New York Attorney General's investigation found that the foundation is little more than an empty shell that functions with no oversight by its board of directors. The foundation, which does not have any employees, delegated its operations to the accounting office of the Trump Corporation Inc., a management company owned by Mr. Trump and located at 725 Fifth Avenue. The Trump Corporation supplies back-office services to the several hundred Trump business entities that make up the Trump Organization. The accounting staff's responsibilities for the foundation are the same as its responsibilities for the businesses in the Trump Organization.

I asked one of the best not-for-profit CPAs I know for thoughts on the violations.

> I do not see a problem with the foundation. I am more of an outcomes-based person. If the money is going to charity I do not care very much about how.
>
> It does highlight the need for good governance that all NFP's need. Multiple non-related board members are a good place to start. Documentation of meetings is a close second.
>
> With the proliferation of NFPs in this country, my experience

> has been that founders are more akin to entrepreneurs than mission-driven warriors. Their ego is immense. When I make suggestions to merge, they balk and claim no one does what they do!
>
> Trump may be many things, but I don't see this PF as a criminal enterprise just a poorly run one.[21]

Reilly's Fourth Law of Tax Planning—*"Execution isn't everything, but it's a lot."* If the two Donalds, Eric, and Ivanka had sat with CFO Allen Weisselberg once a year and had some minutes typed up about the approved donations for the coming year, that would have defused a significant part of the AG complaint. When donations not on the list came up, there could have been an email vote. There is a decent chance that would have prevented the political contribution. Somebody should have been following up on acknowledgments, which would have uncovered the problems with the paintings. Why did it not run that way? Because it is not Trump's style. Again, from *The Art of the Deal*,

> To me, committees are what insecure people create in order to put off making hard decisions.[22]

And of course, a board would have wanted advice on coordinating with a political campaign. Also, not Trump's style.

I like consultants even less than I like committees.

So, what do you do if that is your style? What you do is not have a foundation. Foundations are a bad idea unless you commit to meticulous compliance.◊

Reflection on the First Law

Unless you are extraordinarily rich and or very well connected, there is really not much you can do to change the tax law. So, learn what it actually is and apply it. This principle has much broader application. American theologian Reinhold Niebuhr composed a prayer, that the friends of Bill (AA members) recite in a slightly altered form:

Father, give us courage to change what must be altered, serenity to accept what cannot be helped, and the insight to know the one from the other.

Here is some insight: There are a lot more things you cannot change than there are things you can change.

FIRST LAW OF TAX PLANNING

Footnotes

1. Petitioner F-1 and Petitioner F-12 v. Douglas J. Macginnitie, in his Official Capacity as Revenue Commissioner for the State of Georgia, Georgia Tax Tribunal (No. TAX-IIT-1345974), December 10, 2014, https://gataxtribunal.georgia.gov/sites/gataxtribunal.georgia.gov/files/related_files/document/Petitioner%20F-1%20and%20F-2%20-%20Decision%2C%202014-16%20Ga.%20Tax%20Tribunal%2C%20December%2010%2C%202014.PDF
2. Peter J. Reilly, "The Stickiness of Domicile - Hard To Leave State Income Tax Behind," Forbes, last modified January 9, 2015, https://www.forbes.com/sites/peterjreilly/2015/01/09/the-stickiness-of-domicile-hard-to-leave-state-income-tax-behind/?subId3=xid:fr1605096741010aab.
3. Reilly, "The Stickiness of Domicile."
4. "The American School in London," accessed May 27, 2023, https://www.asl.org/.
5. "Sylvia F. Dion," LinkedIn, accessed May 27, 2023, https://www.linkedin.com/in/sylviadioncpa.
6. "No Foreign Income Tax Exclusion For Army Civilian In Afghanistan," Your Tax Matters Partner (blog), last modified January 6, 2016, https://yourtaxmatterspartner.com/no-foreign-income-tax-exclusion-for-army-civilian-in-afghanistan/.
7. "Figuring the Foreign Earned Income Exclusion," Internal Revenue Service, last modified November 16, 2022, https://www.irs.gov/individuals/international-taxpayers/figuring-the-foreign-earned-income-exclusion.
8. Wendell Wilson and Angelica M. Wilson v. Commissioner of Internal Revenue, Tax Court (No. 16610-13S), April 25, 2016, https://casetext.com/case/wilson-v-commr-49.

9. "Frequently Asked Question Categories," United States Coast Guard, accessed May 27, 2023, https://www.dco.uscg.mil/nmc/faq/.

10. Philip T. Hackney, "Why the I.R.S Should Go After Trump," The New York Times, last modified June 15, 2018, https://www.nytimes.com/2018/06/15/opinion/trump-foundation-new-york-attorney-general.html.

11. Philip Hackney, "Trump's Abuse of Trump Foundation—Criminal Tax Implications?," The Surly Subgroup, last modified October 3, 2016, https://surlysubgroup.com/2016/10/03/trumps-abuse-of-trump-foundation-criminal-tax-implications/.

12. Peter Reilly, "How I Accidentally Impersonated A Veteran," We Are The Future Generations (blog), November 28, 2014, https://activepassivitiesandothermoronicoxen.blogspot.com/2014/11/how-i-accidentally-impersonated-veteran.html.

13. "University Church Chicago," accessed May 27, 2023, https://universitychurchchicago.org/.

14. James Carroll, "Meanwhile: But it sounded so nice in Latin - Opinion - International Herald Tribune," The New York Times, last modified October 30, 2006, https://www.nytimes.com/2006/10/30/opinion/30iht-edcarroll.3332192.html.

15. Peter J. Reilly, "Trump Foundation Imbroglio With New York AG Serves As A Lesson For Small Foundations," Forbes, last modified June 18, 2018, https://www.forbes.com/sites/peterjreilly/2018/06/18/trump-foundation-imbroglio-with-new-york-ag-serves-as-a-lesson-for-small-foundations/?subId3=xid:fr1595069114755ffa.

16. David A. Fahrenthold and The Washington Post, Uncovering Trump: The Truth Behind Donald Trump's Charitable Giving (Diversion Books, 2017).

17. Peter J. Reilly, "Billionaire Stephen Ross And The Ten For One Charitable Deduction," Forbes, last modified July 17, 2017, https://www.forbes.com/sites/peterjreilly/2017/07/17/billionaire-stephen-ross-and-the-ten-for-one-charitable-deduction/#64b348d72bca.

18. Peter J. Reilly, "New IRS Scandal - Syndication Of Conservation Easement Deductions," Forbes, last modified July 24, 2017, https://www.forbes.com/sites/peterjreilly/2017/07/24/new-irs-scandal-syndication-of-conservation-easement-deductions/#7e3aba8e6b33.

19. Charles Mackay, Extraordinary Popular Delusions and the Madness of Crowds: Understanding the Forces Behind Group Mentality, Thoughts and Actions (e-artnow, 2017).

20. Donald J. Trump and Tony Schwartz, Trump: The Art of the Deal (New York City: Ballantine Books, 2009).

21. Reilly, "Trump Foundation."

22. Donald J. Trump and Tony Schwartz, Trump: The Art of the Deal (New York City: Ballantine Books, 2009).

SECOND LAW OF TAX PLANNING

Sometimes You Should Just Pay the Taxes.

A sort of anthem for my generation of tax people was a quote from Judge Learned Hand:

> Repeatedly, courts have said that there is nothing sinister in so arranging one's affairs as to keep taxes as low as possible. Everybody does so, rich, or poor; and all do right, for nobody owes any public duty to pay more than the law demands: Taxes are enforced exactions, not voluntary contributions. To demand more in the name of morals is mere cant.

A couple of sharp attorneys have pointed out to me that Learned Hand was dissenting when he wrote that, but it remains inspiring, nonetheless. It is worthwhile stepping back though and reflecting on why it is that ordinary people seek to minimize their taxes.

There are two reasons I see working at legitimate tax avoidance. One is to have more money to spend now. The other is to build wealth. It is in the wealth-building category a certain sort of analysis is necessary.

Many tax-advantaged vehicles involve investments. Assume that your real estate ship has come in, and you are selling a business property you have owned for a long time, and further, you do not want to be a landlord. One of your options is to structure a 1031 exchange where the target property is a drugstore leased on an exceptionally long lease to CVS or Walgreens. Picture yourself with the after-tax proceeds of your sale. Is that drugstore something you would consider buying? If not, it is better to pay taxes.

This was the origin of the second law. It is a ruling about a tenancy in common in which the "master tenant" went bankrupt and the "in common" tenants had to put together the cash to avoid losing the property.◊

Sometimes You Should Just Pay the Taxes.

PMTA 2010-05 is a taxpayer-friendly statement. It is, however, reasonable to infer that the affected taxpayers are not exactly jubilant. PMTA stands for Program Manager Technical Assistance. The question that the PMTA addressed was:

> ***Whether the temporary pooling of funds on a non-pro rata basis and the appointment of a tenant-in-common owner ("TIC Owner") as a payment and/or communications agent because of the bankruptcy of the primary tenant will cause the tenants-in-common to become partners in a partnership for federal income tax purposes?***

The answer was no. With typical IRS hedging, it qualified the "no" with the assumption that the arrangements weren't partnerships, to begin with.

I suspect there are many sad stories hidden behind this ruling. The TIC structure is a creature of tax law. The most general rule of tax law is that when you exchange one thing for something else, you recognize gain if any. There are, of course, exceptions. Several of them are in Part III of Subchapter O under the heading "Common Non-Taxable Exchanges," including Section 1031 which calls for non-recognition of gain or loss when the properties exchanged are of "like-kind."

Of course, exceptions wouldn't be real exceptions if they didn't have their own exceptions. Among the items that cannot be on either side of a qualified like-kind exchange along with stocks, bonds, animals of different sexes, and "choses in action" (whatever they are) are interests in a partnership.

The 1031 exception is particularly significant in real estate because, for the most part, all real estate in the United States is like-kind to all other real estates in the United States. So, if you trade your stallion for a broodmare that is not like-kind, but if you trade your horse farm for an office building it is. You can even exchange your whole horse farm for part of an office building, which is where the partnership thing comes in.

What is the difference between a piece of real estate diverse persons own and a partnership of diverse persons that owns a piece of real estate? Such questions keep tax attorneys awake at night and also well fed. Revenue Procedure 2002-22 tells you the conditions your arrangement must meet to be worthy of asking the IRS to rule that it is not a partnership.

That revenue procedure was part of the birth of a veritable industry. Someone selling rental or investment property had always had the opportunity to structure the sale as an exchange by inserting a third-party facilitator and can even have time after selling the initial property to identify to the facilitator (45 days) the replacement property and for the facilitator to acquire the property (lesser of 180 days or the extended due date of the taxpayer's return). Someone tired of being a landlord might, however, view that as exchanging one headache for another.

By having a TIC interest as their target there was a broader range of properties available and there would be someone else to deal with all the tenant problems and repairs. Someone else to go bankrupt and leave the TIC members holding the bag.

The saddest part of the PMTA is the reference to the fact that there will be non-pro rata cash contributions. Reading between the lines one can infer that some of the owners are a bit resentful at having to kick money in to straighten out the mess they landed in.

A couple of observations and then a moral. Even if the subsequent events converted the TICs into partnerships, this should not affect the validity of the like-kind exchanges that had the TICs as their targets.

The investors did not have the primary tenant's bankruptcy as part of their plans, and they might want the ruling anyway since preparing a partnership return in these circumstances would be somewhat challenging. Since 1031 defers both losses and gains, some investors might want to argue that the arrangement really was a partnership to begin with, and the partnership interest they received was worth less than their basis in their relinquished properties. That would be a really tough argument to make, though.

The moral is that tax savings are money. If buying something allows you to save taxes, then the thing you buy doesn't cost you as much. It does not make it free. And it is possible that, even with the discount that the tax savings create, the thing is not worth what you are paying for it. I might go so far as to speculate that if the designer had tax savings in mind, then the designer feels entitled to a goodly share of your tax savings. In some cases, it might be your tax savings and then some. In this case, as the title says, it would be better to have just paid the taxes. ◊

In this section, I reflect on what you can do to help a HENRY (High Earnings Not Rich Yet).

Tax Planning for the High Salary Pauper

One of the greatest confusions in discussions of inequality is between income and wealth. This struck me recently when somebody with an extremely high W-2 (low seven figures) asked me what sort of things they could do to manage the income tax that, federal and state combined grabbed roughly half their income.

How the Question Came Up

The person (call him Joe) had contacted me initially to ask about syndicated conservation easements. From his viewpoint, they are really great. The one he was looking at gave a five-to-one charitable deduction, six-to-one if you put in more than $200,000.

So, for $200,000, Joe can cover the $500,000 tax on his second million. I spoke with the consultant that Joe was dealing with, and I am very impressed by the professionalism and how well-thought-out the program is addressing many of the technical deficiencies that have torpedoed these deals and providing for insurance and an audit defense fund.

The Problem With Syndicated Conservation Easements

My coverage of syndicated conservation easements has overall been negative because I think they are fundamentally flawed. There is an IRS announcement[1] that they will be gunning for them, a GAO report[2] and pressure from Congress to look into them.[3]

Another View

My critique of conservation easement syndication sparked a sharp rebuke from one reader.

> What is the difference between a well-meaning "philanthropist" who wants to preserve a $10M property for the good of the public domain, and fifteen neurosurgeons who also want to preserve the exact same $10M property for the good of the public domain? If your answer is anything other than "none," then you are an elitist snob who needs to read the Constitution.

We can get into my elitism and Constitutional literacy some other time, but there is an interesting point that my critic is making in there.

Most of the neat income tax ideas in my bag of tricks relate to people who have some wealth or at the least control how to run their businesses.

What Is Available?

What can you tell somebody like Joe, who has an exceptionally large W-2, but has not yet accumulated any wealth and has no influence over how his employer does things?

I started talking to him about real estate. I am so excited about what a good cost segregation study can do for you. Then, I realized I had gone into a sort of time warp forgetting all about the Tax Reform Act of 1986 and Code Section 469 and the host of Tax Court decisions where guys like Joe fail to convince the Tax Court that they spend more time on real estate than their day job. It was embarrassing.

Naturally, he is maximizing his 401(k). Well, this was all going on while I was in an RV near a national park[4] and Joe wasn't a paying client or anything, so I left it at that, but it nagged at me, so I looked for somebody to talk to.

No Magic Bullet

"No magic bullet" is the answer that I got from Jared Feldman[5], co-leader of the Private Client Group at Anchin[6]. He had a couple of good suggestions. I do not doubt that Joe would get his money's worth if he hired Anchin.

The first one was a Health Savings Account, which can be a good idea, but the savings are really not that significant, although I guess every little bit helps. Next comes putting money in a donor-advised fund, essentially prepaying several years' worth of charity.

And then there is properly managing the timing of itemized deductions. Paying them in December rather than January or vice versa, depending on the AMT or other factors, can be significant, but it is really not that exciting.

Feldman then indicated that they can often get satisfactory results by somehow restructuring the compensation package, but for this exercise, I am ruling that sort of thing out. Remember the Golden Rule. He who has the gold, rules. If you are a working stiff, even a very well-paid one, whoever is paying you can be inflexible if they want to.

Wisdom of the Crowd

Since this is not really a technical issue, I thought it would be worthwhile to reach out to my Twitter crowd. I received a few responses. It may have been the phrasing of my question, but the responses are consistent with the view that there is nothing dramatic for a very high W-2 person, who has no wealth and an employer not inclined to play ball, to do. Here are some of the answers with my commentary:

> "If charitably inclined, make a large contribution to Donor Advised Fund. If on a high deductible health plan, maximize the contribution to HSA. If have children in daycare, maximize dependent care account contribution. To name a few..."

Right. That's what Jared Feldman said. The fact is that if one of my ships (they are more PT boats than aircraft carriers) came in I would jump on the DAF, but I'm 71 and pretty much as rich as I want to be. Somebody who has basically nothing and is now getting some big income probably should and will keep in mind that charity begins at home.

Then there is Andrea Carr who wrote:

> "If someone has a big W-2 (500k plus) but no influence over employer or net worth, what can they do beyond 401(k) to manage tax liability?"

That is Andrea Carr[7] who continues to practice public accounting while waiting for her career as a Twitter comic to take off. "Invest in oil and gas working interest partnership."

Wow. That brings back memories of the '80s. I am not sure that still works, but even if it does, I wouldn't want to put that much into them.

> "A problem I'm running against for clients right now. Directly, I cannot think of much. Feels like the answer is an indirect one by being efficient everywhere else."

Another pessimist like me.

"Become an independent contractor and elect S status? Start your own business? Other than that, maximize itemized deductions."

Again: In a similar situation, by educating client they were able to renegotiate contract to move certain income to contract labor, from there we built a solo-k then non-qualified plan to defer significant portion of income for a 15-year retirement plan. Then unwind it tax efficiently.

Of course, these guys are assuming away one of the constraints in my question.

"Ask their investment manager to harness some losses."

This one was funny. When I pointed out that a capital loss would not shelter salary, he responded with the $3,000. Again, worth doing, but hardly dramatic.

Back to the Syndicated Easement

To be clear, I am not going to recommend these things, but one of my principles is that I work for the taxpayers, not the government. And I have to say I am having doubts about how hard I would push to talk you out of it.

I would have to do a lot more due diligence on the audit insurance and the structure and the like, but I might end up with, "Well, it should not work, but it probably will work for you."

And there is another factor that can make the risk much lower or maybe just different. What can happen in these deals is that there will be some sort of put/call to take you out of the partnership after a couple of years (remember you voted to give away an easement, not the underlying property) for five to 10 percent of your original investment.

Under the new centralized partnership audit regime, the obligation for paying the tax on disallowed deductions falls first on the partnership and then on whoever the partners are when they make the adjustment.

I foresee some very messy tax litigation over how that will work out in six or seven years. When it comes to conservation easement syndication investments, I'm still going to stick with **Reilly's Second Law of Tax Planning — *"Sometimes it's better to just pay the taxes."***

But, if you are among the bold and can do the due diligence and in the taxation is theft school of thought, it is worth considering. Part of the diligence should be making certain that the partnership will not be electing out of the centralized regime. If that is happening, don't walk away, run.

How Times Have Changed

Back in days of very high marginal rates—70 percent federal—people who made their money by working got a break. There was a maximum tax on income from, you know, working. And there were shelters. Many were sketchy and abusive and could get you in trouble, but some like low-income housing had a blessing. You could defer your income, and when the deferral turned around, the IRS taxed it at capital gains rates.

Now it seems that there are breaks for everybody except the high salaried. Of course, if you are prudent with a very high salary, you will accumulate net worth and ultimately can do some fancy stuff, if you are so inclined.◊

***Walgreen Co. v City of Oshkosh*[8] *does not on its face seem to be a case that could have broad reaching federal income tax implications. I happen to think it may, but it may just be me. Nonetheless, my reasoning gives me a chance to explore a sub-sub industry that is kind of interesting. It is the tax tale of why people whose real estate ships come in find themselves buying drugstores of all things and perhaps an illustration of* Reilly's Second Law of Tax Planning—"*Sometimes it's better to just pay the taxes.*"**

Can Walgreens' Stance on Property Tax Hurt Income Tax Position of 1031 Investors?

Like-kind Exchanges—Why Your Farm Is Like a Drugstore

Code Section 1031 (like-kind exchanges) now applies only to exchanges of real property and not to exchanges of personal or intangible property. A 1031 deal is great for someone who wants to go on to bigger and better things in real estate, mainly because the like-kind concept is so broad when it comes to real estate. A cow is not like-kind to a bull, but a cow pasture is like-kind to an office building. Go figure.

But what about people who are tired of being landlords and are looking for passive income and no worries? Something of a sub-sub industry has sprung up to cater to successful real estate operators who want to become what Thomas Piketty would call rentiers without paying capital gains tax. Certain major retailers, drugstores in particular, lease their stores on very long triple net leases, which allows them to tap into that pool of 1031 money that is seeking very passive income.

One of the biggest players in the market is Walgreens. Walgreens has more than 8,000 locations The properties tend to base the price on capitalizing the net lease income.

Walgreens Admits—Nay, Insists—The Buildings Are Not Worth That Much

Since the buildings are triple net leased, the owners don't have a dog in the fight when it comes to real estate taxes, so it is Walgreens that tends to take the matter up. Now, since there is such an active market for Walgreens stores, it would seem that there should not be that much to fight about. Look at the lease and divide with maybe some fancy present value math thrown in. But that's not the way it works, at least not in Oshkosh, by gosh, or the rest of Wisconsin.

In Walgreens/Madison, the court determined that where contractual rights inflate the value of leased retail property, assessors must look to the market to reach their valuations. "An assessor's task is to value the real estate, not the business concern, which may be using the property."

The circuit court found that the City of Oshkosh did not follow this rule in valuing Walgreens properties, as its assessments relied on sale prices and leases that included contractual rights that inflated the properties' values.

There were two properties one sold in 2005 for $2,923,459 and the other for $4,325,000 in 2006. The city valued them at $2,920,500 and $4,093,600 in 2010. I am thinking that might have actually been a good deal given the way cap rates have been moving, but Walgreens was having none of it.

Walgreens' expert appraiser, Paul Bakken, valued the Murdock property at $1,675,000 in 2009 and $1,585,000 in 2010 and the Koeller property at $1,750,000 in 2009 and $1,655,000 in 2010. He based his valuations largely on analyzing what comparable retail properties would receive in rent without considering properties leased by national credit-worthy tenants such as Walgreens.

The Scary Part

The court went with Walgreens, but here is the part of the decision I find very disturbing.

" 'The fact that retail property may be income-producing does not render the contractual benefits of an above-market lease equal to a higher property value. A lease never increases the market value of real property rights to the fee simple estate.' Any **increase in the value of real property attributable to a particular lease constitutes contractual rather than real property rights,** even though those rights may run with the land." (Emphasis added)

Why does this scare me? Well, if I were what I refer to as the agent from hell, and I was auditing somebody who had exchanged into the $4,325,000 Oshkosh Walgreens, I would be inclined to say, "You know, it looks to me as if your exchange facilitator only put about $1.7 million or so into real estate as it is defined under state law in Wisconsin. The balance went into a contractual right, which is property not of like-kind, making it taxable to boot." Yuck.

If my fear is justified, things would not be good for the sub-sub industry that has relied on the pools of 1031 money. ◊

Keeping good records can help you run your business better. If you are not planning on being tax-compliant, it can be self-defeating.

Superior Point of Sale Software Does Not Mix Well With Skimming

The Micros Systems Inc.[9] point of sales system for restaurants seems pretty slick.

Micros provides comprehensive restaurant point-of-service (POS) solutions that can scale to meet the needs of every type and size of restaurant, whether you operate a single restaurant or hundreds. Its modular restaurant POS systems can easily expand as required, and can fit the demands of quick-service, fast casual, and full-service restaurants, as well as catering, pubs, and bars.

That "every type of restaurant" claim is not perfectly accurate. Restaurants where there is significant skimming of cash receipts going on are not well-served by a sophisticated POS system like Micros. That was the lesson that Alaa I. Musa learned in Tax Court[10] in 2017.

The IRS was after him for the seventy-five percent fraud penalty, which is as bad as it gets short of losing your liberty. Unlike the accuracy penalty, where the taxpayer has the burden of providing a good excuse for understatement, the burden is on the IRS to prove fraud. Thanks to the superior POS system, which was less of a challenge for the IRS.

Here's Looking at You, Kid

Mr. Musa's restaurant, Casablanca[11], has Middle Eastern cuisine and the occasional belly dancer. No gambling, as far as I can determine.

The shocking thing is the skimming, I guess. Mr. Musa let the credit card receipts go into his bank account but when it came to actual cash:

> He took the cash received home with him each night and placed it in a safe in his residence. During the years at issue, petitioner never deposited more than a de minimis amount of Casablanca's cash receipts into the operating account or any other bank account.

Some Detailed Records That Went Nowhere

> Casablanca used Micros Systems Inc. (Micros), an industry-standard point-of-sale system, to fulfill customers' food and drink orders. Casablanca's staff entered customers' orders into computer terminals after entering in a four-digit personal identification number unique to each staff member. The Micros computers then routed each order to the kitchen or bar, as applicable. Additionally, each order was recorded by a central computer in an office below the restaurant.
>
> At the end of an employee's shift the Micros system printed a "checkout report" that totaled the gross receipts from an individual waiter's shift, including bills paid by cash or with credit card.
>
> After closing the restaurant each night, petitioner stapled together and retained all of the credit card receipts in the event a customer paying by credit card disputed a transaction. Credit card payments were automatically deposited into Casablanca's business operating account at U.S. Bank. Petitioner threw away the cash receipts and checkout reports.

A Helpful Cousin

Mr. Musa thought it would be a good idea to buy the building he was operating in. He approached his cousin, Jeff, a commercial relationship manager for PNC. When Jeff reviewed Casablanca's tax returns, he was shocked at the restaurant's low profitability. He asked Mr. Musa if he had any other records, and Musa showed him the Micros reports. Jeff noticed some discrepancies. Ya think?

He recommended that Mr. Musa change accountants and recommended a Mr. Sturm to replace Mr. Jobin who had prepared the previous returns without the benefit of the Micros reports.

Mr. Musa did not get around to hiring Mr. Sturm until after he got a notice about the audit. Mr. Sturm prepared amended returns for 2006 through 2008 and original returns for 2009 and 2010 not using the Micros reports, but rather sales tax reports. Although there was significantly more revenue on the amended returns, the final figures agreed to with the IRS were even higher.

Badges of Fraud

Besides the substantial gross receipts' omission, there were some issues about payroll to relatives and expenses, but they were not as dramatic. The IRS still had to prove fraud, though. Mr. Musa was inclined to attribute the understatement of gross receipts to his inexperience and neglect on the part of his accountants. Unfortunately for Mr. Musa, the accountants were not ready to fall on their swords for him.

Just as there are lists of factors for whether a business activity is engaged in for profit or someone is an employee, there is a list of factors that indicates fraud. They are the "badges of fraud."

> Over the years, courts have developed a nonexclusive list of factors that demonstrate fraudulent intent. These badges of fraud include: (1) **understatement of income,** (2) **inadequate maintenance of records,** (3) **implausible or inconsistent explanations of behavior,** (4) **concealment of assets or income,** (5) **failure to cooperate with tax authorities,** (6) engaging in illegal activities, (7) an intent to mislead which may be inferred from a pattern of conduct, (8) lack of credibility of the taxpayer's testimony, (9) **failure to file tax returns,**

(10) **filing false documents,** (11) **failure to make estimated tax payments,** and (12) **dealing in cash.**

The Tax Court found nine of the 12 (the **ones in bold**) in Mr. Musa's case.

That was enough to support the 75 percent penalty.

What Was He Thinking?

I'm really puzzled about why someone would put in a sophisticated POS system if he is not going to be scrupulous about depositing all the receipts. Of course, the other alternative is "zapper" software, illegal in many states, which will allow you to have the benefits of a POS system while being able to manipulate your total sales figure to be consistent with what you decide to deposit.

What we really have here is another illustration of **Reilly's Second Law of Tax Planning—"*Sometimes it's better to just pay the taxes.*"**

Mixing tax evasion with foreign accounts and other sorts of shenanigans can be toxic. ◊

During the Trump Administration, the Mueller investigation led to revealing several of Trump's friends misbehaved, and so the special counsel sought indictments. Finally, after waiting quite some time for the other shoe to drop on the promised indictment in the Mueller investigation[12], it turns out that it was a tax story. The District of Columbia Grand Jury indictment charges that Paul Manafort and Richard Gates hid millions of dollars paid to them by the Ukrainian Party of Regions in foreign corporations, partnerships, and bank accounts.

Manafort and Gates—That's How They Got Al Capone

It's the Disclosure.

That's real exciting stuff, but I'm a tax blogger, you know, so I am more drawn to the mundane. And the most intriguing part of the whole indictment to me comes on page 21:

> For instance, on October 4, 2011, Manafort's tax preparer asked Manafort in writing: "At any time during 2010, did you have an interest in or a signature or other authority over a financial account in a foreign country, such as a bank account, securities account or other financial account?" On the same day, Manafort falsely responded "No." Manafort responded the same way as recently as October 3, 2016, when Manafort's tax preparer again emailed the question in connection with the preparation of Manafort's tax return: "Foreign bank accounts, etc.?" Manafort responded on or about the same day: "None."

What Was He Thinking?

At any rate, I am very intrigued by the scenario outlined in the little bit from the indictment above. I'm wondering if the tax preparer's asking in writing was part of a 30- or 40-page "organizer" that Manafort received. Reading between the lines of the description of the 2016 email exchange, it seems likely that Manafort might not have thoroughly filled out his organizer, and the preparer was trying to confirm that there were no foreign bank accounts. I have to say that if I had been doing Manafort's return, I would have tried to communicate to him how very bad it is to inadvertently fail to report control of a foreign bank account. Given all the running around he was doing consulting with various misunderstood rulers of foreign countries, it would strike me as likely that he would have needed a foreign account to do business.

Of course, the indictment indicates that all those foreign accounts, mostly in Cyprus, were part of a scheme to avoid paying taxes and cover up the existence of the income. Assuming the indictment is accurate, it is a clever scheme. He used the accounts to buy real estate, and then he could tap into the equity tax-free by borrowing against the property. That is only pretty clever. Real estate creates an exceptionally large paper trail.

FBAR Makes for FUBAR

As it works out, in the 12-count indictment, seven of the counts are for failure to file FBAR. For Manafort, it was 2011, 2012, 2013, and 2014. For Gates it was 2011, 2012, and 2013. You may have read in some stories that Manafort and Gates were facing a combined potential of 150 years in prison. If that were true, the FBARs would account for seventy of those years. That is not, however, how sentencing works. The United States Sentencing Commission[13] has a manual on how to compute guideline sentences.

Back in the day, there was this joke that when somebody said the IRS was auditing them the remark would be, "That's how they got Al Capone." Federal authorities had found it easier to convict Capone of income tax evasion than of whatever various crimes he had committed in gathering all that income. Prosecutors have honed that technique. Although, the indictment might imply there was some income tax evasion going on, that was not the charge. Most of the counts are not filing FBARs and that is really easy to prove—kind of like shooting fish in barrel. (That he accepted a Presidential pardon means he admitted his guilt.)

If the charges are true, Manafort has manifested a pretty foolish arrogance. The indictment lists out numerous payments for personal type items, including $520,440 to clothing stores in Beverly Hills, paid out of foreign accounts—mostly in Cyprus. If that is what turns out to be the truth, then next to **Reilly's Second Law of Tax Planning,** there will be a picture of Paul Manafort.

If your job involves people giving you a lot of money, you may want to report it.

I am not a big fan of self-help books, but there is one tip I picked up from *Seven Habits of Highly Effective People* by Stephen R. Covey that I really cherish. "Begin with the end in mind." If you really reflect, paying the least amount of taxes conceivable is not that worthwhile an end. It is a means to having money to use in other ways.◊

SECOND LAW OF TAX PLANNING

Footnotes

1. Peter J. Reilly, "Major Crackdown On Conservation Easements Or IRS Bluff?." Forbes, last modified November 13, 2019, https://www.forbes.com/sites peterjreilly/2019/11/13/major-crackdown-on-conservation-easements-or-irs-bluff/#7478f4b315fb.
2. Peter J. Reilly, "GAO Reports On Charity Tax Abuse," Forbes, last modified October 13, 2019, https://www.forbes.com/sites/peterjreilly/2019/10/13/gao-reports-on-charity-tax-abuse/#23c27e287032.
3. Peter J. Reilly, "Grassley Wyden Take On Sketchy Conservation Tax Shelters," Forbes, last modified March 28, 2019, https://www.forbes.com/sites/peterjreilly/2019/03/28/grassley-wyden-take-on-sketchy-conservation-tax-shelters/#3c44e50da343.
4. Evie Pless, "Nov 26 - 30, 2022 - Post-Thanksgiving," Peter and Evie - Life After RVing (Blog), last modified January 1, 2023, https://peterevierv.blogspot.com/.
5. "Jared Feldman – CPA," Anchin, accessed May 27, 2023, https://www.anchin.com/team/jared-feldman/.
6. "About Anchin," Anchin, accessed May 30, 2023, https://www.anchin.com/about/?view=narrative_1.
7. "Tax Season Therapy the Tweets Of Andrea Carr CPA," Your Tax Matters Partner (blog), last modified June 6, 2019, https://yourtaxmatterspartner.com/tax-season-therapy-tweets-of-andrea/.
8. Walgreen Co. v. City of Oshkosh, Court of Appeals District II (No. 2013AP2818), December 17, 2014, https://law.justia.com/cases/wisconsin/court-of-appeals/2014/2013ap002818.html.
9. "Oracle MICROS POS Systems," Oracle, accessed May 27, 2023, https://www.oracle.com/food-beverage/micros/.
10. Alaa Musa v. Commissioner of Internal Revenue, United States Court of Appeals (No.16-1841), April 26, 2017, https://caselaw.findlaw.com/court/us-7th-circuit/1857948.html#:~:text=Appellant%20Alaa%20Musa%20owns%20and%20operates%20a%20restaurant,Musa%20challenged%20this%20determination%20in%20the%20Tax%20Court.

11. "About Us and Dining," Casablanca, accessed May 27, 2023, https://casablancaonbrady.com/about-us-dining/

12. United States of America v. Paul J. Manafort, Jr. and Richard W. Gates III, United States District Court for the District of Columbia (No. 1:17-cr-00201), October 27, 2017, https://www.justice.gov/file/1007271/download.

13. "2016 Guidelines Manual," United States Sentencing Commission, accessed May 27, 2023, https://www.ussc.gov/guidelines/2016-guidelines-manual.

THIRD LAW OF TAX PLANNING

Any Clever Idea That Pops Into Your Head Probably Has A Corresponding Rule That Makes It Not Work.

The history of tax litigation for as long as I have been in the game is something of an arms race between clever planners and legislation and regulations. If a clever idea pops into your head, there is a decent chance that your head is not the first one it popped into. Sometimes the clever idea will get you in much worse trouble than what you are trying to avoid.

One of those things that "everybody" knows is that banks rat you out to the IRS when you engage in cash transactions of $10,000 or more. A clever response to this reality is to keep your transactions below $10,000. You've got $25,000 in cash to put in the bank? Make three trips, and there will be no reports.

Here is the thing. That is a crime called structuring. And if you get in the IRS sights for structuring, convicting you can be like shooting fish in a barrel. And the really amusing thing is the IRS doesn't generally do much with the currency reports, so you likely just made trouble for yourself in trying to avoid trouble.

The indictment of former House Speaker Dennis Hastert[1] brought new attention to the crime of structuring. The attention is energizing the supporters of Kent Hovind, who finished a long sentence for a large number of counts for structuring a few years ago.

Structuring—First Kent Hovind — Now Dennis Hastert

The Trials of Kent Hovind

Hovind did win a big victory in Pensacola. Filings he made, while in prison, to affect title to property seized as a result of his structuring conviction were contempt of court, conspiracy, and fraud. A trial resulted in a conviction on the contempt charge and a hung jury on the more serious fraud and conspiracy charges. On the eve of his retrial, the government dropped the fraud and conspiracy charges and shortly thereafter Judge Margaret Casey Rodgers reversed the contempt conviction.

What Is Structuring?

Structuring is an illustration of **Reilly's Third Law of Tax Planning**—*"Any clever idea that pops into your head probably has a corresponding rule that makes it not work."* If you deposit or withdraw more than $10,000 in cash at a bank, the bank must file a report to the government. There has been something of a criminalization of cash, a kind of assumption that if you are dealing in a lot of cash, you must be up to something nefarious, low-level tax avoidance at the least. The court convicted Hovind, for example, on 45 counts of structuring and on 12 counts of not filing payroll returns, and one count of interfering with the administration of the Internal Revenue Code. Dealing in cash, of course, facilitated the latter counts.

At any rate, the clever idea is to not take out or deposit, say, $50,000 all at once, which would cause the bank to rat you out to the government by filing a report, but rather to make six or more trips to the bank withdrawing or depositing $8000 or $9000 more or less each time. Section 5324 of Title 31[2] makes that a crime. It is not the deposits or withdrawals themselves that are criminal, but rather the structuring of them to avoid the bank reporting. No really nefarious purpose is necessary—just the desire to avoid the bank reporting requirement. It is the intent to avoid the reporting that makes it criminal, even if the depositor obtained or used the cash lawfully.

How Is Hastert's Case Different from Hovind's?

One difference is that even though the government accused Hastert of withdrawing $952,000 in at least 106 transactions, he was charged with only one count of structuring. Hovind and his wife withdrew just over $400,000 and the charges amounted to 45 counts. This reticence on the part of the Justice Department to stack up the structuring counts may be the result of the Eleventh Circuit decision in the case of Jerry Dwayne Lang[3]. The government indicted Mr. Lang on 85 counts of structuring, each count representing a separate deposit of less than $10,000. The Court ruled that a deposit of less than $10,000 all by itself could not represent structuring. You need at least two deposits that total over $10,000. Under the federal sentencing guidelines, multiple counts of the same thing don't tend to get you much extra time over a single count, so the government does not gain much by multiplying the counts other than possibly impressing the jury with the notion that with all that smoke, there must be a fire somewhere.

The other difference is that the only other thing the government indicted Hastert for is lying to the FBI. He told them that he was stacking up all that cash because he didn't trust banks. Though, he was paying blackmail, which may have been related to sexual abuse from his wrestling coach days.[4] There is irony here. The House Speakership opened up to Hastert when Robert Livingston resigned in the light of a sex scandal while the House was impeaching President Clinton for saying that he had not had sexual relations with "that woman," when maybe he had, depending on how you define sexual relations.

At least in the court of public opinion, it would seem that Hastert could invoke the "everybody lies about sex" defense.

Conspiracy?

I have to say that this prosecution strikes me more as a possible weaponizing of law enforcement for political payback than the interminable Lois Lerner Teapartygate IRS scandal.

Do Structuring Prosecutions Make Sense?

Personally, I am becoming convinced that structuring prosecutions are a bad idea. My inference is that they are attractive to prosecutors because it is a lot easier to prove than the nefarious activity that they think structuring supports. On top of that, the forfeiture provisions can make the effort self-financing. It is too easy for supporters of those prosecuted that way to cast them as victims and increase the amount of alienation in the world.◊

And then there is private life insurance.

Tax Court Nixed Jeffrey Webber's Cayman Insurance Shelter

So here is a truly brilliant, if slightly ghoulish, tax plan.

Jeffrey Webber is a venture-capital investor and private-equity fund manager. His advisor, tax attorney William Lipkind, produced a vehicle that would not only defer gain on some of his investments but also totally avoid income tax when he and his family members cashed in. It's a real shame that the Tax Court agreed with the IRS that the scheme did not work. My only consolation is that it illustrates a couple of Reilly's Laws of Tax Planning.

The Plan

Mr. Webber established a grantor trust that purchased "private placement" variable life insurance policies insuring the lives of two elderly relatives. (That is the ghoulish part.) The premiums paid to Lighthouse Capital Insurance Co.[6] (Cayman Islands) after deduction for mortality risk and administrative costs were placed in separate accounts. The accounts were separated and invested in start-up companies that Mr. Webber was intimately familiar with. They did quite well.

The Third Law

Reilly's Third Law of Tax Planning holds that, ***"Any clever idea that pops into your head probably has a corresponding rule that makes it not work."*** For the clever idea of running your aggressive start-up portfolio with money an insurance company technically owns but meant to benefit you or the natural objects of your bounty, there is Revenue Ruling 1977-850.[7]

> A policyholder of an investment annuity contract issued by a life insurance company must include in gross income, under section 61 of the Code, interest and dividends or other income received by the custodian of the investment account created in conjunction with the contract and over which the policyholder has investment control.

Not exactly Mr. Webber's facts, but pretty close.

The Fourth Law

Reilly's Fourth Law of Tax Planning is ***"Execution isn't everything, but it's a lot."*** The execution of this plan depended on something called the "Lipkind Protocol." An independent manager had to make all decisions relative to the investments in the assets funded by the premiums. The policyholder could set the overall investment philosophy—"high risk" investments, including private-equity and venture-capital assets—and make specific recommendations. The investments were in a special purpose entity, including one called Boiler Riffle.

The "Lipkind Protocol" put a buffer between Mr. Webber and the investment advisor.

> Mr. Lipkind explained to petitioner that it was important for tax reasons that petitioner does not appear to exercise any control over the investments that Lighthouse, through the special-purpose companies, purchased for the separate accounts. Accordingly, when selecting investments for the separate accounts, petitioner followed the Lipkind Protocol. This meant that petitioner never communicated—by email, telephone, or otherwise—directly with Lighthouse or the investment manager. Instead, petitioner relayed all his directives, invariably styled "recommendations," through Mr. Lipkind or Ms. [Susan] Chang.

In the end, though, it was not possible to disguise the fact that Mr. Webber was calling all the shots.

> Although almost all of the investments in the policies' separate accounts consisted of non-publicly traded securities, the record contains no compliance records, financial records, or business documentation (apart from boilerplate references in emails) to establish that Lighthouse or the investment manager in fact performed independent research or meaningful due diligence with respect to any of petitioner's investment directives.
>
> The record includes more than 70,000 emails to or from Mr. Lipkind, Ms. Chang, the investment manager, and/or Lighthouse concerning petitioner's "recommendations" for investments by the separate accounts. Mr. Lipkind also appears to have given instructions regularly by telephone. Explaining his lack of surprise at finding no emails about a particular investment, Mr. Lipkind told petitioner: "We have relied primarily on telephone communications, not written paper trails (you recall our 'owner control' conversations)." The 70,000 emails thus tell much, but not all, of the story.

> The net result of this process was that every investment Boiler Riffle made was an investment that petitioner had "recommended." Apart from certain brokerage funds, virtually every security that Boiler Riffle held was issued by a startup company in which petitioner had a personal financial interest, e.g., by sitting on its board, by investing in its securities personally or through an IRA, or by investing in its securities through a venture-capital fund he managed.
>
> The investment manager did no independent research about these fledgling companies; it never finalized an investment until Mr. Lipkind had signed off; and it performed no due diligence apart from boilerplate requests for organizational documents and "know your customer" review. The investment manager did not initiate or consider any equity investment for the separate accounts other than the investments that petitioner "recommended." **The investment manager received $500 annually for its services, and its compensation was commensurate with its efforts.** (Emphasis added)

To have executed this plan perfectly, it would have been necessary for the investment advisor to perform due diligence on each of Mr. Webber's "recommendations." The added costs would have taken a huge bite out of his superior returns. One of my laws of tax practice, not planning, is: Any reasonably complex tax matter involving significant dollars, **regardless of whatever else it might be, is a white-collar jobs program.**

Still Not Such a Bad Plan

Even though the income tax piece of the plan ended up not working, it appears that the transfer tax aspects were undisturbed. Mr. Webber got all that growth out of his own estate and the income tax bite is coming out of his other assets.

There were no penalties.

> Mr. Lipkind provided petitioner with "advice." Mr. Lipkind did not himself render a written legal opinion, but he reviewed and considered written opinion letters from reputable law firms addressing the relevant issues. Three of these opinion letters specifically

> addressed the "investor control" doctrine; they concluded that the Lighthouse policies, as structured, would comply with U.S. tax laws and avoid application of this doctrine. By informing petitioner that he concurred in these opinions, Mr. Lipkind provided petitioner with professional tax advice on which petitioner actually relied in good faith.
>
> We likewise conclude that petitioner's reliance was "reasonable." Petitioner made multiple filings with the IRS setting forth details about the Trusts and Lighthouse, including gift tax returns filed for 1999 and 2003 and Form 3520 filed when the petitioner transferred the policies to an offshore trust. Petitioner did not attempt to hide his estate plan from the IRS. This supports his testimony that he believed this strategy would successfully withstand IRS scrutiny, as Mr. Lipkind had advised.
>
> For their work preparing trust documents and all other work for petitioner, Mr. Lipkind and his colleagues charged time at their normal hourly rates. Neither Mr. Lipkind nor his firm received from petitioner any form of bonus or other remuneration apart from hourly time charges. Neither Mr. Lipkind nor his firm received compensation of any kind from Lighthouse or the investment manager. IRS Examination and Tax Court Proceedings the IRS examined petitioner's timely filed 2006 and 2007 Federal income tax returns.

The absence of "value billing" distinguishes this transaction from the bogus Son-of-Boss and similar offenses against double entry put on by the erstwhile Big 4 running up to and a bit beyond the turn of the millennium.

From a tax policy point of view, it is clear that this plan should not work. It is taking the favorable tax treatment of life insurance and turning it into the perfect tax shelter. Nonetheless, I admire its elegance. It is also worth noting that if you had a genius investment advisor that was independent, the plan does work. ◊

There is also the idea of manufacturing passive income to absorb your passive losses.

Clever Ideas Cannot Fix Oxymorons in the Tax Law

The Fifth Circuit decision[8] in the case of Larry and Dora Williams has not attracted much attention as it merely confirms a Tax Court decision[9], but I have a passion for the passive activity loss rules (Code Section 469).

Background on the Oxymoron of Passive Activities

When I first started tax blogging in 2009, I named my blog Passive Activities and Other Oxymorons.[10] It was a kind of joke about Code Section 469, which is one of the most challenging sections in the field of individual taxation. The Tax Reform Act of 1986 ushered it in as a way of eliminating traditional tax shelters. TRA 1986 more or less made my career as it, for a time, placed a premium on accountants who could look things up.

What Code Section 469 requires us to do is to put our trade or business activities into buckets. If the activities in the passive bucket net to a loss, the tax preparer suspends that loss until the activity that generated it is totally disposed of or there is income from that passive activity or any other. The regulations that interpret 469 are pretty challenging. They serve as an illustration of **Reilly's Third Law of Tax Planning—*"Any clever idea that pops into your head probably has a corresponding rule that makes it not work."***

A Clever Idea

The clever idea that Larry and Dora Williams had was to generate some passive income to absorb their passive losses. The passive income they generated was rent paid by BEK Medical Inc.[11], a C corporation the couple owned, to BEK Real Estate Holdings LLC, an S corporation. By taking rent out of BEK Medical rather than salary, they transformed otherwise active income into passive income allowing them to currently use passive losses from other activities.

Someone probably first thought of that clever idea about half an hour after TRA 1986 hit the streets. So it's hardly shocking that there is a regulation about it, 1.469-2(f)(6), the so-called "self-rental rule."

> Property rented to a nonpassive activity. An amount of the taxpayer's gross rental activity income for the taxable year from an item of property equal to the net rental activity income for the year from that item of property is treated as not from a passive activity.

It is not the only rule like this, and like similar ones,—land leases, for examples—it is kind of a heads you lose, tails they win type of proposition. An activity subject to rules like this can remain a passive activity with suspended losses. It is only non-passive when and to the extent that it is net positive. Back in the '80s at Joseph B Cohan and Associates, we had a term for rules like that. Sorry, I cannot share it. Contributor guidelines and all.

An Argument Even If Not a Winning One

The taxpayers had an argument. Code Section 469 does not refer at all to S corporations, so the rules could not apply to BEK Real Estate Holdings. The argument went nowhere in Tax Court and the Fifth Circuit agreed.

> As the Tax Court acknowledged, Section 469 does not refer to S corporations at all. The statute specifically applies to "taxpayers" who are individuals, estates, trusts, closely held C corporations, and personal service corporations. An associated regulation defining certain passive activities, including rental activities, specifies:

> This section sets forth the rules for grouping a taxpayer's trade or business activities and rental activities for purposes of applying the passive activity loss and credit limitation rules of Section 469. A taxpayer's activities include those conducted through C corporations

that are subject to Section 469, S corporations, and partnerships.

Citing substantial authority, the Tax Court concluded that Section 469 did not need to specifically refer to S corporations because S corporations are merely pass-through entities, and its individual shareholders are the ultimate taxpayers.

It is worth noting that even though the taxpayers did not have a really good common sense argument, they did have an argument. There are some areas of the Code where partnerships and S corporations are "taxpayers"—making elections, having distinct accounting methods, and engaging in transactions with owners, for example. Who knows maybe if they had gotten this up to the Supremes, the late Justice Scalia, God rest his soul, would have been on their side from a strict textual reading. Or maybe not.

Sometimes you will find that clever tax ideas run afoul of non-tax rules. Are they consistent with local law, partnership agreements, trust instruments, and, sometimes importantly, common sense? Be sure to consider your great ideas holistically. ◊

THIRD LAW OF TAX PLANNING

Footnotes

1. United States of America v. John Dennis Hastert, United States District Court Northern District of Illinois, February 2014, https://s3.amazonaws.com/s3.documentcloud.org/documents/2089608/indictment-of-former-house-speaker-dennis-hastert.pdf.
2. "31 U.S.C. §5324. Structuring transactions to evade reporting requirement prohibited," U.S. Government Publishing Office, last modified 2011, accessed June 1, 2023, https://www.govinfo.gov/content/pkg/USCODE-2011-title31/html/USCODE-2011-title31-subtitleIV-chap53-subchapII-sec5324.htm.
3. United States of America v. Jerry Dwayne Land, United States Court of Appeals (No. 5:11-cr-00207-VEH-PWG-1), October 3, 2013, https://media.ca11.uscourts.gov/opinions/pub/files/201213608.pdf.
4. Michael D. Shear and Michael S. Schmidt, "Hastert Case Is Said to Be Linked to Decades-Old Sexual Abuse," The New York Times, last modified May 29, 2015,

https://www.nytimes.com/2015/05/30/us/politics/hastert-indictment.html.

5. Jeffrey T. Webber v. Commissioner of Internal Revenue, United States Tax Court (No. 14336-11), June 30, 2015, https://scholar.google.com/scholar_case?case=3441219414163278230&q=webber+v.+commissioner&hl=en&as_sdt=2006&as_vis=1.
6. "Lighthouse Capital Insurance Company," Gov.uk, accessed May 27, 2023, https://find-and-update.company-information.service.gov.uk/officers/xyHBLrq3Ke1arC_avl8L2rkSHsc/appointments.
7. Internal Revenue Service, "Rev. Rul. 1977-85," Charitable Planning, last modified March 9, 1977, https://www.charitableplanning.com/library/documents/671868.
8. Larry Williams and Dora Williams v. Commissioner of Internal Revenue, United States Court of Appeals (No. 15-60341), February 2, 2016, http://www.ca5.uscourts.gov/opinions/unpub/15/15-60341.0.pdf.
9. Williams v. Commissioner of Internal Revenue.
10. Peter Reilly, "So You Want To Be A Tax Blogger?," Passive Activities and Other Oxymorons (blog), last modified June 25, 2014, http://riles52.blogspot.com/.
11. "BEK Home Medical Equipment," accessed May 27, 2023, https://www.bekmedical.com/.

FOURTH LAW OF TAX PLANNING

Execution Isn't Everything, But It's a Lot.

When I started out in public accounting, I formed the impression that you could wield immense power with a pencil and green analysis paper as you shifted income and expense around with due to/due from accounts. And I thought nothing of skipping a lot of transaction steps to save time. Peter owed Paul who owed Tom owed Dick who owed Harry. So have Peter cut a check to Harry and make journal entries to square it all away. Then, I had a friend who bought a company from a relative who had died. The probate court was not impressed with all the journal entries, and my friend ended up paying a lot more than he anticipated.

This lesson became quite clear as I read the case law. A corollary of the Fourth Law is that the only people whom an accountant's journal entries impress are other accountants. To judges, the entries "purport" to recognize a transaction. Whenever you see the word "purport" in any of its forms in a Tax Court opinion, you know that things are not going to go well for the taxpayer.

Devil Is in the Details

One of the areas where execution issues show up in the case law a lot is in family limited partnerships. One of my very first posts was about how that played out in some cases. In the FLP case law, it is almost as if execution is everything.

In June 2007, the estate of Sylvia Gore joined the ranks of failed Family Limited Partnership. The case is worthy of consideration because it illustrates clearly why the partnerships fail.

If you plan to set up a family-limited partnership, it is critical that you consult with a well-qualified attorney. The attorney will create a package, thick, of documents, mysterious, and will see that you sign them with witnesses, get them notarized, and store an extra copy in her safe in case you lose yours. That is service. That is follow-through.

Valuation discounts are what tend to be at stake when the IRS attacks Family Limited Partnerships. Having had great service from your attorney, you think that when people lose, it is because they didn't hire a good attorney. The documents did not have witnesses. Maybe one of the incantations in the mysterious documents was missing. Maybe there wasn't an extra copy in the safe after they lost theirs.

The follow-through needed is not the extra hour in the attorney's office. The follow-through will be many hours year in and year out in your accountant's office. The clue to this is in the importance attributed to the extra copy in the attorney's safe. Why doesn't the accountant who has to prepare the income tax return for the partnership have a copy? Why don't you need to look at your copy from time to time too? Here is why:

> … each partner's capital account is increased by (1) the amount of money contributed by him to the partnership, (2) the fair market value of property contributed by him to the partnership (net of liabilities that the partnership is considered to assume or take subject to), and (3) allocations to him of partnership income and gain (or items thereof), including income and gain exempt from tax and income and gain described in paragraph (b)(2)(iv)(g) of this section, but excluding income and gain described in paragraph (b)(4)(i) of this section; and is decreased by (4) the amount of money distributed

> to him by the partnership, (5) the fair market value of property distributed to him by the partnership (net of liabilities that such partner is considered to assume or take subject to), (6) allocations to him of expenditures of the partnership described in section 705(a)(2)(B), and (7) allocations of partnership loss and deduction (or item thereof), including loss and deduction described in paragraph (b)(2)(iv)(g) of this section, but excluding items described in (6) above and loss or deduction described in paragraphs …

This is one of the magic incantations that will appear in your agreement. If you ask your attorney how that partnership's tax return should reflect this paragraph, he is likely to tell you that he doesn't prepare partnership returns. That is what accountants do. Now go to your accountant and ask her what that paragraph means. Among the possible answers are, "That's some stuff the attorneys must put in the agreement. Why don't you ask him what it means?"

So, what did Sylvia Gore and her advisers do or fail to do that cost the estate $1,071,650 in federal estate taxes? Plus, 10 years of interest. Not to mention the cost of their fruitless efforts in the Tax Court.

In 1995, Sydney Gore met with his accountant in the hospital where he expressed to her "his concerns about preserving the wealth he had accumulated through his life's work, protecting his assets from waste, and conserving them for future generations." The accountant had an idea, a very good idea. Form a family-limited partnership. She had never advised any of her other clients to take that step, but it seemed the right thing to do here. She knew that she had limits, though:

> Ms. Bowers had little experience with family-limited partnerships and had never recommended one to a client before she made the proposal to the Gore children, so she recommended that Ms. Powell, Mr. Gore, and the decedent retain an attorney to further advise them about a limited partnership.

Apparently, it didn't occur to anybody that an accountant with more than a little experience with family-limited partnerships might bring something to the table.

What happened from here is not the accountant's fault. The partnership opened a bank account, and it deposited substantial sums. There was an assignment of marketable securities to the partnership. Unfortunately, it did not transfer the title to the securities to the partnership. The dividends from the securities went into the partnership's bank account. When Mrs. Gore needed to pay bills, her personal account sometimes paid them, and other times partnership accounts did.

Eventually, she needed to file returns, which is when Ms. Bowers came back on the scene. What she did was what most competent accountants would try to do. Observing that what happened was nothing near what was supposed to happen, she attempted to fix it all with journal entries. This process relies on one of the great intellectual breakthroughs that built the modern world: double-entry bookkeeping first documented in a mathematical treatise more than 500 years ago. It provides a built-in check that shows that you captured everything. It all must balance. Debits equal credits.

When it is a check, we credit cash. Then, we must debit something. Well, the check went to Mary, so we debit Mary's capital account. Unfortunately, by the terms of the partnership agreement, we were not supposed to make a distribution to Mary. So, we debit "Due from Mary." Joe, on the other hand, was supposed to get a distribution. Well, either we won't worry about that since it's in Joe's capital or, if we want the percentages to be where they should be, we will credit "Due to Joe" and debit his capital account.

When it's all done the amounts on our records will agree to the statements (adjusted for the fact that they may not have the right names on them) and "it will all balance." Mary will owe the partnership, and the partnership will owe Joe. We'll straighten it out next year, or we'll keep making journal entries to keep it straight.

I have learned a hard lesson that many accountants never quite understand. When it comes to this "everything's in balance" routine, almost nobody else cares. Here is some of what the court had to say about Ms. Bower's efforts:

"The GFLP accounting records prepared by Ms. Bowers purport

> to show that decedent transferred…."
>
> "The accounting records also purport to show that after decedent executed the assignment, decedent allegedly sold the Commercial Federal CD, the savings bonds, a Valley National CD, and one of the Treasury notes to GFLP in exchange for a note payable to her from GFLP…."

The word "purport" or one of its forms (e.g., "purporting") occurs six times. Here is the problem. You can get into law school with a liberal arts degree. Law school does not teach double-entry accounting. If it's taught in high school, it's to kids not on the college track. You certainly don't need it for a liberal arts degree. Judges are lawyers. It all balances, and they don't care.

I have no reason to doubt that if I looked at all the statements and agreements, I would have concluded that Ms. Bower's journal entries straightened things out. Likely most other accountants would reach a similar conclusion when they see that the cash ties, and it balances. Much to our professional frustration, almost nobody else, but especially the judge, cares. The meticulous journal entries that straighten everything out in our minds, in the mind of the judge "purport."

In 2007 the Estate of Concetta Rector lost to the tune of $1,633,049 plus about five years of interest. Here is an excerpt:

> The estate attempts to downplay the significance of the direct use of RLP funds to pay the decedent's personal expenses by attributing that use to "errors." Considering John Rector's extensive financial expertise and his testimony that it never occurred to him that RLP should be reimbursed for such "errors" after they were discovered, we find that this argument lacks credibility.

This is nothing new. If you study the cases where taxpayers lose FLP cases, you will, almost always, if not inevitably, find that the failure was not one of a flawed plan. The failure was not following the steps transaction by transaction. If somebody should have a distribution and has bills to pay, you distribute to them and let them pay their own bills. All entities have accounts and the payments in and out are the ones that belong to that entity. If there's a mistake, a transfer of funds fixes it, not a journal entry that creates an indefinite "Due to…."

The story's moral is that for the plan to work you must have coordination between the attorney who prepares the plan and the accountant who will be preparing the relevant returns. If you don't want to trouble yourself with what entity should pay what bill or accept what deposit, etc., let professionals handle that piece, also, but again in an integrated manner. There must be somebody who cares who uses what account because that's their job.◊

Family-limited partnerships seem particularly prone to execution problems. Here is an example of a well-executed plan that stood up.

Tax Court Approves Family Partnership Valuation Discounts

When one of the founding partners of a regional law firm has the firm's estate group handle his planning, they are likely to do a pretty good job. That may well be the moral in the Tax Court decision in the case of the estate of Barbara M. Purdue. I look at the case as another illustration of **Reilly's Fourth Law of Tax Planning—"*Execution isn't everything, but it's a lot.*"**

The IRS was looking for more than $4 million in estate and gift tax from Mrs. Purdue's estate. She died at the age of 95 in 2007. During WWII she was a Red Cross hospital aide on the USS Comfort[1], the only hospital ship ever struck by a Kamikaze. Her husband Robert, one of the founders of the Seattle law firm Montgomery Purdue Blankinship & Austin PLLC[2] died in 2001. They had five children, and in the words of the decision "multiple grandchildren and great-grandchildren." As of 1999, their net worth was approximately $28 million, mostly marketable securities and an interest in a commercial building in Hawaii (the Hocking Building).

The Plan

Mr. and Mrs. Purdue had engaged Alan Montgomery to work on their estate plan in 1995. The decision refers to them as "the parents." Montgomery recommended a family-limited partnership to centralize management and take advantage of valuation discounts. In 2000, he created and capitalized the PFLLC with $22 million in marketable securities and some other assets, including the interest in the Hocking Building valued at $900,000.

Also in 2000, he formed PFT, a trust. The trust beneficiaries were the descendants and their spouses. The agreement provided the beneficiaries with Crummey withdrawal rights. From 2002 till 2007, Mrs. Purdue made annual exclusion gifts of interests in PFLLC to PFT based on the number of beneficiaries on January 1 of each year and additional gifts on December 31 if there were more beneficiaries or the LLC value had dropped. At the time of her death, Mrs. Purdue owned about 25 percent of the LLC, 42 percent was in a QTIP, 5 percent in a Bypass Trust, 7 percent was owned outright by the children, and 21 percent by PFT.

Conflict

The problem with family-limited partnerships is that they involve, you know, families. The five siblings had some issues to work out when it came time to pay the taxes.

> Montgomery sent a letter to the Purdue children dated August 18, 2008, explaining the options for paying the estate tax liabilities, including a $6,245,744 loan from the PFLLC to the estate and the QTIP Trust or a $9,863,571 dividend from the PFLLC. The Purdue children had limited rights. The members of the PFLLC could not transfer their interests without unanimous consent by the other members. Beverly refused to approve a PFLLC dividend sufficient for the estate and the QTIP Trust to pay their estate tax liabilities with their proportionate shares to induce her siblings to approve a large

> lump-sum PFLLC dividend that she wanted but that they opposed (deadlock). For the same reason, she also refused to approve PFLLC dividends necessary for the QTIP Trust and the Bypass Trust to pay their income tax liabilities. The $5,040,090 of combined PFLLC dividend shares of the estate and the QTIP Trust were insufficient to pay their estate tax liabilities. The remaining distributees aggregated their distributions and made loans totaling $1,233,897 to the estate and the QTIP Trust.

The IRS challenged the estate's deduction of $20,891 in interest on the loan. The Court allowed the deduction.

IRS Attack

The IRS argued that the transfer of property to the LLC was not a bona fide transfer for adequate consideration. The Court did not buy that. And this is the part that you should really look at.

> Other factors, however, support the estate's argument that a bona fide sale occurred. First, the **decedent and Mr. Purdue were not financially dependent on distributions from the PFLLC.** The decedent retained substantial assets outside of the PFLLC to pay her living expenses. Second, aside from a minimal dollar amount across three deposits to the PFLLC account, there was **no commingling of the decedent's funds with the PFLLC's funds. Further, the Court respected the formalities of the PFLLC.** The PFLLC maintained its own bank accounts and held meetings at least annually with written agendas, minutes, and summaries. Third, Mr. Purdue and the decedent transferred the property to the PFLLC. Lastly, the evidence shows that the decedent and Mr. Purdue were in good health at the time they made the transfer to the PFLLC. **(Emphasis added)**

There were other signs of good execution mentioned.

> Since 2001, the Purdue children have held annual meetings in their capacities as trustees and beneficiaries of the PFT and the Purdue Testamentary Trusts, personal representatives and beneficiaries of

the parents' estates, attorneys in fact for the parents, and individual members of the PFLLC. They discussed the Purdue family's accounts and assets, ratified prior PFLLC distributions, approved annual cash distributions, heard presentations from the Rainier Group investment manager, and received estate tax planning updates and advice from Mr. Montgomery.

The IRS also attacked the Crummey gifts arguing that interests in PFLLC were not "gifts of a present interest." The Court did not buy the IRS argument mainly because the LLC was producing income.

First, the PFLLC held an interest in the Hocking Building, subject to a 55-year lease, expected to generate income, as well as dividend-paying marketable securities. Second, the PFT made annual distributions from 2000 through 2008, totaling $1,997,304. Further, the PFLLC operating agreement and applicable state law impose a fiduciary duty on the PFLLC to make proportionate cash distributions sufficient for the QTIP Trust and the Bypass Trust to pay their income tax liabilities. ◊

One of the best ways to create a small fortune is to have a large fortune of appreciated property inside a C corporation, sell the property, and liquidate the corporation. A company called Midcoast purported (remember that word) to help people with that problem. There was something called transferee liability that could get in the way and whether it did or not depended on good execution.

Solid Due Diligence Shields Trucking Heirs from IRS Attack

The Tax Court decision in the case of the John Alterman Trust[3] is one of the best positive examples I have seen of **Reilly's Fourth Law of Tax Planning**

—*"Execution isn't everything, but it's a lot"* in a while. (Negative examples abound.) The Alterman family found itself caught up in the Midco swindle, but the diligence of the family advisers saved them from the fate of others. The decisions have other features of interest; I think it shows the dynamics of the companies whose shareholders ended up having to pay for corporate taxes arising from business shutdowns.

The Problem

Back in the day—the day being before 1987—you could sell the assets of a C corporation without recognizing any gain pursuant to a plan of liquidation. This was known as the General Utilities doctrine[4] named in honor of a 1935 Supreme Court decision, but I had always thought of the rule as a doughty old soldier with an impressive mustache and a riding crop in his hand. The Tax Reform Act of 1986 made other significant changes, but the court-martial of General Utilities was probably what made the biggest impression in the world of closely held companies.

There was now a new recipe for making a small fortune: having a large fortune in appreciated assets inside a C corporation.

I remember devoting feverish study to the Tax Reform Act of 1986. One of the things that came out of that was a project to examine every corporate return done by Joseph Cohan and Associates to see if there were any compelling reasons for them to not make S elections. There were some compelling reasons: net operating loss carryovers, for example. There were also some really stupid reasons like, "They'll never sell the business."

There were very few JBC clients that should have made S elections in 1987 that did not thanks in part to my dogged persistence in challenging the stupid reasons, but the subsequent decades would show that there were many corporations that missed the boat in 1987. They had significantly appreciated assets and the "they will never sell" prediction turned out to be false.

The Solution, Kind Of...

Midcoast Investments (Midco) offered help to companies that were in this pickle. They had their own secret sauce to avoid corporate tax. So, before the year in which selling the assets ended, when the corporation had on its balance sheet only cash and a tax liability, the shareholders would sell stock to Midco at a premium over what the net liquidation would be. In the case of the trust's sale of Alterman Corporation stock, the price was cash in the till less 44.5 percent of the projected corporate tax liability.

About Alterman

The business of the Alterman Corporation commenced in 1938 with the acquisition of a single truck by the eponymous Sidney Alterman. AC was incorporated in 1986 as a holding company for Transport Realty Co. and Alterman Transport Lines which had a subsidiary called Reefer Division. The primary assets were trucks, trailers, and real estate for the terminals. As with all of these decisions, there is no discussion as to why all those assets were in C corporations.

One clue might be that the founder liked to do things his way. I picked up this colorful story about him from a trucking website.

> Sidney just was one tough cookie and probably wouldn't succeed today. The PC police would be on him constantly, and he would be sued constantly. I know that he always had a running battle with the ICC and Florida PSC, he loved defying authority. I remember when there was a federal court order to allow the Teamsters to organize in Miami. Sidney blew a gasket and really launched into a tirade. I told him, "Sidney this is one battle you cannot win, if you ignore that court order, you will go to jail." He said, "Tony, I don't really care."

He died in 2001 at the age of 89. According to his obituary, he built his company to be the second largest carrier of refrigerated "less than truckload" shipments in the nation with 17 terminals and more than 1,400 employees.

He had transitioned management to his son Richard, who gave up an academic career to join the company, but the hit to working capital from having to borrow more than $12 million from the company to pay estate taxes and deteriorating business conditions led to a decision to begin liquidating[5] in late 2002.

The story is a lot like that of Frank Sawyer who shined shoes and sold newspapers to save money to buy his first taxicab, whose company would end up being the largest owner of Boston taxi medallions. After the death of his widow in 2000, the family sold the medallions for about $36 million and availed themselves of a Midco deal to help with the corporate tax problem.

About Midco's Secret Sauce

Midco did not really have a legitimate way to avoid the corporate tax liabilities that they "bought" for 50 cents or so on the dollar. Of course, the people who were selling to Midco would, quite reasonably, adopt the position that was not their problem. The IRS did, however, have a way of making it their problem—transferee liability.

Due Diligence

That the IRS couldn't assert transferee liability against the Alterman family is due to great work on the part of their advisers. The main attorneys that worked for the Altermans on the sale of AC were Robert Barron, Nick Jovanovich, and Sheldon Polish. Their CPA was Jeffrey Lefcourt.

> Mr. Polish understood Midcoast's plan to include[6] "startup phase" write-offs. Midcoast's representatives explained that "over the years that they have been doing this business, that at the time of the acquisition of this, that there were certain things that could be written off in the startup phase of the business that wouldn't be actually worth anything in the future." Then after the initial write-off, the business would begin generating income in the subsequent years and then "they'd have to pay the tax." Mr. Polish, a seasoned and experienced tax lawyer and C.P.A., thought that Midcoast's tax deferral plan "sounded reasonable."

The Altermans' advisers told Midcoast about Diversified's bid. In response, Midcoast in a letter dated September 30, 2003, told the Altermans that Midcoast "has no competitors" and that other transactions were tax shelters. In this letter Midcoast also promised it would provide the Alterman shareholders with a post-closing cash pro forma showing how the new asset recovery business would operate, which it did. Midcoast wrote in this letter that the pro forma financial statement was "based on actual historical experience, as well as industry-wide data." At this point, the Altermans' attorneys did further research into transferee liability and determined that Diversified's offer lacked economic substance and business purpose.

The final share purchase agreement included the following promises by Midcoast:

- Midcoast would not allow AC to dissolve or liquidate for at least four years and had no intention of allowing that after four years either.
- Midcoast would reengineer AC into an asset recovery business.
- Midcoast would ensure that AC invested at least $1,450,000 into delinquent receivables and would reinvest the proceeds into more delinquent receivables for the next 10 years.
- Midcoast would ensure that AC maintained a net worth of at least $1.5 million for at least four years.
- Midcoast would "cause to pay the deferred tax liability to the extent that the deferred tax liability is due given the company's post-closing business activities and shall file all federal and state income tax returns on a timely basis related thereto."
- Midcoast would indemnify the former shareholders against any and all claims, including any damages, losses, deficiencies, liabilities, costs, and expenses resulting from and relating to any "misrepresentation, breach of warranty, or nonfulfillment of any agreement or covenant on the part

of any purchaser under this Agreement."

- Midcoast would represent that the "combined net worth of purchasers exceeds $10,000,000 as of the date hereof and as of the closing date."

You might not be shocked, *shocked* that Midco did not follow through on its representations.

Nick Jovanovich's shock was much more genuine than that of Captain Renault in Casablanca, when he learned that Midco true to its name was, well, a middleman.

> Mr. Jovanovich nearly "fell off the chair" when he heard the news. Mr. Jovanovich testified that the immediate purchase by Sequoia was something with which he "would never associate myself or allow clients to associate themselves with." As noted by Mr. Barron, Sequoia's immediate purchase of AC was "completely opposite of what we were told." Midcoast concealed its intended sale of the AC shares to Sequoia from the Altermans and their advisers, and Midcoast's intent was not reasonably discoverable by the Altermans or their advisers.

Not My Circus, Not My Monkeys

The decision goes on at some length as to why the IRS cannot tag the Alterman's with transferee liability, but the bottom line is extensive due diligence saved them. ◊

In this one, we see what happens when charitable contributions run through an "officer loan" account.

Corporate Advances Kill Individual Charitable Deduction

Larry Zavadil, founder and CEO of American Solutions for Business[7], may have gotten a raw deal from the IRS and the Tax Court on his 2005 charitable contributions and the Eighth Circuit is not cutting him any slack in its decision[8]. There is a useful lesson to accountants in the decision. The lesson is that life is easier if you have everybody pay their own bills. It is really a variation of **Reilly's Fourth Law of Tax Planning**—***"Execution isn't everything, but it's a lot."***

More Month Than Money

Mr. Zavadil founded ASB in 1981 and was the sole owner until 2000 when he sold to an ESOP, remaining, without compensation, as CEO and a member of the board of directors. One of the little benefits he maintained was that the company would pay some of his personal expenses subject to his reimbursing the company. This sort of thing is quite common. Many charts of account will have an "officers' loan account" where expenses for which no plausible business connection is discernible and will have charges. Sometimes the amount converts to salary at year end, depending on the type of entity. In this case, it was a "ledger balance."

The creditors of ASB required that ledger balances zero out at the end of every month. So, Mr. Zavadil wrote a personal check to ASB at the end of every month. Some months, though, his personal account was a little light. The solution to that problem was one that would have given me heartburn.

> At the end of certain months[9] in 2004 and 2005, however, Zavadil's personal bank account had insufficient funds to reimburse American Solutions for the amount recorded on the ledger. For those months, Zavadil and American Solutions employed a system of advances that allowed the ledger to reflect a zero balance at the end of the month. At the end of each month, Zavadil wrote a personal check to the company, and the company brought the ledger balance

> to zero. At the beginning of the next month, however, American Solutions advanced funds to Zavadil's personal bank account to cover some or all of the amount of the check, recorded the advance as an expense on the ledger, and then cashed the personal check received at the end of the previous month.

I'm not certain it would be accurate to describe this practice as kiting[10], but it certainly has some of the attributes of that practice.

Who Really Made the Contribution?

Rather than being exceptional, the practice of a month beginning advance to cover the check that had represented the month end repayment became the rule with advances following repayments for all the months in the second half of 2005. So, the Tax Court ruled the Zavadils could not deduct charitable contributions run through the ledger account during that period.

> As relevant to this appeal, the tax court ruled in favor of the Zavadils[11] on charitable contributions made prior to July 2005, ruling that they were deductible because Zavadil reimbursed American Solutions for those contributions and thus bore the economic burden. The tax court, however, disallowed charitable deductions made from July 2005 through December 2005, because the Zavadils did not demonstrate that they—not American Solutions—bore the economic burden of those contributions. Because the record did not establish that Zavadil bore the economic burden of paying the entire ledger balance in any of those months, the court found that the Zavadils failed to prove "what portion, if any, of the charitable contributions made after June 2005 Mr. Zavadil effectively paid with his own funds and not funds advanced by [American Solutions]." The court also found no evidence that the ledger account balance at the end of 2005 represented Zavadil's bona fide indebtedness.

The final sentence is telling. It is not out of the question that properly executed notes would have salvaged the situation for Mr. Zavadil.

However, as noted, the Eighth Circuit was not inclined to cut Mr. Zavadil a break. It maintained:

> [t]hat Zavadil repaid all funds in the first half of 2005 did not necessarily show that he was obliged to do so, especially when there was no evidence that he did so in the second half. The court permissibly declined to accept accountant Carlson's testimony, given that the system of advances undermined the claim that Zavadil actually repaid the company in full at the end of every month. The requirement imposed by creditors that the company show a zero-ledger balance at the end of each month did not exclude the possibility that American Solutions nonetheless bore the economic burden by reimbursing Zavadil for some or all of his end-of-month payments through advances at the beginning of the next month. And the company's obligation to make installment payments to Zavadil in exchange for his sale of the company does not establish that Zavadil was required to repay the advances. Zavadil points to no evidence that the company deducted the advances from its installment payments on the note, or that the note was designated as collateral for the advances. It was not clear error for the tax court to find Zavadil's evidence wanting.

The Moral

The other moral of this story might be, "Oh what a tangled web we weave, when first we practice to deceive." That work-around in order to show the zero-ledger balance might have been not so bad to do just once, but once it became a habit, it was bound to create trouble. Accountants tend to think they can create reality by what accounts they charge things to, but a lot of case law indicates that the courts do not think the accountant's pencil is that mighty an instrument. It really is much more prudent to have a clean transaction trail with deductible items paid directly by the person or entity deducting them. ◊

Establishing basis and at-risk is also a matter of having all your ducks in a row.

Florida Man Runs Afoul of IRS Basis Rules for S Corporations

You will rarely see a better illustration of **Reilly's Fourth Law of Tax Planning**, than the Tax Court's decision in the case of William and Amaryllis Tinsley. The Tinsleys were hoping to post a good-sized negative number ($110,480) from their S Corporation (Command Computers of West Florida Inc.) on their individual return. The court disallowed the loss because of lack of basis. The Tinsleys thought they had solved the problem of basis. Maybe they had in some sense, but not to the satisfaction of the Tax Court.

Jumping Through the Hoops

> As I explain here[12], to post a negative number to the front page of your Form 1040, you have to jump through a series of hoops. The business generating the loss must be a real business, and the loss has to be properly allocable to you. You have to have sufficient basis[13], be "at-risk" and satisfy the passive activity loss rules—in that order.

Command Computers financed its money-losing activities with a loan guaranteed by Mr. Tinsley. A reasonable person might argue that Mr. Tinsley was thereby "at-risk" for the borrowing. (There is a technical problem with that argument.) It really does not matter, though. The basis hoop comes before the "at-risk" hoop. And, unlike partnerships or single-member LLCs, the obligations of S corporations do not provide basis to S corporation shareholders.

But What Happens When You Liquidate?

We know that Tinsley suspended the losses of Command Computers because of loss of basis, but what happens when the company liquidates, and Mr. Tinsley becomes personally liable on the debt? The Tax Court indicated that could create the basis that would free up the loss.

> ...the Court of Appeals held that a shareholder's guaranty of a loan to an S corporation "may be treated for tax purposes as an equity investment in the corporation where the lender looks to the shareholder as the primary obligor."

And that is what Mr. Tinsley claims happened at the end of 2010. Command Computers liquidated, making him personally liable.

Only You Have to Prove It

This is where the execution problems come in. The business continued to operate under the name Command Computers, and when the bank renewed the note in 2011, it did so in the name of Command Computers. Mr. Tinsley argued that it was merely a matter of administrative convenience. That argument went nowhere.

> There is insufficient evidence[14] in the record to permit us to make, with confidence, a finding that in both 2006 and 2011 the loan was made to Mr. Tinsley personally, as opposed to Command Computers, and that Mr. Tinsley, as the borrower, advanced the loan proceeds to Command Computers. Because petitioners failed to establish that the bank looked primarily to Mr. Tinsley to satisfy the debt obligation or that Mr. Tinsley made an economic outlay with respect to the loan, they failed to prove they had a basis in Command Computers as of December 31, 2010, sufficient for them to deduct the reported business losses.

A detail that is worth noting that was not in the decision is that Command Computers of West Florida is on the record as having been administratively dissolved for not filing its annual report. The effective date[15] of the dissolution is September 23, 2011. I believe it is a common practice to not do a formal filing for a liquidation and just let non-filing take care of the matter, but here we see that could be an expensive way of saving legal work. It is also worth noting that the Tinsleys were representing themselves in Tax Court.

The Moral

If you are starting a business and have income that initial losses might shelter, you are probably better off starting out as a limited liability company, which will be a partnership or disregarded. This should avoid most basis and at-risk problems. Consider becoming an S corporation, which can save you a bit of self-employment tax after you have achieved consistent profitability. That and try to get your documentary ducks in a row. Execution is not everything, but it is a lot. ◊

IRA Withdrawal Penalty a Cost of Do-It-Yourself Divorce

In the tax aspects of divorce from Tax Court Memo Decision 2017-125[16] is an illustration of **Reilly's Fourth Law of Tax Planning—*"Execution isn't everything, but it's a lot."*** The name of the petitioner is there for you if you want to know, but I figure he does not need me to help make him famous. I'll call him Robin and his wife Terry, my favorite mythical couple.

Robin got a pat on the head from the Tax Court and even a tad of sympathy from the IRS, but he is still going to have to pay the $1,738 early withdrawal penalty that the IRS hit him with on his IRA distribution.

Robin wanted to save money on legal fees. He may well have on net, but that early withdrawal penalty really hurts. Here is what happened. Robin and Terry had four children. They considered their marriage irretrievable but wanted to minimize difficulties for the kids. As Judge Lauber puts it:

> To their credit they were determined to do this in the least acrimonious manner possible. And to minimize costs they decided to accomplish their divorce without involving lawyers.

They reached agreement on child custody, visitation rights, child support, spousal maintenance, and division of property. Robin filed a petition for dissolution that incorporated the agreements. Among the assets was an IRA account with about $17,000.

As these matters were working out, Terry had debts. Robin cleaned out the IRA withdrawing $17,378. He used $8618 to pay down Terry's car loan. Subsequently, he sent her $71 to true-up. I have to say I admire that kind of precision.

A couple of months later the court entered a consent decree for the dissolution of the marriage incorporating the agreements that Robin and Terry made. Since the IRA account was empty, there was no mention of it. Robin reported the $17,378 on his return but did not report any "additional tax" on line 58. The custodian of course, ratted him out, by sending a 1099 to the IRS with "early distribution, no known exception" indicated.

The IRS admitted that with respect to the portion that had gone to Terry, he could have structured things to avoid the penalty under Section 72(t)(2)(C) ("Payments to alternate payees pursuant to qualified domestic relations orders"). Woulda, coulda, shoulda. Robin failed to meet the exception for two reasons. Terry did not receive the money directly, and as it worked out there was no QDRO.

> [T]he distribution was not made "pursuant to a qualified domestic relations order." Although Robin's petition for dissolution of marriage requested a 50-50 division of the IRA, any judicial action on that request was pretermitted by his well-intentioned decision to divide the IRA with Terry a month before the divorce decree. That decree accordingly recited that "either party has a retirement, pension, deferred compensation, Section 401(k) plan and/or benefits." The

IRA distribution was not made "pursuant to" that order or any other judicial decree.

Believe it or not, my spell-checker, to the contrary notwithstanding, "pretermit" is a word. It means "omit to do or mention." Here I am, 65 years old and still improving my vocabulary.

Poor Robin got the, "You are a mensch, but we are still dinging you," treatment from the Tax Court.

"We have considerable sympathy for petitioner's position: In effect, his willingness to help minimize stress on his soon-to-be ex-wife disabled him from satisfying the statutory requirements. But we are not at liberty to add equitable exceptions to the statutory scheme that Congress enacted, and we thus have no alternative but to sustain the 10 percent additional tax that respondent has determined."

So, this is also an instance of **Reilly's First Law of Tax Planning—"*It is what it is. Deal with it.*"** ◊

Nobody cares about journal entries except accountants.

Do Not Try to Create Tax Basis with Journal Entries

Companies should pay their own bills[17]. That is probably the real lesson to be learned from the Eleventh Circuit[18] upholding of the Tax Court decision in the case of developer Homero Meruelo. The stakes were high, a deficiency over $2.6 million. The controversy was about the scintillating topic of S corporation stock basis. We will start with a brief primer the professionals may want to skip.

About Basis

Basis is a fundamental[19] tax and accounting concept. When you sell something, you pay tax not on gross receipts but on your gain, which is the amount received less basis. And if you are eligible for a deduction because something becomes worthless, your loss will usually be your basis.

The simplest situation is when you obtain something by paying money for it. Your basis, at least to start off, will be the amount of money you pay for it. That is the case with S corporation stock that you buy. If you are a founder, your basis will be your initial capital contribution. From there it starts getting complicated.

S Corporations

S corporations don't pay tax on their income. The income passes through to the shareholders increasing stock basis. Additional capital contributions will also increase basis. Losses that flow through will decrease basis as will distributions.

Here we have another complication and the problem that Meruelo ran into. Basis in S corporation stock never goes below zero. A loss that would run basis below zero is suspended. Meruelo was a 49 percent shareholder of Merco of the Palm Beaches Inc. (Merco). In 2008, Merco had a loss of $27 million. That loss wiped out Meruelo's income from other S corporations and created a carryback to 2005.

The IRS is only allowing about $5 million of the $13 million loss allocable to Merulo, because that is what it determined Meruelo's basis in the Merco stock to be, but there is more. A flow-through loss from an S corporation can also reduce the basis in the corporation's indebtedness to the shareholder and according to Meruelo's accountant, Merco owed enough to Meruelo to absorb the loss.

The problem was that there was not a straightforward transfer of cash from Meruelo to Merco, supported by a promissory note from the corporation to the shareholder.

A Complicated Schedule

It turns out that Merco was one of a family of companies that Meruelo had an interest in. And despite the disparate ownership, the companies supported one another when it came time to pay the bills.

> From 2004 to 2008, Merco entered into hundreds of transactions with various partnerships, S corporations, and limited liability companies in which Meruelo held an interest. These Merco affiliates often paid expenses, such as payroll costs, for each other or for Merco to simplify accounting and enhance liquidity. The payor company recorded these payments to its affiliates as accounts receivable, and the payee company recorded them as accounts payable.

The accountant who prepared all the returns then went through a process that only another accountant could love. There was a line of credit promissory note from Meruelo for $10,000,000 at 6 percent interest. A schedule was prepared showing his share of each of the intercompany balances effectively treating the transactions as if the advancing entities had loaned the money to Meruelo who then loaned to Merco thereby giving him indebtedness basis to prevent the loss from suspension.

The Arguments

There are two theories under which this sort of thing might work. One is "back-to-back loans," and the other is "incorporated pocket-book."

"Back-to-back loans" fail because the taxpayer is stuck with the form of the transaction, which the taxpayer controls. And the form of the transaction was transfers among the companies not transfers to the shareholder who then transferred to the company.

> Because the transactions were contemporaneously classified as transactions between the affiliates and Merco, the designation Meruelo's accountant gave them at the end of the year does not govern.

The "incorporated pocket-book" theory did not work, because there were multiple companies making advances and Meruelo did not own 100 percent of all of them.

> Meruelo failed to establish that the Merco affiliates constituted his incorporated pocketbook. Unlike the shareholders in Yates and Culnen—who used a single, wholly owned entity to pay third parties on the shareholder's behalf—Meruelo seeks to treat eleven distinct Merco affiliates, many of which he only partially owned, as his incorporated pocketbook.

The Lesson

The lesson is a discouraging one for accountants. I went digging in PACER and found the schedule that Meruelo's accountant prepared, and they are really good work. A good bit of effort must have gone into them. But they end up meaning nothing.

Those of us who think in double entry might believe that Meruelo should have gotten his basis and the loss. Throughout most of my career, I would have thought there was no problem. But years of reading decisions like this have caused me to conclude that the only people impressed by an accountant's entries are other accountants.[20]

Reilly's Fourth Law of Tax Planning—"*Execution isn't everything, but it's a lot.*" Here we have an exception. Execution was everything. If the money that Meruelo loaned to Merco had actually passed through his hands and had a record as a loan or a distribution to him, he would have had his basis and his loss.

One of the sad realities of public accounting is that meticulous close attention is not what brings people to the top. We are supposed to be entrepreneurial and develop sales personalities. That is all well and good as far as it goes, but we still need to cherish the nose to the grindstone people if we want to keep our clients out of trouble. ◊

Footnotes

1. "USS Comfort (II) (AH-6)," NavSource Online, last modified August 9, 2019, http://www.navsource.org/archives/09/12/1206.htm.
2. Montgomery Purdue, accessed May 27, 2023, https://www.montgomerypurdue.com/#1.
3. John M. Alterman Trust v. Commissioner of Internal Revenue, United States Tax Court (No. 6936-10), December 1, 2015, https://casetext.com/case/john-m-alterman-trust-v-commr.
4. Andrew Mitchell, No Gain on In-Kind Corporate Distributions (Centerbrook: Andrew Mitchell LLC, 2006), https://www.andrewmitchel.com/charts/general_utilities.pdf.
5. "Class A Drivers," accessed May 27, 2023, https://www.classadrivers.com/.
6. John M. Alterman Trust v. Commissioner of Internal Revenue.
7. "History & Mission," American Solutions for Business, accessed May 27, 2023, https://home.americanbus.com/ABOUT/HistoryMission.aspx.
8. Larry Zavadil and Diane Zavadil v. Commissioner of Internal Revenue, United States Court of Appeal (No. 14-1053), July 16, 2015, https://caselaw.findlaw.com/court/us-8th-circuit/1707971.html.
9. Zavadil v. Commissioner of Internal Revenue.
10. "Check kiting," Wikipedia, last modified May 1, 2023, https://en.wikipedia.org/wiki/Check_kiting.
11. Zavadil v. Commissioner of Internal Revenue.
12. William Reilly, "Through the Hoops," Your Tax Matters Partner (blog), last modified June 17, 2014, http://ytmp.blogspot.com/2014/06/through-hoops.html.
13. "What Is Basis And Why It Is Important," Your Tax Matters Partner (blog), accessed May 27, 2023, http://ytmp.blogspot.com/p/what-is-basis-and-why-it-is-important.html.
14. William H. Tinsley and Amaryllis E. Tinsley v. Commissioner of Internal Revenue, United States Tax Court (No. 6698-14S), February 28, 2017, https://www.courtlistener.com/opinion/4563355/william-h-tinsley-amaryllis-e-tinsley-v-commissioner/.

15. "Detail by Entity Name - Florida Profit Corporation Command Computers of West Florida, Inc.," Divison of Corporations, accessed May 27, 2023, http://search.sunbiz.org/Inquiry/CorporationSearch/SearchResultDetail?inquirytype=EntityName&directionType=Initial&searchNameOrder=COMMANDCOMPUTERSWESTFLORIDA%20P060000417970&aggregateId=domp-p06000041797-6a72536b-93a6-4688-9209-b6cc76b6bdd5&searchTerm=COMMANDCOMPUTERSWESTFLORIDA&listNameOrder=COMMANDCOMPUTERSWESTFLORIDA%20P060000417970

16. Jeremy Ray Summers v. Commissioner of Internal Revenue, United States Tax Court (No. 32259-15), June 26, 2017, https://casetext.com/case/summers-v-commr-3.

17. Peter J. Reilly, "Don't Try To Create Tax Basis With Journal Entries," Forbes, last modified May 21, 2019, https://www.forbes.com/sites/peterjreilly/2019/05/21/dont-try-to-create-tax-basis-with-journal-entries/?subId3=xid:fr1593549025753cjb.

18. Homero F. Meruelo v. Commissioner of Internal Revenue, United States of Appeals (No. 18-11909), May 6, 2019, https://media.ca11.uscourts.gov/opinions/pub/files/201811909.pdf.

19. "What Is Basis And Why It Is Important."

20. Reilly, "Don't Try To Create Tax Basis With Journal Entries."

A Tax Plan That Ignores AMT or SALT is Not Much of a Tax Plan.

When I was working for a national firm, I always felt sad for the SALT people. They came after the federal tax people who came in after the auditors. Usually, they bore unwelcome news. If you have your head caught up in federal regular taxes issues, there can be some nasty surprises coming from state and local.

If you invest in an LLC (Limited Liability Company), you probably think your liability is, you know, limited. When it comes to sales tax in New York maybe not so much.

New York Springs Sales Tax Trap on Passive LLC Members

The limited liability company has been the entity of choice for many for quite a while. A domestic limited liability corporation is taxed as a partnership unless it elects to be a corporation. Generally, if you are not working in the business and trying to beat SE tax, an entity taxed as a partnership is a better deal than an S corporation. Among the reasons are that not just anybody can be an S corporation shareholder, income allocation rules are rigid, and S corporation shareholders do not get basis from their share of the corporation's liabilities.

Of course, if it turned out that the limited liability of the LLC was not so limited, people might start taking another look at that entity choice. A decision by the State of New York Division of Tax Appeals[1] in the case of Eugene Boissiere and Jason Krystal might give investors pause as to the exposure they might take on by becoming LLC members—at least when they are investing in cash businesses in New York.

Tim Noonan of Hodgson Russ[2] represented the taxpayers in this case. Tim told me that the underlying business of Ask 244 LLC was a night spot on West 14th Street in Manhattan called The Plumm. According to this story[3], the Plumm closed in April 2009. New York assessed Ask 244 sales and use tax for the period June 1, 2004, through May 31, 2009, in the amount of $735,899.91. Then, there was an unusual turn. Both Eugene Boissiere and Jason Krystal have assessed a total of $429,014.06 on November 15, 2010, for Ask 244's sales and use tax for the period September 1, 2007, through May 31, 2009. The dates make me think that was what was open on the statute when the state decided to start chasing them for the tax.

Mr. Boissiere had a 14.9044 percent membership interest in the LLC and Mr. Krystal's was 13.522 percent. After some negotiating the revenue department agreed to just chase them for "their share," $20,202.81 from Mr. Boissiere and $18,510.42 from Mr. Krystal. What, to me, is very unusual about this case is that it is not a "responsible person" case. "Everybody" knows that if you are in charge of paying bills and you pay money withheld for taxes to vendors and the like, you can be required to pay the withholding. Those cases tend to be rather fact-intensive and get into the fine points of how much authority the "responsible person" actually had and how much they knew and when they knew it. None of those issues matter in this case.

Neither Mr. Boissiere nor Mr. Krystal had managerial responsibility, the ability to hire and fire employees, knowledge of or control over the LLC's finances, or the authority to sign returns. They did not participate in the audit of the LLC and did not know how the auditor computed the tax. The assessment depended purely on their membership. By statute, the state could have assessed each for the whole tax, as they were initially, but the Department of Taxation and Finance issued a policy statement[4] in 2011 that recognized that the 100 percent liability can result in:

> … unfortunate consequences for certain partner and members who have no involvement or control of the business's affairs.

You think?

It Is What It Is

Mr. Boissiere and Mr. Krystal tried to argue that the tax statute contradicted the statutes governing limited liability companies. The argument went nowhere; Administrative Law Judge Arthur Bray found the statute clear and unambiguous.

> Having chosen to proceed as members of an LLC, petitioners must accept the consequences of their choice of business organization.

The judge there is, unwittingly, restating **Reilly's First Law of Tax Planning—"*It is what it is. Deal with it.*"**

How Aware Are People of This?

I have not found any coverage of this case, so I went looking for coverage of this trap that members of New York LLCs face. I found this article in the *New York Law Journal* by Timothy Lewis.[5]

Tim Noonan said there was a flurry of this type of activity by New York—i.e., chasing passive investors for sales tax—a couple of years ago, which seems to have subsided to some extent. Nonetheless, the law has not changed so that passive investors in businesses with significant sales tax exposure such as restaurants and bars need to be extremely cautious about getting involved as LLC members or limited partners, because, by statute, their liability has no limitations when it comes to sales tax. Tim did not think that investors had any idea they were taking on this type of exposure when they signed up. Brian Gordon of Sanders Thaler Viola & Katz agrees that the sales tax exposure should incline investors in New York restaurants and bars to favor S corporations.

If the only thing you have to consider is federal income tax, entity choice can still be a fairly complicated matter. This case shows that there are other issues that can sneak up on you that have nothing to do with federal income tax. Robert Redford was in the news about a New York state income tax issue that turned on someone not being aware of how having an S corporation in the chain of ownership affected allocations. Something tells me that when the decision to organize Ask 244 as an LLC rather than an S corporation, nobody was thinking about personal liability of members for sales tax. ◊

It can come as a surprise to people that they might be a resident of more than one state.

What Happens When You Are a Full-Year Resident of More Than One State

The challenge of Samuel and Louise Edelman to the state of New York is a protest against double taxation. I covered it here a while ago[6], and even came up with a workaround for people in their situation. I had a nice talk with Tom Corrie of Friedman LLP[7]. He directs Friedman's State and Local Tax Group (SALT). He threw cold water on my workaround and had other great observations. I also have some more reflections on the issues.

The Issue

The beef that the Edelmans have is that they had to pay both Connecticut and New York income tax on the gain from the sale of their business (and probably other income). They live in Connecticut, which is where their domicile (their true home) is. However, they also had an apartment in Manhattan in the years in question. That "place of abode," along with being in New York for at least a part of a day for more than 183 calendar days, made them statutory residents.

Had they worked in Boston with a place in the North End, they'd be statutory residents of Massachusetts. But it would have been much less onerous, not only because Massachusetts has a lower rate, but also because of a 1996 multi-state agreement, to the effect that the state of statutory residence should credit taxes paid to the state of domicile on income not sourced to the statutory resident state.

The New York legislature did not follow through on the agreement, because, I guess, it is New York. If you make it there, they will take it there, and if you are a statutory resident, they will take it from everywhere.

My Solution

I put myself in the shoes of the Edelmans and thought about what I would do if I lived in, say, Greenwich, Connecticut, and worked in Manhattan and wanted to have a place to stay over but did not want to be a New York statutory resident.

I would get a waterfront apartment in Jersey City. You have the ferry that will take you to either the financial section or Midtown. You have the PATH train, and if you must drive, you are close to the Holland Tunnel. I was inspired, in part, by my covivant and I capping off our four-month RV tour of the Southeast with a stay in Liberty Harbor RV Park.[8]

Mr. Corrie told me that sort of thing is a nonstarter. There is this certain cachet to having an apartment in Manhattan, and despite the relative convenience, Jersey City does not cut it. That confirms a similar sentiment I got from an attorney on Twitter. That fellow tends to think that most of the people caught as statutory residents actually domicile in New York. And in a way, the notion that being on the opposite side of a not very wide river makes such a big difference is evidence of that.

Get Help

Mr. Corrie indicated that it is not that unusual for people to feel blindsided by the statutory resident rule and other subtleties and special issues that are peculiar to New York. If you are dealing with significant dollars, you really need someone on your team who can get into the New York weeds. And practitioners with just a couple of New York clients should be sure to get help from someone with strong expertise. This is true of every state with an income tax, but New York has more nasty surprises than most of them. Except for New Hampshire. Do not get me started.

Then, There Is Domicile

New York is one of the states that will fight hard to hang onto somebody who wants to escape its clutches. Mr. Corrie referred me to the Nonresident Audit Guidelines[9] to get a sense of what is going on. The problem with domicile is that it is an almost mystical concept. In a domicile argument with a state, a state that you are claiming to leave has a presumption in its favor. If you are new to the state, the presumption favors you.

A lot of people focus on things like voter registration, car registration, and driver's licenses.[10] That is wise since failure in that area will hurt you, but those are secondary factors to the auditor. The primary factors are home, active business involvement, time, items near and dear, and family connections. "Items near and dear" is my favorite. A good example of that is your pet.[11] I was pleased to see that the manual included book collections. That is definitely one of the things that keep my distant condo my home rather than the RV that we are roaming the country in.

The idea of a domicile is becoming obsolete. It is based on intent, but of course, actions are the evidence. Here is how the guide puts it.

> The actual process of ascertaining an individual's intentions regarding domicile, the crucial question in a residency audit, is a subjective inquiry for the auditor and often a difficult one. How does one determine what was in a taxpayer's mind?

It is worse than that. I think quite a few people with multiple residences really don't have one that is predominant, and if the auditor examines the evidence of their actions, it will be possible to craft different narratives.

And if someone can afford to take on the trappings of two different domicile identities, sophisticated New Yorker and Connecticut Yankee or whatever, maybe it is fair they pay full tax to each state. Manhattan has much infrastructure to support. If you want to make out you're a New Yorker, pay up. ◊

How the payment of state income taxes by trusts can become optional.

How Wealth Accumulators Can Use Trusts to Avoid State Income Tax

"Put not your trust in money, but put your money in trust"[12] comes from the *Autocrat of the Breakfast Table* by Oliver Wendell Holmes Sr. The context was advice to young women about to be married and is probably reflective of the legal concept of coverture, which put the property and earnings of a married woman under the control of her husband. The law was changing in that regard even in 1858 when Holmes penned the advice, but the advantages of putting your money in trust have multiplied since then.

We now have a new social group—trustafarians—created by the forethought of previous generations putting their money in trust. The Urban Dictionary defines them as:

> Privileged white kids who subscribe to the hippie lifestyle (because they can) since they have no worries about money, a job, etc. They can then devote their lives to eating organic, following Phish, and wearing dreadlocks (no need for job interviews).

A Victory for the Trustafarians

And the Supreme Court handed a victory to tomorrow's trustafarians in North Carolina Department of Revenue v Kimberly Rice Kaestner

1992 Family Trust.[13] For the very wealthy, trust arrangements can make the payment of state income taxes largely optional. As an individual, it can be extremely challenging to establish domicile in a tax-free state and avoid being a statutory resident. Accomplishing this with a trust requires professional expertise, but you can hire an expert and that won't affect your day-to-day life.

I got some great feedback about the decision from people at the international law firm Withers.[14] Withers had filed an amicus brief on behalf of organizations representing professional trustees, bankers, and attorneys in South Dakota, New Hampshire, Delaware, Nevada, and Tennessee.

The lawyers at Withers like the decision, which, of course, went the way they recommended and have some pro tips I will share, but the overall practical takeaway is that you need really sharp legal work with a national, if not international perspective to take advantage of the favorable state income tax treatment of trusts. And you will need to be alert or more likely to pay somebody to stay alert to avoid nasty surprises.

Why This Is Not Such a Great Thing

The state income tax treatment of trusts that can afford and benefit from the counsel of firms like Withers is one of those things that fuel inequality. One of the biggest differences between the very wealthy and even the quite prosperous is that the very wealthy don't spend all or even most of their income to live. Another big difference is that most of the income of the non-wealthy comes from working. If you have income generated by the wealth that you don't need to spend to live on, sharp trust legal work can avoid state income tax on that income regardless of where you live.

The benefit goes not to today's trustafarians who are living in Williamsburg. They might end up paying through the nose on their distributions if they come out of trust income. It is their children and grandchildren whom the state tax-free accumulations will support. Regardless, that is why I see this decision as not such a great thing, but rather as one more brick in the wall that the new American gentry is building .[15]

How Does It Work?

Now that I have gotten my inner anarchist out of my system, let's look at the practical points.

To grossly oversimplify, trusts don't get a really good deal for federal income tax purposes. If they have certain attributes, they are "grantor trusts." They are disregarded, and what they do hits an individual's return like a single-member LLC, or they may be mere title holding devices that they altogether ignore. And some things called trusts are corporations for tax purposes.

There are, however, entities called trusts that are taxed as entities. They must file Form 1041.[16] Doing Form 1041 correctly for a trust that has a decent amount of stuff going on is beyond most tax preparers. Fortunately, nobody seems to care much that a large percentage, perhaps the majority, of 1041s are wrong[17]. It usually does not matter that much.

Again, oversimplifying for federal tax purposes, a trust's taxes are much like an individual's with a less generous rate table and smaller exemptions. That's the whole deal if the trust is just accumulating income. If the trust makes distributions, it can, with all sorts of limitations and special rules, deduct those distributions from its taxable income. Then the beneficiary who received the distribution has taxable income, reported on a K-1, much like a partnership or an S corporation.

The Trust Triad

The Withers amicus brief refers to the trust triad, settlor, trustee, and beneficiary. Let's say the Tommy Atkins Fantasy Family Trust has a million in interest income. Tom is the settlor. His friend Richard is the trustee. And Tom's son Harry is the beneficiary. Depending on the terms of the trust and actions Dick takes, someone will report that whole million dollars for federal income tax purposes by some combination of Tom, Dick (in his capacity as trustee), and Harry.

When it comes to state income taxes, it is a different story. Assume that Tom, Dick, and Harry all live in states with state income taxes—three different states. Let's also assume that Tom has made the trust irrevocable and has not retained any of the powers that would make it a grantor trust. If Dick distributes to Harry and deducts the distribution, Harry will have state taxable income on the distribution. (There might be an exception to that, but I don't know of any.)

The interesting question is what happens if Dick does not make a distribution. If the million is the only thing going on, Dick will pay, out of trust assets, federal income tax. And what about state income taxes?

State Income Tax—Who Pays? If Anybody

North Carolina wanted to tax the trust merely because the beneficiaries lived there. The Supreme Court has now ruled that is not enough at least in the case of a trust that is wholly discretionary. What about the state where the trustee is? Well, you will probably find a state that will not tax on that basis, because the states are competing for trustee business. That was the biggest takeaway from my discussion with William Kambas[18]. Then, there is the state where Tom was living when the trust became irrevocable.

In 2014, I wrote[19] about a trust that traced to an Illinois trust A.N. Pritzker funded in 1961. The trust in question had A.N.'s granddaughter Linda as its primary beneficiary. The trustee relocated it in Texas. (That is a simplification.) The remaining tenuous connection to Illinois was not enough to allow Illinois to tax the trust.

Mr. Kambas had something to say on that:

> For those looking for what will happen for taxing regimes not addressed by Kaestner[20], the focus should now be on the case of Bauerly v. Fielding, which has a pending petition as of today. This is a case where the state is seeking to levy an income tax on trusts based primarily on the fact that the settlor domiciled in Minnesota when the trusts became irrevocable. This is a second case where there is potentially only a "single factor" that could establish nexus between the state and the trust.

Let the Games Continue

How to tax trusts for income tax purposes is a matter that screams out for a simple uniform rule. (I have no idea what that rule would be.) Mr. Kambas does not see that happening anytime soon.

Instead, states have rules based on the trust triad in various degrees. Massachusetts will consider a trust resident if it has a Massachusetts settlor and a Massachusetts trustee. So, switch to a Connecticut trustee. Connecticut does not consider the residence of either trustees or beneficiaries.

Thanks to the Supreme Court decision, a Massachusetts settlor can set up a trust with a Connecticut trustee, and the only way any state can tax any of its income is if the trust does business in that state or distributes to a beneficiary in that state. Throw in that capital gains are generally not distributable income.

A Caveat

The Kaestner Trust was a discretionary trust. The discretion is with the trustee. What that means is that if you set up a trust with a view to having your beneficiaries taken care of, you have to select somebody that you can, you know, trust. Giving the beneficiaries rights to demand distributions may create enough nexus to allow a state to tax the trust. At least, that seems to be the concern.

Other Withers Comments

David Lehn[21] sees the decision as confirming a general belief.

> Historic jurisprudence remains the same. Confidence retained. The Court (both the majority and concurrence) were clear that historic cases supported the conclusion that mere presence of a discretionary beneficiary is not sufficient to meet constitutional standards for state income tax nexus.

James Dougherty emphasizes why you don't want to just download a trust form from a free internet site if you want it to work.

> Careful drafting. One important takeaway is that absolute discretion trusts bring real advantages. Often absolute discretion standards are touted for the creditor protection and flexibility they provide. Today's decision highlights that it also limits the ability of a state to claim there is nexus over the trust for tax purposes. If there was an enforceable right, such as under a HEMS standard, this case could have turned out differently.

Ivory Tower

The oddest thing to me about Justice Sonia Sotomayer's decision is what I see as stunning naïveté.

> Finally, the State urges that adopting the Trust's position will lead to opportunistic gaming of state tax systems. There is no certainty, however, that such behavior will regularly come to pass, and in any event, mere speculation about negative consequences cannot conjure the "minimum connection" missing between the State and the object of its tax.

I would be inclined to replace "certainty" with "doubt" in that sentence.

About Trust Lawyers

When you are talking about large wealth, there are, of course, a great number of non tax considerations, but I can't help you much there other than to tell you what I know based on what I have observed throughout my career, which is that it is about 50-50 whether inheritance is good or bad for people, which is a little demoralizing for estate planning.

As to the lawyers who work on these issues, I would observe that there is a danger that they can get into ruts. They may only know the state they practice in. That narrows your options. Also planning in this area tends to focus on transfer taxes, which is really big money for large estates, but not something that happens every year. Income tax planning can get short shrift sometimes, or it's possible to overlook the income tax implications of estate planning techniques.

Finally, state income taxes tend to be at the bottom of the list. The money is not as big, but it looks to me that trusts that pay substantial state income tax might likely be missing out on savings opportunities. If a trust is paying substantial state income taxes, particularly in light of Kaestner, take a close look at the planning. ◊

Just because your organization qualifies as a federal exempt organization does not mean that you will get state and local benefits.

Pennsylvania Court Denies Property Tax Exemption to Another Religious Camp

501(c)(3) status confers several benefits on an organization, including, for example, the ability of donors to deduct charitable contributions. Recognition under 501(c)(3) does not, however, automatically confer exemption from local property taxes, even for property used for the organization's exempt purpose. The recent decision by the Commonwealth Court of Pennsylvania in Camp Hachshara Moshava of New York v. Wayne County[22] illustrates this well.

Despite its corporate name, Camp Moshava[23] is in Pennsylvania, although its office is in New York. Founded in 1936, its current location is in Wayne County since 1969. Here is its mission:

> Camp Moshava aims to educate all members of its camping community to make Aliyah and to establish a model society in Eretz Yisrael, which will serve as an Or La Goyim. At the heart of this endeavor is Bnei Akiva's[24] ideology of Torah Va'Avodah and Religious Zionism. Permeating all aspects of camp life, Torah Va'Avodah[25] emphasizes the importance of interpersonal relations, social justice, and contributing to community within the framework of Torah and Halacha. Camp Moshava will support and inspire the social,

> emotional, intellectual, and religious growth of its members within a fun camping environment.
>
> Camp Moshava is a religious Zionist camp sponsored by Bnei Akiva of the U.S. and Canada for the purpose of furthering the educational and ideological goals of Bnei Akiva.

According to its 2010 Form 990, it runs on about $4 million per year, almost entirely fees from the camp, with less than $200,000 per year in contributions. The only paid board member Alan Silverman, Camp Director, drew a salary of $192,500 in 2010 for his average 80-hour work week. The organization seems to have been roughly breaking even for the past few years. Somebody must have raised some money at some time in the past, as the $7 million in net book value of property on the assets side is matched mainly by net worth and an unsecured note of $1.5 million. DDK & Company prepared Form 990, and Mr. Silverman signed it.

Under the Pennsylvania Constitution, for an organization to qualify for property tax exemption, it must be an "institution of purely public charity." The term, at the time, was undefined in the Constitution, but the Pennsylvania Supreme Court has ruled that an "institution of purely public charity" does all of the following:

(a) Advances a charitable purpose;

(b) Donates or renders gratuitously a substantial portion of its services;

(c) Benefits a substantial and indefinite class of persons who are legitimate subjects of charity;

(d) **Relieves the government of some of its burden;**

(e) Operates entirely free from private profit motive.

Qualifying under 501(c)(3) is much less challenging. Glossing over a variety of technical points, the first and last items on the list are sufficient for 501(c)(3) status. Since failure on any of the points denies the property tax exemption, the focus on the case was whether Camp Moshava relieves the government of some of its burden. As noted, the Camp provided extensive assistance to local firefighters:

> Specifically, Camp Moshava allows an ambulance to be stored on its premises and owns its own fire truck, which is available for use by firefighters in the community. Camp Moshava also provides its facilities to the local volunteer firefighting company and other firefighting companies for the purpose of staging training exercises.

That did not do the trick, though, because it is unrelated to the core mission of running a summer camp.

There is one issue that Moshava raised that I found rather intriguing, although as usual beyond my investigative resources:

> Camp Moshava's final argument is that the trial court and the Board have inconsistently applied the eligibility standards for charitable tax exemption contrary to the uniformity clause of the Pennsylvania Constitution and the express purposes stated in section 2 of Act 55. In support, Camp Moshava contends that the Board has granted tax exempt status to two other charitable organizations that are purportedly similar to Camp Moshava in many material respects and that the Board has erroneously applied the law in granting the exemptions to the other organizations.

Wayne County appears to be rich in summer camps, as this site of the Wayne County Camp Association[26] shows. Camp Moshava serves roughly 1,000 campers drawn from all over the United States, Canada, Europe, and Israel. Probably not so many from Wayne County. Is it possible that camps with a strong local constituency get easier treatment from the county?

The Pennsylvania Supreme Court decision in Mesivta Eitz Chaim of Bobov, Inc v Pike County[27] in April invites comparison. Here is a comment in one of the earlier decisions in that case:

> However, Mesivtah did not present any evidence that the camp's recreational and food facilities alleviate any local community burdens in Pike County like the Sewickley Valley YMCA.

The "burdens of government" test applied from a local perspective would appear to disadvantage religious minorities. The Bobov case was something of a major precedent in that it indicated that the legislature could not loosen the "purely public charity" standard that the Supreme

Court of Pennsylvania had previously defined. Whether a case ends up going to court, though, will hinge on local decisions to grant or not grant exemptions. Any group that is thin on the ground will not have much of a local constituency wherever it decides to set up camp. Pennsylvania's roots come from principles of religious toleration. Presumably, the fact that the first decision using the Bobov case as a precedent in a case about another Jewish summer camp is just one of those awful coincidences. ◊

Leaving a partnership open after selling its main asset might not matter for federal income tax purposes, but state results might vary.

Real Estate Partnerships and State Income Tax—Nasty Surprises

State tax computations will quite often follow federal computations closely. Not infrequently, though, there are nasty surprises. The decision in New Jersey Tax Court in the case of Constance Dinallo[28] is an example. New Jersey does not care for tax shelters. The numbers you enter on the Gross Income Tax return form designating the various categories of income must all be positive. If a category is negative, you enter zero. New Jersey only wants to partner with you when you are making money.

Coordinating this with your federal return is a little tricky. If you are a partner in a partnership, your losses reduce your basis in your partnership interest. Someday, if you are lucky or good, your ship might come in. The positive number that flows through on your federal return might be larger due to those past losses New Jersey did not give you credit for.

> N.J.S.A. 54A:5-2 mandates that any losses in any category of income incurred in a given taxable year must be applied as a deduction against income in that same category in the same taxable year. Thus, losses may not be carried forward into taxable years in which they were not incurred.

So, it seems as if you are out of luck. There is a glimmer of hope, though.

> However, the New Jersey Supreme Court held that the Director cannot use a federal adjusted basis if it results in a taxpayer being taxed on a return of capital. In other words, a taxpayer can only be taxed on the economic gain resulting from a sale.

In 2004, Empire Ltd. flowed a $2,533,468 gain through to Ms. Dinallo. Following the logic above, she offset the gain with losses from prior years of $1,749,716.

There was a problem:

> In this case, Director contends that plaintiff could not offset losses from prior years for NJ GIT purposes in her tax year 2004 return as her interest in Empire continued through 2005 (i.e., there was no sale, exchange, or other disposition terminating plaintiff's interest in Empire in 2004). On the other hand, plaintiff contends that she was able to offset the prior years' losses because her interest in Empire dissolved in the year 2004 with the sale of the partnership's land.

Apparently, the partners of Empire Ltd. kept the partnership open for several years after the land sale in 2004. New Jersey only allows the accumulated losses in the year when the partnership no longer exists. Since the big gain was in 2004, when those losses are finally allowed for New Jersey purposes, they might do no good.

State Taxes—Nasty Surprises

It would not be at all unusual to keep a single purpose partnership alive for a year or two after selling its main assets. There will frequently be contingent liabilities or escrows and the like. Absent special circumstance (such as a transfer without a 754 election), the continued existence of the partnership will have little significance to the partners. They recognized income in the year the partnership earned it and as long as they get the bulk of their distributions, the remaining entity will not cause them any trouble for federal tax purposes. State taxes, at least in New Jersey, are a different story.

When it comes to New Jersey Gross Income Tax, keeping the partnership alive cost Ms. Dinallo $166,049 plus penalties and interest. I have written about worse outcomes. Robert Marshall invested about $150,000 in a partnership that invested in the iconic U.S. Steel Tower in Pittsburgh, Pennsylvania. He received about $6,000 in distributions over 20 years. When the deal unwound with no further distributions in 2005, he ended up with a Pennsylvania state income tax liability of $165,055.

In planning flow-through investments, it is important that you consider state income taxes, both in the state of operation and the investors' states of residence. This is particularly important when dealing with states that have significant variations from federal principles in their computations.

Commentary From Another Jersey Boy

Bob Flach, the Wandering Tax Pro[29], like me is a New Jersey native, but he stayed a lot longer than I did and has much more experience with New Jersey returns than I do. So, I asked him for his take on this case:

> My former home state of New Jersey is indeed a unique one when it comes to state income taxes. It has a "Gross" Income Tax—and losses in one category of income cannot be applied against income in other categories of income.
>
> Most states with income taxes follow the federal 1040. However, when the N.J. state income tax was created, they decided to borrow from neighbor Pennsylvania rather than neighbor New York. Pennsylvania has a true gross state income tax, with losses from one category not being allowed against income from another category. N.J. did make some adjustments just to be different—it allowed for personal exemptions and a couple of deductions (excess medical expenses and real estate tax).
>
> For N.J. Gross Income Tax purposes income from a sub-S corporation has been a different category of income than income from a partnership, which is a different category from income from a sole proprietorship. This is different from the PA state income tax, where all types of business income and losses (Schedule C, sub-S,

and partnership) are combined in a single category. N.J. has only recently decided to allow losses from one type of business activity to offset gains from another type of business activity, and is phasing in this change beginning with the 2012 Form NJ-1040.

And, as Peter points out, N.J. does not permit the carry forward of any net losses that are not allowed to be claimed in the current year. This is also true for capital losses from the federal Schedule D. So, the N.J. taxpayer is royally screwed (something he has become very used to).

Where I have seen this royal screwing most is with the sale of rental real estate. The federal basis must be used in the calculation of gain or loss, including the recapture of depreciation allowed or allowable on the federal Schedule E. So, the N.J. taxpayer, who received no state tax benefit from much if not all of the annual depreciation deductions when the property was being rented, because this deduction created a rental loss for the year, still has to reduce his basis for gain by the federal depreciation.

There is some relief if the annual depreciation by itself, without taking into consideration any other rental deductions, reduced the gross rental income below 0. In years when this was the case, the depreciation deduction in excess of gross rents does not have to be recaptured when determining the N.J. state tax basis of the property.

Peter's takeaway from this post is very important. When doing tax planning, you must always take into consideration the state tax implications of whatever actions you are considering. Or more appropriately, don't live in N.J. ◊

This was an utter nightmare as investors in a tax shelter that had losses that had not benefited them for state tax purposes reverse in the year of sale. They suffered a state tax liability in the vicinity of their total investment. It was a 2005 transaction, and as late as 2018, I was getting calls from people Pennsylvania was chasing.

The Tax Shelter from Hell—U.S. Steel Tower in Pittsburgh

Investing in a partnership that owned an iconic building in Pittsburgh, The U.S Steel Tower,[30] has turned into a tax nightmare for out-of-state investors. When people invested in real estate shelters in the early to mid-1980s, they usually did not give a lot of thought to state income taxes. In many states, it would be safe to assume that the state income taxes would tag along with the federal income taxes—benefits in the early years and costs in the later years after the dreaded crossover with perhaps a large cost on disposition of the property. They never thought about the implications of the underlying real estate being in a different state from the investor.

The partners in 600 Grant Street Limited Partnership are finding this lack of forethought rather expensive. Among them is Robert Marshall who does not live in Pennsylvania. He recently received bad news from the Commonwealth Court of Pennsylvania[31]. The Court told him that although the computations need a bit of fine tuning, the position of the Commonwealth's Department of Revenue is essentially correct.

Mr. Marshall put about $150,000 into the partnership and received a little more than $6,000 in distributions over the roughly 20 years he owned an interest in the partnership. The real estate, sold at a sheriff's sale in 2005, generated no net proceeds for the limited partners. In 2008, Revenue (as the Court refers to the department) informed Mr. Marshall that he owed Pennsylvania $165,055.24 for 2005. I think his reaction was something to the effect of that does not even make good nonsense. Over 20 years on net, he lost more than $140,000 in Pennsylvania. For that, the state thinks he owes them in income tax somewhat more than he lost. To understand how that might be, you need to know just a bit about old-fashioned real estate shelters.

How Real Estate Shelters Worked in the Good Old Days

When you buy a piece of real estate by taking out a mortgage, it is almost certain that your taxable income from the property will be different from your cash flow. Principal amortization on the mortgage requires cash but does not produce a deduction. Depreciation, on the other hand, is deductible, but does not require a cash outlay. So, a building that is breaking even on cash flow after debt service will produce a taxable loss if the depreciation is greater than the principal amortization on the mortgage.

Buildings placed in service between 1981 and 1986 could be depreciated over less than 20 years. So, in the early years at break-even cash flow, there would be losses. Eventually, you "crossover" and the mortgage principal payments would exceed the depreciation giving you "phantom income." On top of that, your basis in the building would be less than your mortgage balance, which some people refer to as negative basis. There was generally the assumption that the building will have appreciated, since everybody knew that real estate only went up. On top of that, even if you had to walk away from the building and recognize phantom income on the disposition, the gain would be a capital gain. Since your losses would have sheltered income subject to a 50 percent tax rate, you would still be ahead. That is, if you put your tax savings in excess of your investment into tax exempt bonds. There must have been somebody, somewhere, who actually did that. He probably flossed regularly, too.

Some Bells and Whistles

That was the basic engine that made things work. There were a lot of bells and whistles available. One of them, which Mr. Marshall seems to have taken advantage of, is an extended pay-in period of about seven years for his investment. A well-structured shelter would give you 2 for 1. That is, the losses for a year would be twice your payment for that year. With a 50 percent rate, it was like you were getting the investment for free. The other technique, which was a little less common, was that the 14.55 percent purchase money mortgage did not have to have all the interest paid if there was not enough cash flow. So not only were you getting depreciation deductions, but you were also getting negative principal amortization. This was the feature that would bite the out-of-state investors in an uncomfortable place. In 2005, at the sheriff's sale, the original $308 million purchase money mortgage had grown to $2.6 billion.

Blame it on Dan Rostenkowski?

Mr. Marshall went into this deal in January 1985. Little did he suspect he was at the end of the era. The Tax Reform Act of 1986 changed the landscape. No more short lives for real estate. A lower top marginal rate. The Passive Activity Loss rules would suspend most of his losses unless he had other passive income. I'm not an economist, but I believe that the act reduced the value of commercial real estate by removing its inherent tax shelter characteristics.

Blame it on the General Partners?

It turns out that the "sheriff's sale" transaction generated a little bit of publicity in 2005. According to this story, the foreclosure was a friendly transaction. A new entity, 600 GS Prop LP, controlled by the same group (but likely not the same limited partners), acquired the mortgage. By structuring the transfer as they did, they avoided substantial transfer taxes, but also may have created interest on the part of the Department of Revenue. The possibility that someone would come to the sale and bid $2.6 billion didn't trouble them. (The Tower has 2.3 million square feet. I do not think you are going to see values in excess of $1,000 per square foot in Pittsburgh any time soon.) One wonders if the departing limited partners knew about their potential liability to Pennsylvania.

It is What It is. Deal with It.

Mr. Marshall received a K-1 showing losses every year for 20 years. Since he apparently had no other income from Pennsylvania, he did not need to file a return there. If he did not have other passive income, those losses would have been suspended after the first few years of transition into the new regime of the Internal Revenue Code of 1986. So, when the phantom income hit all at once in 2005, there may have been substantial losses released. Conceivably because the phantom income was capital gain, Mr. Marshall would have actually come out ahead in 2005. Since Mr. Marshall did not get anything in 2005, why is there a gain? The balance of a non-recourse mortgage is proceeds in the sale of a property. So, for the tax purposes of the partners in 600 Grant Limited Partnership, it is as if somebody did bid $2.6 billion for the property.

The rather lengthy decision gets into the $2.6 billion deemed proceeds. It then discusses how things are different in Pennsylvania. Pennsylvania does not suspend losses. So even if Mr. Marshall had filed every year in Pennsylvania, he would not have a store of losses to use in the big income year. It is even worse, though. Pennsylvania does not have an extremely high rate—3.07 percent—but it only wants to be partners with you when you are winning. Even if he stuffed the whole 21 years of activity into 2005, Mr. Marshall would have the same problem. The interest deduction that built up the $2.6-billion-dollar debt and the depreciation deductions that reduced the basis in the building created rental losses. The gain on the building's sale is a different class of income under Pennsylvania law. When you compute your total taxable income in Pennsylvania, you take each of the classes and add the ones that are positive. You do not subtract the ones that are negative.

What About the Allocations?

Mr. Marshall threw out several arguments all of which the Court knocked out. There was one, however, that I think deserved more scrutiny:

> Marshall argues that application of the PIT to him in this instance is unconstitutional, because it treats him differently from the partners

> who reside in Pennsylvania. Marshall contends that he cannot be liable for PIT in an amount greater than what a Pennsylvania resident partner would be liable to pay. Marshall contends that Revenue permitted resident partners in the partnership to offset any taxable gain from the foreclosure of the property with the loss incurred by the partner upon liquidation of the partnership. ... Thus, Marshall was assessed a tax more than 11 times the tax imposed on a resident.

Since the partnership interest is an intangible asset, gain or loss on its disposition will not enter into the computation of a non-resident tax. There are two interesting things about this. One is whether Mr. Marshall had an unused escape hatch from this nightmare. If he had abandoned the interest before the foreclosure, would he have escaped the Pennsylvania tax? More to the point, though, is the question of how the Pennsylvania partners had a loss on the partnership liquidation. Did Revenue allocate the foreclosure gain on a straight percentage basis rather than using substantial economic effect principles? If the limited partners were getting no money, their share of the gain allocation should have brought them to zero, not to a positive basis in their partnership interests. Given all the other defenses they used, it is hard to believe they overlooked this one, but I really wish I had a chance to study the K-1s.

The Moral

The state taxable income in most states tracks federal taxable income pretty closely. That is not true in all states. Pennsylvania appears to be one of the more peculiar states in this regard. I would be very cautious about highly leveraged real estate deals in Pennsylvania.

Here is another example of unwelcome news for an out-of-state partner.

AMT died down as a major concern during my writing career. In practice, I had seen its existence as an entirely parallel tax system cause quite a bit of grief. A limited focus to federal regular tax in planning was the source of the troubles as it is in the SALT area. ◊

Footnotes

1. Arthur S. Bray, In the Matter of the Petitions of Eugene Boissiere and Jason Krystal (New York: Division of Tax Appeals, 2014), https://www.dta.ny.gov/pdf/determinations/824467.det.pdf.
2. "Timothy P. Noonan," Hodgson Russ Attorneys, accessed May 27, 2023, https://www.hodgsonruss.com/professionals-Timothy-Noonan.html#profile.
3. Amanda Kludt, "The Shutter Report: Jeeb, Plumm, Cafe Zest, and More," Eater New York, last modified April 17, 2009, https://ny.eater.com/2009/4/17/6769867/the-shutter-report-jeeb-plumm-cafe-zest-and-more.
4. Taxpayer Guidance Division, New Policy Relating to Responsible Person Liability under the Sales Tax Law (Albany: New York State Department of Taxation and Finance, 2011), https://www.tax.ny.gov/pdf/memos/sales/m11_6s.pdf/.
5. Timothy Lewis, "Personal Liability of LLC Members for Unpaid Sales Taxes," New York Law Journal, accessed May 27, 2023, https://www.twllaw.com/articles/LLC_Member_Sales_Tax_080509.PDF.
6. Peter J. Reilly, "Voraciousness of the New York Income Tax and the Jersey City Solution," Forbes, last modified Jul 29, 2019, https://www.forbes.com/sites/peterjreilly/2019/07/29/voraciousness-of-the-new-york-income-tax-and-the-jersey-city-solution/#be7c77e4764c.
7. "Tom Corrie," Thomson Reuters, accessed May 27, 2023, https://www.thomsonreuters.com/en-us/posts/authors/tom-corrie/.
8. "Liberty Harbor RV," accessed May 27, 2023, https://www.libertyharborrv.com/.
9. State of New York Department of Taxation and Finance, Nonresident Audit Guidelines (New York: Department of Taxation and Finance, 2021), https://www.tax.ny.gov/pdf/2021/misc/nonresident-audit-guidelines-2021.pdf.
10. Peter J. Reilly, "Hard For Snow Birds To Avoid New York Tax," Forbes, last modified July 29, 2013, https://www.forbes.com/sites/peterjreilly/2013/07/29/hard-for-snow-birds-to-avoid-new-york-tax/#f94d6f0440b2.
11. Peter J. Reilly, "Match Group CEO Wins Tax Case By Arguing His Heart Was In Texas With His Dog," Forbes, last modified February 19, 2017, https://www.forbes.com/sites/peterjreilly/2017/02/19/match-group-ceo-saves-state-income-tax-by-convincing-judge-he-was-a-texan-for-a-while/#79dabdbe23d1.

12. Peter J. Reilly, "How Wealth Accumulators Can Use Trusts To Avoid State Income Tax," Forbes, last modified July 20, 2019, https://www.forbes.com/sites/peterjreilly/2019/07/20/how-wealth-accumulators-can-use-trusts-to-avoid-state-income-tax/?subId3=xid:fr1593525899323acj.

13. North Carolina Department of Revenue v. Kimberly Rice Kaestner 1992 Family Trust, Supreme Court of the United States (No. 18-457), April 16, 2019, https://www.supremecourt.gov/opinions/18pdf/18-457_2034.pdf.

14. "Withersworldwide," accessed May 27, 2023, https://www.withersworldwide.com/en-gb.

15. Peter J. Reilly, "Republican Tax Cuts And The New Gentry," Forbes, last modified November 6, 2017, https://www.forbes.com/sites/peterjreilly/2017/11/06/republican-tax-cuts-and-the-new-gentry/#221608b41930.

16. Internal Revenue Service, Form 1041: U.S. Income Tax Return for Estates and Trusts (Washington D.C.: Department of the Treasury, 2022), https://www.irs.gov/pub/irs-pdf/f1041.pdf.

17. Reilly, "How Wealth Accumulators Use Trusts."

18. "William J. Kambas," Withersworldwide, accessed May 27, 2023, https://www.withersworldwide.com/en-gb/people/william-kambas.

19. Peter J. Reilly, "Pritzker Trust Dodges Illinois State Income Tax," Forbes, last modified January 2, 2014, https://www.forbes.com/sites/peterjreilly/2014/01/02/pritzker-trust-dodges-illinois-state-income-tax/#3e287b5be51a.

20. The American College of Trust and Estate Counsel, "North Carolina v. Kaestner: The Recent US Supreme Court Case on State Fiduciary Income Tax," The ACTEC Foundation, last modified July 23, 2019, https://actecfoundation.org/podcasts/state-fiduciary-income-tax-nc-v-kaestner/.

21. "David M. Lehn," Withersworldwide, accessed May 27, 2023, https://www.withersworldwide.com/en-gb/people/david-lehn.

22. Camp Hachshara Moshava of New York v. Wayne County Board for the Assessment and Revision of Taxes, Commonwealth Court of Pennsylvania (No. 1016 C.D. 2011), May 23, 2012, http://riles52.blogspot.com/2012/06/pennsylvania-camp.html.

23. "Camp Moshava," accessed May 27, 2023, https://moshava.org/.

24. "Bnei Akiva ," Wikipedia, last modified May 17, 2023, https://en.wikipedia.org/wiki/Bnei_Akiva.

25. "Ne'emanei Torah Va'Avodah," Wikipedia, last modified February 27, 2023, https://en.wikipedia.org/wiki/Ne%27emanei_Torah_Va%27Avodah.

26. "Wayne County Camp Alliance," accessed May 27, 2023, https://www.waynecountycamps.com/.

27. Mesivtah Eitz Chaim of Bobov, Inc. v. Pike County Board of Assessment Appeals, Supreme Court of Pennsylvania Middle District (No. 16 MAP 2011), April 25, 2012, http://riles52.blogspot.com/2012/06/orthodox-camp.html.

28. Constance Dinallo v. Director, Division of Taxation, Tax Court of New Jersey (No. 017895-2009), August 16, 2013, https://casetext.com/case/dinallo-v-dir-div-of-taxation.

29. The Wandering Tax Pro (blog), accessed May 27, 2023, http://wanderingtaxpro.blogspot.com/.

30. "U.S. Steel Tower," Wikipedia, last modified May 25, 2023, https://en.wikipedia.org/wiki/U.S._Steel_Tower.

31. Robert J. Marshall, Jr. v. Commonwealth of Pennsylvania, Commonwealth Court of Pennsylvania (No. 933 F.R. 2008), March 1, 2012, http://riles52.blogspot.com/2012/02/penn-foreclosure-gain.html.

SIXTH LAW OF TAX PLANNING

Don't Do the Math in Your Head.

Although some tax computations are straightforward, others are not. Individual income tax, for example, has a host of thresholds and interactions of various parts of returns. I realized this once when I had a client recognize gain, and their tax went down. There were passive activity loss carryovers and capital loss carryovers. So really, the only way to test a plan is to run multiple versions of the same return. With software nowadays it's not that hard, but it is easy to get into a rut and think you know how things will turn out.

These stories with a bit of a celebrity angle illustrate some arcane estate tax computations.

Tom Clancy's Widow Prevails Over Kids from First Marriage in Estate Dispute

Before his death in 2013, Tom Clancy wrote some of the most exciting novels I have ever read. My personal favorite is *Red Storm Rising*. Alas, since I'm just a tax blogger, I only get to write about the litigation around his estate. There was a decision this week in the case of Michelle Bandy et al v Alexandra Clancy[1]. It concerns, don't get too excited, the estate tax marital deduction and, stay calm, iterative computations. Or you can look at it as a fight between a widow and Clancy's children from his first marriage, which probably makes it sound more interesting.

The Iterative Computation

I often remark that you learn all the math you need for tax work by the fourth grade. The math issue in this case is one of the rare exceptions. If a share of an estate is exempt from estate taxes because it will benefit a surviving spouse, as in this case, or a charity, and you use some of that share to pay the estate taxes, then that much does not qualify for the exemption.

So now, you have a higher estate tax, and if you pay some of that additional tax from the exempt share, you have an even higher tax, and so on. A real accounting Einstein could solve the problem with algebra, but you can also grind it out by doing the computation over and over till it does not change. Thanks to Goal Seek in Excel[2], it is not that hard, but still, I would want at least an eighth-grader handling it.

The Dispute

Tom Clancy's will gave the real and personal property to Mrs. Clancy (that may mean she got the honest-to-goodness tank he owned) with the residue divided into trusts. One-third went to a marital trust, and the remainder after that split between a family trust benefiting Mrs. Clancy and her child and Older Children's Trusts to benefit Clancy's four children from his first marriage.

Somebody had a brainstorm and drafted a codicil to the will to tweak the first family trust for Mrs. Clancy and the minor child so it would also qualify for the marital deduction. (Basically, the income must go to Mrs. Clancy for her life and the trustee can invade the principal if someone blows through the marital trust.) There are no numbers in the appellate decision. According to Scott Calvert's Wall Street Journal[3] story on the original decision, the older children's trusts gross $28.5 million will be hit with $11.8 million in tax. The alternative would be to divide a higher tax of $15.7 million (remember the iterative computation) between the family trust and the older children's trusts.

Given that the estate is in the highest bracket, it seems likely that if the family trust did not qualify for the marital deduction, it would also pay about $11.8 million, and there would have not been anything to fight about. Although maybe they would have thought of something else.

QTIP Is Not Free

On top of everything else in the will, there is a savings clause that is meant to protect the marital deduction:

> ITEM TWELVE
>
> D. Anything in this will to the contrary notwithstanding, and whether or not any reference is made in any other provision of this will to the limitations imposed by this Paragraph D, neither my representative nor my trustee shall have or exercise any authority, power, or discretion over the marital share, or the income thereof, or the property constituting the marital share, nor shall any payment or distribution by my representative or my trustee be limited or restricted by any provision of this will that would in any way prevent my estate from receiving the benefit of the marital deduction as hereinbefore set forth.

So, what was more important to Tom Clancy? Equality between the family trust and the older children's trusts or minimizing immediate estate taxes? It is worth remembering that qualifying the family trust for the marital deduction is not a free lunch. When Alexandra Clancy dies, the value of that trust will be in her estate. Of course, because she was 21 years younger than Tom Clancy, that age difference mitigates that concern somewhat.

The Decision

Like the lower court, most of the appellate court focused on the primacy of the savings clause:

> The second codicil did not, however, specifically address, in any way, the will provision that instructed that taxes were to be paid out

> of the residuary estate of which the family trust was a part.
>
> To resolve the ambiguity and apparent conflict, we rely on the interpretive aid of the savings clause to elucidate Mr. Clancy's intent. In so doing, we determine, as did the Orphans' Court, that the savings clause contained in the second codicil, which prevented the personal representative from exercising any "authority, power, or discretion" to disqualify any portion of the family trust from the marital deduction, such as the payment of federal estate taxes, "trumps" ITEM THIRD of the will relating to the payment of taxes from the residuary estate. We reach this conclusion for several reasons, the first of which is because of the decisions in similar circumstances by other courts, as well as the Internal Revenue Service's decision in Revenue Ruling 75-440.

The majority noted the non-free lunch aspect of qualifying the family trust for the marital deduction.

> Moreover, was the family trust to bear the burden of federal estate taxes, at the time of Mr. Clancy's death, the corpus of that trust would be subject to the imposition of federal estate taxes twice, at the time of Mr. Clancy's death as well as when Mrs. Clancy dies. The establishment of the QTIP trust in Mr. Clancy's will ensures that the younger child will have to pay estate taxes when Mrs. Clancy dies (26 U.S.C. Section 2044). Certainly, as each party agrees, Mr. Clancy intended to minimize the impact of federal estate taxes in the entirety of his will, an intent that would be eviscerated by double taxation.
>
> Finally, the older children question having the burden of federal estate taxation placed on them, to the benefit of Mrs. Clancy. Mr. Clancy, however, clearly intended, by the establishment of the QTIP trust, to benefit Mrs. Clancy to the detriment of the younger child, whose remainder could be diminished by Mrs. Clancy's invasion of corpus for need. As a result, all of Mr. Clancy's children are burdened for the benefit of Mrs. Clancy and to avoid federal estate tax.

An exercise that in my mind would have proved useful was to compute the estate tax hit that would fall on the older children's trusts without the codicil to qualify the family trust. I think it is likely that it would be what they are ending up paying.

Dissent

Three of the judges did not agree with the majority opinion. I have to give them credit for the cleverest part of the overall document.

> The majority opinion appears to be based on the premise that the preeminent value for any testator is the avoidance of taxes. Perhaps there are people like that. If so, one would expect them to have bought a Yugo years ago and scrupulously maintained it to minimize and thereafter avoid the automobile excise tax.

The Lesson

It seems as if someone should have noticed this issue when they bolted the codicil onto the original will. Another sentence or two would have given direction on how to allocate the estate tax savings and avoid some costly litigation. Commenting on an earlier stage of the struggle, Mark Harbin of Greenbaum Doll [4] blog wrote:

> This case presents a compelling example of how quickly an estate plan can go awry when dealing with a blended family once the single link between otherwise disparate elements is removed—the late Mr. Clancy. It is hard to tell right from wrong when all parties are acting in self-interest. Attorneys and clients should retain the essential drafting lessons from this case that the testator's intent must be expressed as clearly as possible; vague or arguably conflicting provisions can cause a clear and present danger to the estate. Also, the language of a provision as seemingly banal as a savings clause can have a profound impact. Choose your words wisely. ◊

My account[5] of the Court of Appeals of Maryland's decision[6] on the division of Tom Clancy's estate generated a good bit of interest, so I thought it would be worthwhile to share some expert opinions on the decision to see whether any lessons in the story might be broadly applicable.

Experts Comment on Tom Clancy's Estate Litigation

When in Doubt Go with the Lower Estate Tax

I reached out to a few experts for comment. Keeping with the literary nature of this chapter first up is the late Howard Medwed[7] who was with Burns & Levinson, whose late wife, Mameve Medwed was a novelist, who managed to sometimes slip arcane tax references into her novels, which I would view as romantic comedies. Howard focused on the merits of the case and general estate planning principles. In his reply, he said:

> I'm on the widow's side. Virtually, all clients (and their advisers) want the marital share to (a) pass unencumbered by taxes on the first death, (b) minimize current taxes, and (c) avoid the iterative calculation. If that overweighs the marital trust, then the amount passing in the marital trust has to be set out to reach that result.

It Might Have Been Real Expensive

Hubert Klein[8] of Eisner/Amper in New York focused on the expense of the litigation, which is one of the things I was wondering about.

> I suspect this estate litigation was more than $1 million, based on the size of the estate, the type of litigation, and the need for legal, tax, and consulting experts. It was a sizable issue, and the meters were running on this matter on both sides.

As with all estate planning, even the best of planning and intentions can go awry. It appears that Mr. Clancy's estate was complicated by having blended family members as beneficiaries. Generally, the desires or expectations of biological children are not always completely aligned with that of the surviving stepparent.

When this happens it generally leads to costly litigation issues, specifically when trying to settle a sizable estate. Even in situations where all family members have been advised of the wishes of the deceased before death disagreements can arise. There have been many instances of high- and low-profile cases involving estates with significant value in which it appears all the proper planning steps may have taken place before death, and there is still conflict between the beneficiaries.

Often, an estate disagreement is driven by the belief that one side has been disadvantaged as a result of undue influence, improper planning, or both. Other times, it is greed: One side believes they are entitled to something regardless of the wishes of the deceased. When this happens, the disgruntled parties may believe they may be able to squeeze more money out for themselves, or a class of beneficiaries, knowing that many disputed estate matters settle as opposed to going to trial.

Either way, whether or not an estate dispute is litigated or tried in court it can cost, at the low end, tens of thousands of dollars to several hundreds of thousands of dollars and in some cases millions between lawyers and expert fees. The fees are generally driven by the complexity of the issues in dispute and the amount of the potential expected recovery at stake.

Codicils May Not Be Such a Great Idea

Matt Erskine[9] has an estate planning and trust administration practice that includes a focus on unique assets. Matt is in Worcester, Massachusetts (heart of the Commonwealth), and full disclosure, is responsible for part of my not-very vast fortune. Despite his focus on unique assets, even he has never run into somebody who, like Tom Clancy, had an honest-to-goodness M4 Sherman tank. Matt did run into a collection of machine guns, though.

Matt focused on practical suggestions, which might have avoided the litigation.

> Never, ever use a codicil. A codicil requires just as much formality as does a will, and so the better practice is to sign an entirely new will rather than use a codicil. In this case, if Tom Clancy revoked the prior will (with the language making the family trust taxable) and only had the language that makes it qualify for the marital deduction, there would be much less ambiguity. This is also true not only for technical corrections like this but also when you change your mind about bequests in a will. For example, Aunt Mabel may make Nephew Phil very happy with a $10,000 gift under her new will or very mad if she reduces a $50,000 gift under her prior will using a codicil.
>
> Use models and flow charts to illustrate what the plan should do when explaining the effects to the client. This case revolves around intent. If you could clearly illustrate the cash flow (and tax effect) of the revised language as explained to Clancy before he signed the new document, it is ancillary evidence of his intent in executing the document. Even though for you this is elementary math, for us medieval history majors, it is about as clear as mud. A picture is worth a thousand words (or a will contest).

I found Matt's passionate rejection of codicils interesting. On reflection, though, I think he is on to something. I mean, codicils probably made a lot of sense in the days of *Bartleby the Scrivener*[10] (by Herman Melville), when documents had to be tediously hand-copied, but we have made some technical progress since then.

His second suggestion reminds me a bit of this **Law of Tax Planning**—"***Don't do the math in your head.***" To ordinary mortals, it is not intuitively obvious that qualifying the second trust for the marital deduction would create tension between minimizing tax and keeping the shares in the same proportion.

Matt is not alone in rejecting codicils as this article by Mary Randolph[11] indicates.

> The witness requirement, plus the ease of using computers to prepare, modify, and print documents, erase any reason to make a codicil. When legal documents were painstakingly written out with quill pens, it made sense not to rewrite a whole will if you could just tack on a brief codicil. But these days, there's no advantage to a codicil.
>
> There is, however, a drawback: A codicil is unlikely to seamlessly fit with the original will. Is it a pure addition, or does it negate something in the original document? If it's supposed to replace part of the first will, which part?

So, the lesson from the case is that if you want to change your will, just redo it rather than tweaking the existing one and then take a good look at how all the parts fit together.

I experienced the dawn of hands-on computer use by accountants. We had a couple of Kaypros in the early 80s, and I was amazed by their power. Working on a seven-figure estate and gift tax audit, I could show that a very large dollar adjustment that the attorneys were heavily focused on had no bottom-line dollar effect. They were not entirely pleased with me, but so it goes. Given the easily available software, there is no excuse nowadays for seat of the pants tax planning. ◊

SIXTH LAW OF TAX PLANNING

Footnotes

1. Michelle Bandy et al. v. Alexandra Clancy, Courts of Appeals of Maryland (No. 93), August 24, 2016, https://caselaw.findlaw.com/court/md-court-of-appeals/1746772.html.
2. "Use Goal Seek to find the result you want by adjusting an input value," Microsoft, accessed May 27, 2023, https://support.microsoft.com/en-us/office/use-goal-seek-to-

find-the-result-you-want-by-adjusting-an-input-value-320cb99e-f4a4-417f-b1c3-4f369d6e66c7?redirectSourcePath=%252fen-us%252farticle%252fUse-Goal-Seek-to-find-a-result-by-adjusting-an-input-value-ef3495fe-9ddc-4249-89b4-0e24406b7fcb.

3. Scott Calvert, "Tom Clancy's Widow Wins Legal Battle Over Taxes on $86 Million Estate: Judge rules trust for grown children must shoulder the bill," The Wall Street Journal, last modified August 24, 2015, https://www.wsj.com/articles/tom-clancys-widow-wins-legal-battle-over-taxes-on-86-million-estate-1440438903.

4. Mark E. Harbin, "Court battle rages over the estate of a prominent military novelist Tom Clancy," Lexology, last modified January 28, 2016, https://www.lexology.com/library/detail.aspx?g=3937f5f0-acc1-415a-85c0-0faced2a0eca.

5. Peter J. Reilly, "Tom Clancy's Widow Prevails Over Kids From First Marriage In Estate Dispute," Forbes, last modified August 28, 2016, https://www.forbes.com/sites/peterjreilly/2016/08/28/tom-clancys-widow-prevails-in-estate-dispute/#5fe86d326a90.

6. Michelle Bandy et al. v. Alexandra Clancy.

7. Mameve Medwed

8. "Hubert Klein," EisnerAmper, accessed May 27, 2023, https://www.eisneramper.com/hubert-klein/.

9. "Matthew F. Erskine," Erskine & Erskine, accessed May 27, 2023, https://www.erskineanderskine.com/.

10. "Bartleby, the Scrivener," Wikipedia, accessed May 27, 2023, https://en.wikipedia.org/wiki/Bartleby,_the_Scrivener#Plot.

11. Mary Randolph, "Why Not Make a Codicil to Amend Your Will? : It's often better to make a new will, rather than using a codicil to amend your old one," NOLO, accessed May 27, 2023, https://www.nolo.com/legal-encyclopedia/why-not-make-codicil.html.

SEVENTH LAW OF TAX PLANNING

Read the Instructions.

In the 80s, before the Clarence Thomas confirmation hearings, my favorite review note was RTFI, which stood for "Read the instructions." Even in those raunchier times, the "F" remained silent. Back in the day when preparers did returns by hand, people would be inclined to "follow last year." But at least they would generally have the instructions handy. Once software became predominant, preparers would often just focus on what box to check or what letter to put in a particular field.

By reading the instructions and following them, you are generally showing compliance. It is even possible to lose a large deduction by not filling in the form thoroughly.

Billionaire Stephen Ross had a great plan that gave him a $33 million deduction while only going $2 million out of pocket. Although it likely would have failed for other reasons, the mere failure to thoroughly fill out Form 8283 was enough.

Billionaire Miami Dolphins Owner Gets Shut Out at Tax Court

Billionaire Stephen Ross[1], owner of the Miami Dolphins, who, thanks to a $200 million donation (largest in the history of the school), earned the description of leader, visionary, philanthropist, and Wolverine from the University of Michigan, is inherently more interesting than filling out Form 8283 properly[2], so I will lead with his part of the story in the Tax Court's decision RERI Holdings I, LLC[3]. Don't forget about the form, though, because we have here an illustration of **Reilly's Seventh Law of Tax Planning—"*Read the instructions.*"**

About Stephen Ross

Stephen Ross is a billionaire. He is a big-time New York real estate developer. His project, Hudson Yards[4], does not sound like that big a deal when you consider that it is 28 acres, but given that those 28 acres was more or less an expansion of midtown Manhattan, it is something. Location, location, location. Quite interesting to me is that Mr. Ross got his start in real estate based on his knowledge of federal tax garnered as a tax attorney for Coopers and Lybrand. His first deals were affordable housing deals. That business was very tax-driven. What is extraordinary is a tax attorney becoming a developer and succeeding. Usually, when people in the ancillary trades dive into development, they go broke. I have to wonder whether the name of his flagship Related Companies[5] is a tax geek joke.

What Ross Donated

As noted, Mr. Ross is a big supporter of the University of Michigan. And it is a donation to UM that is the subject of the decision. You have to dip into it to see Mr. Ross. What was being donated was a successor member interest (SMI) in an entity that owns the land and a building in Hawthorne, California, leased to AT&T as a data center. When Red Sea Tech acquired the building, it created H.W. Hawthorne Holdings, LLC. The building's purchase price of $42,350,000 Branch Banking & Trust Co. financed the purchase 100 percent. The final balloon payment on the mortgage of $11.8 million corresponded with the end of the initial term of the AT&T net lease in May 2016. AT&T had three renewal options of five years each.

Of course, that is not complicated enough. There were two interests in Holdings. One was for a term of years and the other was the successor member interest that kicked in in 2021 around when AT&T would have its second renewal option if it exercised its first one. RERI bought the SMI for $2,950,000 in March 2002. The cash flow net of expenses was roughly equal to the debt service. There was also an insurance policy to guarantee the balloon's payment. In the event the insurance company paid the balloon, it got the building.

The SMI was something of a bet in 2002 on what circumstances would be in 2016. If AT&T did not renew the lease and the specialized building, which went up in 1963, did not have an alternative use that justified a value over $12 million, the SMI would be worthless. We here in 2023, of course, have the benefit of hindsight and can see that it worked out well. Red Sea Group sold the data[6] center for $79.5 million to Carter Validus Mission Critical REIT in 2016. That didn't do the Wolverines any good, as we will see.

Given that the Holdings had, in principle, zero equity in the building then nearly $3 million seems like a pretty nice sum. That's why we have capital markets, I guess.

The Gift

Mr. Ross pledged $4 million (later raised to $5 million) for a University of Michigan athletic center. RERI's donation of the SMI was under an agreement that provided there would be a $1 nominal credit to the pledge, that the university would hold the interest for two years and then sell it crediting Mr. Ross's pledge with whatever it received for the interest. The appraised value of the SMI used for charitable donation purposes was $32,935,000.

Wash, Rinse, Repeat

After two years went by, UM sold the interest as contemplated. Despite an appraisal of $6.5 million, UM received only $1.94 million from HRK Real Estate Holdings LLC, which the "petitioner and one of his associates" owned indirectly. (HRK had presold the interest to another individual for $3 million. That individual donated the property and took a charitable contribution of nearly $30 million.)

So now using round numbers, the partners in RERI (mainly Mr. Ross, apparently) bought something for $3 million and gave it to UM. People they knew bought the item from UM a couple of years later for $2 million and sold it to somebody else for $3 million. That puts the Related crew out of pocket $2 million, which is what went to UM. For that somebody, probably mostly Mr. Ross gets a charitable deduction of $32,935,000.

According to a footnote in one of the decisions, this was not an isolated transaction:

> As a result of the petitioner's donation of the SMI to the university and other donations of similar successor member interests in other LLCs arranged by Mr. Ross, the university derived sale proceeds of $4,276,604, which it credited to Mr. Ross' $5 million pledge. Respondent alleges that, in at least some of those cases, the amounts realized by the university on its sales of the donated successor remainder member interests were far less than the appraisal thereof for which the donor, presumably, claimed a Section 170 deduction.

One of the things that is disturbing to me is that it seems likely the university development people must have been aware that these shenanigans were going on. If so, at least these transactions are not philanthropy. They are a tax scam out of which the university gets a cut.

The Valuations

The fig leaf covering this naked tax grab was Code Section 7520 and the related regulations that give instructions on how to value remainder interests. The Court found that the 7520 rates are meant to value things that are a good bit more certain than the SMI interest was in 2002.

> ... because of the limitation on remedies available to the holder of the remainder interest for breaches of protective covenants, the agreement that created that interest did not provide adequate protection to its holder, for purposes of Section 1.7520-3(b)(2)

(iii), Income Tax Regs.; the standard actuarial factors provided under Section 7520 thus do not apply in valuing the remainder interest; instead, the value of that interest is its "actual fair market value," determined without regard to Section 7520, of based on all of the facts and circumstances. Section 1.7520-3(b)(1)(iii), Income Tax Regs.

The discussion of the appraisals in the final decision is rather mind-numbing. Thankfully, Judge James Halpern boils it down for us. (I'm thinking his bachelor's from Wharton might be paying off).

A future interest such as the SMI is extremely sensitive to the discount rate selected. I would have thought the bought and sold price of the interest within a couple of years was a pretty good indication of its value, but I guess they needed an opportunity to show off their math skills.

But the Value Didn't Matter Mostly

The valuation discussion was only relevant to determine whether there would be a 20 percent accuracy penalty or a 40 percent accuracy penalty. Since $33,019,000 is more than 400 percent of $3,462,886, the 40 percent accuracy penalty will apply.

Appraiser	2021 Cashflow	Growth%	Discount%	SMI Value
Mr. Myers	$8,107,588	3.00	11.01	$16,550,000
Dr. Cragg	$6,663,522	3.29	18.99	$2,090,000
Mr. Abraham	$6,586,595	2.50	16.44	$3,382,000

How much the penalty turns out to be will depend on what kind of a year Mr. Ross and his compatriots had overall in 2003, since the penalty applies to the extent that the transaction created an understatement of tax of greater than 10 percent.

The reason the court disallowed the deduction entirely, rather than just reduced by $30 million, is rather mundane. If you study Form 8283[7], you will note that it asks you when and how you acquired the donated property and what your basis is. They didn't fill that part of the form thoroughly.

> The Form 8283 appraisal summary that RERI attached to its 2003 return indicates that it acquired the SMI by purchase on March 22, 2002. It shows no amount in the space provided for the "Donor's cost or another adjusted basis."

If you are giving away something you inherited from your great-grandfather, it is understandable that you might not have a good handle on the basis, but something purchased a little more than a year ago should not be that challenging. Given the difference between basis and value claimed, the Tax Court was not inclined to give the taxpayer a "substantial compliance", "No harm, no foul" sort of break. ◊

Read on to learn how Luke Chiarelli, a tax attorney, thought his substantial compliance was enough to save his deduction. The Tax Court thought otherwise.

Mortal Sin or Venial Sin?

Luke Chiarelli[8] is the only child of an only child. So, when his mother died not long after his father, he ended up with a lot of stuff, not only from his parents but indirectly from his grandparents. Nice stuff—vintage clothing, furniture, antiques, and the like. He got Tarquinio F. Durante of Cedarburg Auction and Estate Sales[9] to help him with it. Although a lot sold at estate sales, Mr. Durante recommended that Chiarelli donate quite a bit to charity.

Mr. Chiarelli is a tax attorney and a veteran of the Arthur Andersen tax department, so he prepares his own returns. His 2012, 2013, and 2015 returns included a noncash charitable deduction of $89,110, $93,087, and $77,300, respectively. The resulting audits resulted in notices of deficiency for all three years, including penalties for 2012 and 2013. Mr. Chiarelli ended up in Tax Court arguing about just shy of $65,000 (not including interest). It did not go well for him.

A Good Sport

We can use this opinion to illustrate three of **Reilly's Laws of Tax Planning: the Fourth—"*Execution isn't everything, but it's a lot*", the Seventh—"*Read the instructions*", and the Sixteenth—"*Being right without substantiation can be as bad as being wrong.*"** You can quibble about the 16th since there was a good bit of substantiation. It was just not quite enough. A corollary exists with large charitable contributions, where you should always aim for more substantiation.

Mr. Chiarelli, although gracious and dignified in defeat, has a problem with the IRS approach to cases such as this that I think is worth considering. He compliments IRS attorneys George Bezold, Laurie Downs, and Mark Miller on their honor and professionalism, and Judge Nega and the staff at the Tax Court, and the overworked IRS people who were second to none even when they were yelling at him. His problem is that he thinks the IRS has let go of the concept of substantial compliance.

In explaining his theory to me, Mr. Chiarelli inadvertently outed himself as having an old-fashioned Catholic education. (It takes one to know one.) In his view, none of the deficiencies in his reporting were mortal sins. Mortal sin would have been not giving the property away during the relevant tax year, not using a qualified appraiser, or having the appraisal not include the relevant information. With that in mind, we can look at Mr. Chiarelli's venial sins and decide whether he deserved absolution. I confirmed with Mr. Chiarelli that he agrees that the opinion is accurate as to facts.

Form 8283

The opinion gets into the detailed instructions of Form 8283[10]. For items or groups of items over $5,000, the form calls for a summary of physical condition, appraised fair market value, date acquired, manner of acquisition, and cost or adjusted basis. On the 2012 form, the $89,110 was "miscellaneous household items" in "excellent" condition with an aggregate fair market value of $89,110. The manner of the acquisition was as a purchase with a basis of $251,800 but no information on how they arrived at that number.

The 2013 form was similar except that method of acquisition was "inheritance." The 2015 form was also similar going back to purchase as a method of acquisition. Most significantly, Parts II, III, and IV, which call for signatures by the taxpayer, the appraiser, and the donee were all unsigned. Mr. Chiarelli might have saved himself a lot of grief here if he had gone to a CPA or EA with a substantial tax practice. There are very few such that would have let the return out of their office without all the signatures.

The opinion gets into the nitty gritty of the audit relating to how additional substantiation was in response to IRS requests. One sentence is very telling:

> The 2015 appraisal grouped **purported** donation items into generic categories and did not provide identifying information about the individual items donated, such as the age or condition. **(Emphasis added)**

Whenever any form of the word "purport" appears in a Tax Court opinion, you know that things are not going to go well for the taxpayer.

Substantial Compliance

Mr. Chiarelli's arguments are based on the notion of substantial compliance. He provided the IRS enough to establish that he donated the property and that he had it appraised. Rather than challenging the appraisal, the IRS threw out the deduction on technical grounds. This is very common in charitable cases, particularly conservation easements. Judge Nega notes, "As a general matter, taxpayers have had great difficulty in meeting the substantial compliance standard for charitable deductions."

Judge Nega also noted that taxpayers cannot meet the 170(f)(8) requirement for "contemporaneous written acknowledgment" (CWA) with substantial compliance. The Code requires that you have the CWA in your hot little hand by the earlier of the due date of the return or when filing the return. In the high net worth group where I spent much of my career, calling charities for our clients to get the CWA was a routine part of our service. That included making sure the wording was correct.

Judge Nega could have left it at that, but he went into some detail on the insubstantiality of the compliance. The IRS had conceded the penalty for 2015. Judge Nega upheld the 20 percent penalty for 2012 and 2013. Mr. Chiarelli argued that he relied on Mr. Durante on the appraisal matters, but Judge Nega held him to a higher standard since he was a tax attorney qualified to practice in the Tax Court.

Don't Know If There Will Be an Appeal

When I spoke to Mr. Chiarelli, he indicated he wasn't sure whether he would appeal, but he remains passionate about the "substantial compliance" notion. As a practical matter, once your charitable contributions break into the high-five to mid-high-five figures, plan on rigorous compliance. I doubt that Mr. Chiarelli has much chance on his appeal, but it would be entertaining if he won, because then he would have to duke it out on the merits of the appraisals. Regardless, I give him high marks in sportsmanship for his kind comments about his IRS adversaries. ◊

Chad and Dana Loube thought that they had found a great deal. They purchased a property that was a teardown. They learned that there was a more tax-efficient socially responsible step on the way to achieving the vacant lot they wanted to build on.

Deconstruction—The Real-World Kin

Before final demolition Second Chance Inc[11], a 501(c)(3) organization, would send in a team to "deconstruct" salvaging material that might be re-purposed. The social good is manifold.

The team, composed largely of recently released prisoners who need, you know, a second chance, was to learn how a building is put together by helping to take it apart. Second Chance calls the work created to be green-collar jobs. There is less stuff going into the landfill, and Second Chance can sell the material at affordable prices to those in need.

On top of the satisfaction of helping the community, the Loubes get a tax deduction for the fair market value of the material salvaged.

Deduction Denied

Only they didn't get the $297,000 deduction claimed on their 2013 tax return. They got an IRS audit resulting in a deficiency notice for $117,612, which Judge Elizabeth Copeland's Tax Court decision upheld on January 8, 2020.

I spoke with Mr. Loube, and he thinks he got a raw deal. He was dealing with a not-for-profit that had IRS approval and relied on their assurances and had a bad outcome. You and I both know that the IRS has close to zero capacity to regulate the not-for-profit sector, but I can still sympathize with Mr. Loube's point of view.

About Second Chance

I spoke with Mark Foster, founder and executive director of Second Chance Inc. (salary of $254,000 for 2017, if you care about that sort of thing). His inspiration for starting the organization was trying to find items to do an authentic renovation, but from there he saw the opportunity to employ people who had a great deal of trouble finding work and have a positive environmental impact.

A tax subsidy fuels all this significantly, which frankly puts my bs detector on high alert. I asked Mr. Foster whether Second Chance will sell the items from a deconstruction project for the appraisal price, and he allowed that they might not be. It reminds me just a little bit of what was going on with used cars quite a few years ago.

The IRS Has a Problem

The fair market appraised value of the salvage does not seem to have a real-world anchor. The taxpayers pay cash for the deconstruction and the appraisal, but there does not appear to be the option to just sell the stuff to somebody, which, in principle, would dictate the amount of the charitable contribution.

So, there are indications that the IRS has an overall problem with the deals. Second Chance Inc. faced a class-action lawsuit from a disgruntled donor who had a bad experience with the IRS and thought it was part of a larger pattern.

The lawsuit fell apart, though, and Second Chance pressed for an apology as part of the dismissal. Mr. Foster provided me with a copy. I have not heard back from the plaintiffs or their attorneys.

Go for the Gotchas

It appears the IRS is taking a similar approach to what it has been doing up until recently with easement donations. Rather than tackling valuation, they go over deals with a fine-tooth comb looking for technical faults to deny the deduction altogether.

> We conclude that petitioners failed to strictly comply with DEFRA Section 155[12] and the regulations thereunder because **they failed to provide, among other information, the basis and the acquisition date of the contributed property** on the appraisal summary. Petitioners also failed to attach to the appraisal summary an explanation of the reasonable cause for their inability to provide the basis, acquisition date, or other information related to the contributed property. **(Emphasis added)**

So, at the end of the day, the disallowance falls on the return preparer. Two of **Reilly's Laws of Tax Planning** come into play here. **The Fourth Law—"*Execution isn't everything, but it is a lot*",** and the purpose of this chapter is **The Seventh Law—"*Read the instructions.*"** Implicit in the Seventh Law is the notion that you should answer all the questions or to put it another way, fill out the form thoroughly.

Another Disallowance

This is not the first IRS rodeo with Second Chance Inc. Lawrence and Linda Mann sued for a refund in district court[13] over a $675,000 deduction for the donation of their house. That one turned on another execution failure:

> As to the house, even though taxpayers sought to convey their undivided interest to org. via private contract, because they never recorded their transaction in accordance with Maryland law, the house wasn't properly severed from the underlying property, and ownership wasn't transferred to org., leaving donation as more in nature of license to org. and not valid transfer of an entire interest in real property …

It Might Work Even If It Should Not

I hold two seemingly contradictory opinions on Second Chance Inc. I think what they are doing is good and that their leadership is sincere. And I think that their deductions are fundamentally unsound.

If the salvageable material from deconstructing your house is worth hundreds of thousands of dollars, you should not need to pay somebody to take the house apart so that you can give the pieces to charity. There should be people waving money in front of your face to come in and take it apart.

As it happens, though, the IRS has won in court only against taxpayers who did not execute well. So, if you are thinking about using this technique, see that you dot all the i's and cross all the t's and use a substantial firm for the preparation. And set aside your tax savings, just in case. I'm not going to recommend it, but I probably wouldn't try that hard to talk you out of it. ◊

When it comes to due dates, the instructions are usually clear, which means no excuses.

The Hits Just Keep Coming—Assuming Leads to Costly Late File Penalty

Lesley West, Peter West, and John West were the executors of the estate of their mother (June West). The IRS hit the estate with pretty nasty late file/late pay penalties: $317,821.05. The executors were in district court seeking a[14] refund because they thought they had a reasonable cause for being late. Things did not go well for them.

When to File

If you ever are wondering whether, where, and when to file a particular tax form, here is what you should do. Go to the instructions, which generally you can find online, and scan the first couple of pages. You will likely find paragraphs with labels like "When to File." For the United States Estate (and Generation-Skipping Transfer) Tax Return Form 706, "When To File" is on page 2 of the instructions[15], and it tells you that the form is due within nine months of the date of the decedent's death and that you can use Form 4768 to apply for a six-month extension.[16]

If you are responsible for an estate that must file (see Which Estate Must File on page 1), you may well need professional assistance, which the estate more than likely can afford. Nonetheless, that due date thing is something that is not hard to find, and it is very precise, not at all vague.

Another Approach

June West died on December 27, 2009. (If only she had held on for a few more days, they would have avoided all these problems.) Peter West sent an e-mail on January 3, 2010, to John Rodgers, June West's attorney seeking guidance as to "what legal follow-ups are needed in the short term." Rodgers responded that they would:

> "…need to pay final bills, and…possibly file a Federal Estate tax return, final 1040, and a trust income tax return." Rodgers went on to explain that "this all takes as short as a few months or (if an estate tax return is required) as long as years." The following day,

> Peter West, again via email, responded that he was sure there will be tax due on the estate and that he assumes that John Renner, the accountant hired to do June West's 2009 taxes, "would also take care of preparing estate taxes."

Heads up, here. Estate tax returns are not something that the preparers of income tax returns just kind of throw in with the final income tax return.

Another Assumption

Peter got back to John Rodgers in November 2010, which you and I know was a bit past the due date, which was in September.

> In November, Peter West met with his siblings around Thanksgiving and thereafter emailed Rodgers inquiring as to what plaintiffs "need to do next to start work on the estate taxes." Rodgers interpreted this question as Peter West's hiring him to prepare the estate taxes, and Rodgers began work preparing the estate tax return in December 2010. Rodgers was not concerned that the deadlines had already passed, and he never mentioned this fact to plaintiffs, as he mistakenly assumed that Renner, the accountant, had obtained the appropriate extensions, as Peter West had earlier advised Rodgers that Renner would "take care of preparing estate taxes."

This is the part that is a little difficult to understand. The final income tax return of the decedent (Form 1040), the estate's fiduciary income tax return (Form 1041), and the estate tax return (Form 706) interact with one another in a variety of ways. Ideally, the people doing these things need to coordinate. And if I were to prepare a return that I "assumed" had an extension, I would be inclined to ask for a copy of the extension, but maybe that's just me.

Rodgers prepared the return and informed the Wests that the federal estate tax due was $1,258,019. Lesley West filed the return on March 28, 2011, which I think would have been spot-on timely if there had been an extension since the 27th was a Sunday. Although frankly, I tend to avoid cutting it that fine on things like this. Regardless, the estate had to hand over $275,032.72 in late file and $42,783.33 in late payment penalties.

Reasonable Cause?

The refund claim was based on the theory that the e-mail that stated that it could take as long as two years "constituted legal advice as to the required deadlines for filing and paying estate tax on which plaintiffs could reasonably rely." The Court found that it was not.

Simply put, Rodgers' January 4, 2010, email to Peter West was not legal advice as to the date of a filing or payment deadline. The language on which plaintiffs seize is Rodgers' comment that "this all takes as short as a few months or (if an estate tax return is required) as long as years." This is insufficient as a matter of law to constitute legal advice as to tax filing or payment deadlines for several reasons. First, nothing in the record indicates that plaintiffs ever asked for a deadline, even before the January 4 email was sent. Indeed, Peter West's January 3 email that prompted Rodgers' January 4 response email simply asked what needed to be done in the "short term." Thus, Rodgers was not responding to a request for specific information about a deadline. Moreover, the email does not contain the language characteristic of advice as to deadlines, e.g., "pay by," "due on," or "file within." Finally, there is no objective basis to determine from what date Rodgers would even calculate a two-year deadline.

Lessons

I think that the result, in this case, is rather harsh. Given how compliant the taxpayers were once they got their act together, I think the government should have been satisfied with the late pay penalty. They could have easily avoided the problem if they had been more proactive in communicating with their professionals and if the professionals had been communicating with one another. You can't tell from the decision why the activity was not happening. There may have been an understandable desire to minimize fees. If that is the case it was kind of a penny-wise, pound-foolish result.

I think that you could use this case as an object lesson in why you might want to consider involving a professional as at least a co-executor if you have a significant estate. At any rate, you should try to arrange things so that your advisers and heirs/executors will work as a team. ◊

And then there is that NAICS code mentioned in the instructions that does not get enough attention.

Defining Construction and Reconstruction

If you are involved in construction and reconstruction, you may get a better deal on your losses from rental real estate. But what exactly is construction and reconstruction? The Tax Court had to look it up in the dictionary. Here's the story.

Some Background

The stake in the heart of the tax shelter vampire provided by the Tax Reform Act of 1986 was Code Section 469, which introduced the oxymoronic concept: passive activities. Other sections of the Code, like those concerning S corporations discuss "passive income"—interest and dividends and the like—but such investment income is not the passive activity income that 469 refers to. Passive activity income and, more significantly, loss comes from a trade or business activity in which you do not materially participate. We must divide our trade or business income from proprietorships, partnerships, and S corporations into two buckets. If the passive bucket is a net loss, the act allows a suspension of the loss and a carryforward to use if there is passive income in the future or when the underlying activity is entirely disposed of.

The rules about how you classify your activities and measure material participation are mind boggling in their complexity. Don't get me started. There is one rule that created a lot of angst, though. Rental activities are per se passive. This was troubling to people in the real estate industry who might, for example, have rental losses on a development while making money on the sale of property. So, there's a special rule for people involved in real estate trades or businesses. If you spend more than 750 hours per year in real estate trades or businesses, and the amount of time that you spend in the real estate trades is greater than the amount of time you spend doing anything else, then the per se passive rental income rule does not apply to you. Rental losses are not passive if you materially participate in the related properties.

Not Easy for People with Day Jobs to Be Considered Real Estate Pros

For some reason, the IRS is particularly zealous in enforcing Code Section 469. If you have substantial income and are posting losses from rental activities, you still have a better than average chance of a challenge. At least that is my inference from the cases I read and some discussions with other practitioners.

People with non-real estate day jobs who claim that they spend more time on their amateur landlord activity find the IRS almost always accuses them of having insufficient records of their time. "Ballpark guestimates" is a colorful term that the Tax Court seems to have reserved for 469 cases. Even in the cases where people have logs, the authorities often find them to be improbable. You don't see "pants on fire" in the decisions, but you suspect the judges are whispering it under their breath.

Construction And Reconstruction

Howard Cantor's trip to Tax Court[17] introduces a seldom explored angle. What exactly qualifies as a "real property trade or business"? The legislative and regulatory guidance is a little sketchy.

> A real property trade or business means any real property development, redevelopment, construction, reconstruction, acquisition, conversion, rental, operation, management, leasing, or brokerage trade or business. Section 469(c)(7)(C). The determination of whether a taxpayer's activities constitute a real property trade or business "is based on all of the relevant facts and circumstances."

Mr. Cantor was involved in the ownership of four rental properties. The IRS conceded that he materially participated in the operation and management of the properties. He had a demanding day job, though. He spent 40 to 50 hours a week running his proprietorship called ABS Glass. The NAICS code on his Schedule C was 811120, which stands for "Automotive, Paint, Interior, and Glass Repair." The NAICS classification of business is a return question that, in my experience, seldom receives much deep thought. Actually, people copy it over from one year to the next. That may have been what happened on Mr. Cantor's return, because there is a wrinkle to his business that he thought would allow his rental losses.

ABS Glass started out doing automotive glass replacement, but then it expanded its services. There was a residential division.

> Obviously, the services performed by petitioner in connection with the automotive division of ABS Glass are not services petitioner performed in a real property trade or business. According to petitioners, the services petitioners provided in connection with the residential division of ABS Glass are "construction" or "reconstruction" activities that qualify the residential division of ABS Glass as a real property trade or business under Section 469(c)(7)(C) for both years in issue. As the petitioners view the matter, the time petitioner spent performing services in connection with the residential division of ABS Glass qualifies him as a real estate professional as described in Section 469(c)(7)(B).

Mr. Cantor argued that all the time he spent on residential glass work qualified as construction or reconstruction. The Tax Court was not so sure.

Webster's II New Riverside University Dictionary (1984) defines the term "construction" as "the act or process of constructing" and defines the term "constructing" as "put together by assembling parts." This dictionary defines the term "reconstruction" as "the act or result of reconstructing" and defines the term "reconstructing" as "construct again." Nothing in the dictionary definitions limits the terms to real property construction or reconstruction, but the statute expressly imposes such a limitation.

Keeping that limitation in mind, we assume without finding that installing original or replacement windows in newly built or existing buildings constitutes "construction" or "reconstruction" within the meaning of Section 469(c)(7). On the other hand, we find that cutting and installing mirrors and tabletops, cutting, and installing shower and bath glass enclosures, and replacing windowpanes do not.

No Logs

It was good to try. The Tax Court seems to have agreed that Mr. Cantor could count some of the time that he spent on ABS Glass as a real estate trade or business. Presumably, he could add that to the time he spent on the properties, and if the total was more than 750 hours and more than he spent on other aspects of his glass business, he wins. As it happens, he did not have any detailed time records, so he lost.

What About That NAICS Code?

Most tax preparers won't pay a lot of attention to numbers that don't enter the tax computation. One of those numbers is the code for the Schedule C business. The instructions point you to a list[18] that is from the North American Industry Classification System. Generally, it is the same from one year to the next, particularly if you are using the software. If you are claiming your client is a real estate professional, maybe you should pay more attention to it. Would we have had a different outcome or maybe no audit at all if the code had been 28150 Glass & Glazing Contractors?

Does the Tax Court Have a Favorite Dictionary?

The reference to *Webster's II New Riverside University Dictionary* made me wonder if that is somehow the official Tax Court dictionary. I found the Tax Court cited it 20 times, which is twice as often as the Oxford English Dictionary. The higher courts seem to favor the OED.

In some ways the **Seventh Law** is really an extension of the **Fourth Law**. Ethereal thinkers at the highest level of the profession conceive brilliant tax plans and convey them to entrepreneurs who have great practical business skills. Ultimately, though, they need to transmit them to the IRS, and there is where the need for boring accountants who can follow instructions comes into play. Those are my people. ◊

Footnotes

1. "Stephen Ross," Forbes, accessed May 27, 2023, https://www.forbes.com/profile/stephen-ross/.
2. Internal Revenue Service, Form 8283: Noncash Charitable Contributions (Washington D.C.: Department of the Treasury, 2022), https://www.irs.gov/pub/irs-pdf/f8283.pdf.
3. RERI Holdings I, LLC
4. "Hudson Yards, Manhattan," Wikipedia, last modified November 28, 2022, https://en.wikipedia.org/wiki/Hudson_Yards,_Manhattan.
5. "Related," accessed May 27, 2023, https://www.related.com/.
6. Katherine Clarke, "Kansas City REIT nabs Hawthorne data center for $79.5M," The Real Deal, last modified October 11, 2016, https://therealdeal.com/la/2016/10/11/kansas-city-reit-nabs-hawthorne-data-center-for-79-5m/.
7. Internal Revenue Service, Form 8283.
8. Luke J. Chiarelli, Mawicke & Goisman, S.C., http://mawickelaw.com/profiles/luke-j-chiarelli/
9. Tarquinio F. Durante of Cedarburg Auction and Estate Sales
10. Internal Revenue Service, Form 8283-2012 https://www.irs.gov/pub/irs-prior/f8283--2012.pdf
11. "Second Chance," accessed May 27, 2023, https://www.secondchanceinc.org/.
12. Refer to Section 155 of "H.R. 4170 (98th): Deficit Reduction Act of 1984," GovTrack, last modified July 18, 1984, https://www.govtrack.us/congress/bills/98/hr4170/text.
13. Lawrence P. Mann and Linda S. Mann v. United States of America, United States District Court of Maryland (No. TDC-17-0200), January 31, 2019, https://casetext.com/case/mann-v-united-states-59.
14. Lesley A. West, et al. v. John Koskinen, Commissioner of the U.S. Internal Revenue Service, United States District Court for the Eastern District of Virginia (No. 1:15–cv–131), October 19, 2015, https://casetext.com/case/west-v-koskinen.
15. Internal Revenue Service, Instructions for Form 706 (Washington D.C.: Department of the Treasury, 2022), https://www.irs.gov/instructions/i706.

16. Internal Revenue Service, Form 4768: Application for Extension of Time To File a Return and/or Pay U.S. Estate (and Generation-Skipping Transfer) Taxes (Washington D.C.: Department of the Treasury, 2020), https://www.irs.gov/pub/irs-pdf/f4768.pdf.

17. "Docket Number: 20858-11S," Welcome to DAWSON, accessed May 27, 2023, https://dawson.ustaxcourt.gov/case-detail/20858-11.

18. Internal Revenue Service, "2022 Instructions for Schedule C," accessed May 30, 2023, https://www.irs.gov/instructions/i1040sc.

Both Before and After Thinking Outside the Box, Look Inside the Box.

This is one of the laws I learned more from practice than from case law. One example shows up in the partnership area. The way the 704 regulations work you are likely to allocate losses to the people who put in money rather than those who didn't without doing anything really fancy. And that is likely the result you want.

The planners for mystery writer Karin Slaughter came up with a very clever argument to avoid SE tax. It did not go that well. In fact, an S corporation might have been a better plan for her.

K Slaughter v Commissioner

There can be good money in crime fiction. That is the first lesson in K Slaughter v Commissioner[1]. The second lesson is that there is a lot more than writing involved in accessing that money. Finally, there is a tax lesson, an illustration of **Reilly's Eighth Law of Tax Planning**[2]—"***Before thinking outside the box, take a good look inside the box.***" Slaughter's advisers passed up a well-known planning technique for their own clever plan. It did not end well.

Who Is K Slaughter?

K Slaughter is Karin Slaughter[3] author of the Grant County series[4] and the Will Trent series[5]. The Grant County series is from the viewpoint of a woman who is a pediatrician and part-time coroner in a small Georgia town and her chief of police ex-husband. Will Trent is with the Georgia Bureau of Investigation.

I'm a fan of crime fiction, but my covivant is much more dedicated than I. I commissioned her to read *Blindsighted,*[6] which kicked off the Grant County series. CV thought the character, plotting, and pace were good, but found the graphic violence and gruesome details too much. *De gustibus non est disputandum.*[7]

Big Dollars

Ms. Slaughter was challenging deficiencies of $155,931 and $110,670 for the years 2010 and 2011. What makes these numbers dramatic is that they are deficiencies in self-employment tax. As you read the case, you will see that she ran through the Social Security maximum with income on which she did pay self-employment tax. If you do the math (i.e., divide by 0.0295), you'll get that she had income excluded from SE tax of over $5.1 million in 2010 and over $3.7 million in 2011. (The computation may be a little more complicated than that. Regardless, the income is, as we say, a number.)

Samuel Johnson remarked, "No man but a blockhead ever wrote except for money."[8] No evidence that Karin Slaughter is a blockhead.

So, You Want to Be an Author

Another interesting part of the case is a pretty extensive discussion of what is involved in becoming the sort of branded author that can make that kind of money. Writing is one of those careers that calls to many. You can find in this decision some advice on how to become one of the chosen.

> A brand author is one who provides prestige or reliable profits to a publishing house. When she decided to become a writer, petitioner set out in a businesslike fashion to obtain stationery, a reputable agent, and a contract with a New York publishing house. She succeeded in working with a media coach and publishers to develop her name and likeness into a successful brand. Therefore, in addition to writing, she spent time during 2010 and 2011 meeting with publishers, agents, media contacts, and others to protect and further her status as a brand author.

I checked in with my high school friend Thomas A. Burns author of the Natalie McMasters[9] Mystery Series. (Natalie is a millennial private detective trainee college student. Being Natalie's friend is more hazardous than vacationing in Cabot Cove, Maine.)[10] Tom confirmed that the work of building a brand is partly writing consistent stories so that your readers keep coming back for what they have come to like and also quite a bit of promoting. There can be a lot more time spent promoting than writing.

The Tax Lesson

Slaughter's CPA firm was sensitive to the fact that there were two aspects to her job. One was actually writing the books, and the other was her brand. They took the position that the income attributable to the latter was essentially the return on an intangible asset making it not subject to self-employment tax.

I can see some merit in the argument. The Tax Court has recognized the value of an author's brand for purposes of the estate tax in at least one case.[11] Virginia C. Andrews wrote a series of novels in the "children in jeopardy" genre beginning with *Flowers in the Attic* in 1978. After her death, the series continued under the V.C. Andrews name with Andrew Niederman doing the actual writing.

The estate of Virginia C. Andrews did not include the V.C. Andrews name as an asset, but the IRS insisted it had economic value. The Tax Court agreed with the IRS in principle, although it carved back its valuation.

According to the decision, Ms. Slaughter's advisers came up with their own methods for splitting the income into two pieces. (They reported all the income onto Schedule E and then transferred a portion to Schedule C.)

> The accounting team did not have copies of petitioner's publishing contracts. To calculate the amount reported on petitioner's Schedule C, the preparers used a calendar-based approach. They applied the percentage of the year which petitioner spent writing to the total payments she received for the year. Petitioner did not provide the preparers with a work calendar. Instead, the preparers relied on petitioner's statement that it took her roughly 12 to 15 weeks to produce a manuscript for a publisher. The preparers applied a 12-week period and assumed a five-day workweek because petitioner told them she occasionally took time off from writing. For the 2011 tax year, the percentage reported was higher than that for 2010 because petitioner spent more time writing.
>
> No other adviser recommended apportioning the income in the foregoing manner, and no appraiser was employed to value petitioner's contracts or opine on the calendar-based approach.

The Tax Court was not buying it.

> The statute provides that "net earnings from self-employment" includes income derived from any trade or business. An allocation within petitioner's contracts is beside the point if all elements are to be allocated to a trade or business. We conclude that petitioner's brand is part of her trade or business. We construe "trade or business" broadly, and, examining all of the facts, find that petitioner was engaged in developing her brand with continuity and regularity for the primary purpose of income and profit.

The Other Way

In my Monday morning quarterbacking, I have to be sensitive to the notion that there may be some factor constraining the available choices —state income tax or perhaps a business constraint, for example. Barring that, however, it seems that Slaughter could have achieved her goal with an S corporation that paid her a reasonable salary. I don't know how many authors do it that way, but as I mention in this chapter[12], one of them was Newt Gingrich.

The exposure comes in this technique when your salary is unreasonably low. The case law indicates that the IRS only goes after people whose salary is way unreasonably low. The problem the IRS has is that in the case of C corporations, they are going after salaries being unreasonably high.

So, if Slaughter had been working for her own S corporation drawing a salary of say $400,000, she could have avoided most of the SE tax that way. And it is an "in the box" technique.

Now More Than Ever

Section 199A supercharges the S corporation as a vehicle for authors like Slaughter, which allows a 20 percent income tax deduction for the flow-through income, provided the W-2 is sufficient. Writing is not one of the specified fields like health or performing arts excluded from 199A for high-income people.

Assuming she does not have a team of minions writing for her, she would need an S corporation so she can pay herself W-2 wages. I discuss the optimal amount here.[13] You would absolutely not want to argue that she is getting paid for the brand rather than the writing since that might fall under one of the dreaded SSTB categories that don't qualify for the deduction. The example in the regs is not a writer, but you can get the idea.

> L is a well-known chef and the sole owner of multiple restaurants each of which is owned in a disregarded entity. Due to L's skill and reputation as a chef, L receives an endorsement fee of $500,000 for the use of L's name on a line of cooking utensils and cookware. L is in the trade or business of being a chef and owning restaurants and such trade or business is not an SSTB. However, L is also in the trade or business of receiving endorsement income. L's trade or business consisting of the receipt of the endorsement fee for L's skill and/or reputation is an SSTB.

On The Bright Side

The good news in the decision was that the Tax Court threw out the accuracy penalty.

> Petitioner engaged the services of several qualified professionals to prepare her tax returns, including a certified public accountant with many decades of experience. Petitioner provided everything requested from her, and the preparers were satisfied with the information. It was reasonable for petitioner to rely on her preparers' expertise, considering that she has no background in finance, law, or tax.

Other Coverage

I picked this up from Lew Taishoff who titled his post *The Brand.*[14]

> But, no books, no brand. Perhaps a more carefully drafted publishing contract might differentiate between royalties for brand enhancement, and just plain literature.

Janet Novack covered this case at an earlier stage, "Tax Thriller: Best Selling Crime Writer Karin Slaughter Versus the IRS."[15]

Karin Slaughter's latest novel *False Witness*[16] focuses on a lawyer in a prestigious Atlanta firm gearing up for a criminal trial. Coincidentally, we have this week the outcome of her own legal drama, which likely only excites the tax blogosphere. Her appeal to the Eleventh[17] Circuit of a 2019 Tax Court decision confirming that she owed almost $190,000 in self-employment tax for 2010 and 2011 was unsuccessful. ◊

Footnotes

1. "Docket Number: 13256-14," Welcome to DAWSON, accessed May 27, 2023, https://dawson.ustaxcourt.gov/case-detail/13256-14.
2. Peter J. Reilly, "Laws Of Tax Planning Updated For Tax Cuts And Jobs Act," Forbes, last modified Jan 4, 2018, https://www.forbes.com/sites/peterjreilly/2018/01/04/laws-of-tax-planning-updated-for-tax-cuts-and-jobs-act/#34110cb25ee5.
3. "Karin Slaughter," accessed May 27, 2023, https://www.karinslaughter.com/.
4. "The Grant County Series," Karin Slaughter, accessed May 27, 2023, https://www.karinslaughter.com/grant-county-series.
5. "The Will Trent Series," Karin Slaughter, accessed May 27, 2023, https://www.karinslaughter.com/will-trent-series.
6. Karin Slaughter, Blindsighted (New York City: Harper, 2015).
7. "De gustibus non est disputandum," Wikipedia, last modified May 22, 2023, https://en.wikipedia.org/wiki/De_gustibus_non_est_disputandum.
8. Samuel Johnson, "No man but a blockhead ever wrote except for money," Brainy Quote, accessed May 27, 2023, https://www.brainyquote.com/quotes/samuel_johnson_170103.
9. "Thomas A. Burns," Amazon, accessed May 27, 2023, https://www.amazon.com/stores/Thomas-A.-Burns/author/B07FF2Z13D?ref=ap_rdr&store_ref=ap_rdr&isDramIntegrated=true&shoppingPortalEnabled=true.
10. "Where the Heck is Cabot Cove, Maine?," Jesmaine Tripod, accessed May 27, 2023, https://jesmaine.tripod.com/mswcabotcove.html.
11. Estate of Virginia C. Andrews, Deceased, etc. v. United States of America, United States District Court for the Eastern District of Virginia (No. 2:92cv97), May 10, 1994, https://www.leagle.com/decision/19942129850fsupp127911978.
12. Peter J. Reilly, "S Corporation SE Avoidance Still A Solid Strategy," Forbes, last modified August 25, 2013, https://www.forbes.com/sites/peterjreilly/2013/08/25/s-corporation-se-avoidance-still-a-solid-strategy/#4cca7b9161fe.
13. Peter J. Reilly, "How Much Owner Salary Should S Corp Pay To Maximize Qualified Income Deduction?," Forbes, last modified, December 28, 2017, https://www.forbes.com/sites/peterjreilly/2017/12/28/how-much-owner-salary-should-s-corp-pay-to-maximize-qualified-income-deduction/#7173405772ef.

14. "The Brand," Taishoff Law, last modified June 4, 2019, https://taishofflaw.com/2019/06/04/the-brand/.

15. Janet Novack, "Tax Thriller: Best Selling Crime Writer Karin Slaughter Versus The IRS," Forbes, last modified September 5, 2014, https://www.forbes.com/sites/janetnovack/2014/09/05/tax-thriller-best-selling-crime-writer-karin-slaughter-versus-the-irs/#32d7aca7e4a7.

16. Karin Slaughter, False Witness: A Novel (New York City: William Morrow, 2021).

17. K. Slaughter v. Commissioner of Internal Revenue Service, United States Court of Appeals (No. 13256-14), August 3, 2021, https://www.taxnotes.com/research/federal/court-documents/court-opinions-and-orders/eleventh-circuit-affirms-author-is-liable-for-self-employment-taxes/76zkq.

NINTH LAW OF TAX PLANNING

Tell the Preparer What the Plan Is.

There is a certain tendency to scorn pure compliance work. An effect of this can be that the preparers do not have all the information they need to memorialize the magnificent work of the brilliant planners. And oddly enough, the planners seem to rarely look at the returns to see if they came out the way they were supposed to. This seems to happen a lot in the partnership area.

When I spoke with Ken Weissenberg[1] about GKK 2 LLC's appeal of its Real Estate Transfer Tax,[2] his best comment was that taxes, like ogres, are like onions.

Many Layers

Ken is co-chair of real estate services of the Real Estate Services Group of Eisner Advisory Group. He seemed to be the right guy to ask about this decision since he's both a lawyer and a CPA. He also indicated that he has been around long enough not to be overspecialized, which may be the lesson in this case, because taxes are like, you know, onions.

Three Million in Transfer Taxes

The stakes were pretty high. GKK was looking for a refund of more than $3 million (including interest). That struck me quite a bit for real property transfer taxes, but this was the Big Apple where the real property transfer tax can get as high as 2.5 percent. And there was an iconic building involved, 2 Herald Square (also known as 1328 Broadway and the Marbridge building). That is the very Herald Square that George M. Cohan wished to be remembered to.

A Creative 1031 Deal

The LLC was a disregarded entity Gramercy Capital Corp.[3] (now known[4] as Gramercy Property Trust, Inc.) owned. GKK acquired a 45 percent interest in the building in 2007. SL Green Realty Corp., which had acquired 100 percent of a leasehold interest acquired the other 55 percent. The arrangement referred to in this story as a joint venture was not considered a partnership between the two entities. The interest, a 1031 (like-kind exchange) target, probably dictated the co-ownership structure (sometimes referred to as a tenancy in common) as noted in this release.

> Andrew Mathias, Chief Investment Officer of Gramercy Capital Corp. and SL Green, stated: "Our success in Manhattan is due to our extensive network in the real estate community, and our proven ability to creatively structure value-add situations for buyers, sellers, and co-investors. In this acquisition, we connected with Sitt Asset Management, a savvy New York City real estate investor with whom SL Green has transacted on several occasions and devised and executed a transaction in which the joint venture and Sitt were able to accommodate tax-free 1031 exchanges. We believe this acquisition in particular will deliver secure debt-like returns with the potential for equity upside."

I have to tell you that the transaction strikes me as just a bit dubious. The co-owner has a 100 percent leasehold interest in the underlying property, so the 45 percent interest appears to behave a lot more like debt than equity, but that is not what the case is about.

Substance and Form

In 2010, SL Green bought out Gramercy's interest in 2 Herald Square as part of a larger deal. Well, that's the way the real estate press[5] puts it, but to the tax geeks, here is what happened. On December 22, 2010, GKK2 LLC contributed its 45 percent interest to the newly formed 2 Herald Owner LLC. SLG 2 LLC did the same thing with its 55 percent interest. Assuming that 2 Herald Owner LLC did not elect corporate taxation (something exceedingly improbable in these circumstances), there is now a partnership. That is probably a decent enough interval from the acquisition not to cast doubt on the exchange back in 2007.

As it turns out, the new partnership (for income tax purposes) was extremely short-lived. Also, on December 22, 2010, GKK2 LLC sold its 45 percent membership interest in 2 Heald Owner LLC to SLG2 LLC. To have a partnership, you have to have partners (plural), so 2 Herald Owner LLC transformed, most likely, to a disregarded entity. What gives me a serious headache is wondering whether 2 Herald Owner LLC needed to file a Form 1065 for its mayfly existence as a partnership. In my experience, none of the deal meisters who designed this whole thing would have thought about that. There is a serious gap between people who design structures and people who do returns. I used to think that businesspeople must do it better when it came to nine-figure deals, but my brief term with a national firm makes me suspect otherwise.

No Step Transaction Doctrine for Transfer Taxes

Believe it or not, those extra steps do not seem to have any income tax significance. By converting what was for income tax purposes an interest in the real property into a partnership interest, Gramercy couldn't do a like exchange. The extra steps were for transfer tax purposes. If it had been effective for federal income tax purposes, the IRS could have collapsed the transaction into a sale, just as the real estate press reported it. Different story for transfer taxes, though. Follow along (https://www.dta.ny.gov/pdf/determinations/826402.det.pdf).

The first step was the transfer of the co-tenancy interest to 2 Herald Owner LLC. There is no argument there.

> The Division concedes that the petitioner's contribution of its 45 percent tenant-in-common interest to Owner LLC in exchange for a 45 percent interest in Owner LLC, and SLG's contribution of its 55 percent tenant-in-common interest to Owner LLC in exchange for a 55 percent interest in Owner LLC, standing alone, are exempt from the RETT as a mere change in form of ownership. Indeed, the Division's regulations provide that the RETT does not apply to "the conveyance by tenants-in-common of their interest in real property to a partnership or a corporation, the partnership or corporation interests being in the same pro rata shares as the tenants-in-common held before the conveyance. Such conveyance is not taxable as there is no change in beneficial ownership."

What New York wanted to do was apply something like the step-transaction doctrine.

> The Division attempts to "aggregate" three nontaxable transactions, namely (1) the transaction between SLG and Owner LLC, which effectuated a mere change in form of ownership, (2) the transaction between petitioner and Owner LLC, which effectuated a mere change in form of ownership, and (3) the transaction whereby petitioner transferred its 45 percent interest in Owner LLC to SLG, to impose a tax under the RETT on the transfer of a minority interest. However, the third transaction does not meet the definition of a transfer of a "controlling interest" because the petitioner did not own more than 50 percent of the Owner LLC. As such, that transaction, by definition, cannot be a transfer or acquisition of a controlling interest in an entity with an interest in real property.

The court was not buying it. Their message to the Division of Taxation was a lengthier version of **Reilly's First Law of Tax Planning—"*It is what it is. Deal with it.*"**

> The issue in the present case does not involve an understanding of the physical or social sciences, obscure regulatory practices, complex

> markets or industries, expert analysis of voluminous factual data, or subtle policy determinations outside the competence of ordinary persons. Indeed, the issues are so purely legal in nature that the parties stipulated the facts and submitted the case without a hearing. The Division's interpretation herein is inconsistent with the plain language of the statute, regulations, and its publication and as such is not entitled to deference.

LLC Is Not Always the Right Answer

Ken Weissenberg told me that this is an illustration of exactly what he has been saying over the years about holding co-tenancy interests through LLCs. But do not forget the onions. He also told me about a couple who lost favorable real estate tax rates on their cooperative apartment because they held it through an LLC. I recently wrote about a school in New Jersey[6] that lost its property tax exemption.

The people who designed these transactions were pretty slick, and I have to take my hat off to them. 2.5 percent might not sound that large. But you must remember that it is on the whole value of the real estate interest, including the leveraged portion. That would have pulled a pretty big chunk out of the "debt-like" return the 1031 acquisition was to achieve. The planner's ability to drill down below the federal income tax issues and have their position sustained shows some really good work. An illustration of **Reilly's Fifth Law of Tax Planning—"*A tax plan that ignores AMT of SALT is not much of a tax plan.*"** SALT stands for State and Local Tax, a specialty that is quite underappreciated.

If somebody told me that the planners figured out in advance whether a one-day return was necessary for 2 Herald LLC, I'd be impressed because almost no planners follow **Reilly's Ninth Law of Tax Planning—"*Tell the preparer what the plan is.*"** ◊

It goes without saying that if you are preparing a return for a trust or a partnership, you need to refer to the governing documents. Well, it should go without saying, but actually, it needed saying a lot. Expecting that your preparer reads and understands the instruments is another hurdle.

IRS Penalizes Plan of Minister to Donate House to Ministry While Continuing to Live There

By all appearances, Presley Family Ministries is an admirable organization.

> Each summer, Presley Family Ministries travels overseas to share the love of Christ and provide glasses to 1000s of people. In 2017, we traveled to northern Peru and provided free eye care and glasses to approx. 1,200 people while also planting a church in Canasbamba, Peru, and praying with nearly 300 to receive Christ!

There are also regular services and family retreats. Some of the support for all this comes from a pick-your-own blueberry farm and donations from supporters, but a large proportion seems to have come from Richard Presley who runs an optometry practice[7]. The tangled relationship between Richard Presley and the ministry is what had him and his spouse, Martine, in Tax Court. It did not go well for them.

About Presley Family Ministries

Detailed financial information about PFM is available for 2005 and earlier at Guidestar[8]. That stops in 2006, because, as Guidestar notes, "This organization is not required to file an annual return with the IRS because it is a church." At the end of 2005, total assets were $472,957, mostly fixed assets. The public support percentage was 38 percent, barely keeping the organization out of private foundation status. That is how it stood when it disappeared into church status. According to the Tax Court decision, in the years at issue (2010 and 2012), 95 percent of the support for the ministry came from Mr. Presley.

Conversion to church status involved ordaining Mr. Presley. In June 2004, there was a certificate of ordination from the Universal Life Church[9]. This put Mr. Presley in a distinguished company. He can count among his fellow ULC ministers Conan O'Brien, Paul McCartney, and Lady Gaga.[10] There was also a certificate from World Christianship Ministries[11]. They are a little less ecumenical than ULC:

> What is the difference between the WCM's ordination, and the ordination provided by other ordaining ministries on the internet like Universal Life Church, the Monastery, and the American Marriage Ministry AMM?
>
> We, the WCM, are a Christian Ministry and ordained Christian Clergy only, and we only authorize Christian services.

One of my theories is that given their education requirements, I can think like a revenue agent. And I started thinking that maybe we don't have an actual church here, but it turned out that would not have been fair. There was much church-like activity.

Mr. Presley spent about 20 hours each week on certain activities and certain events relating to PFM, which took place in the petitioners' residence. For example, he conducted weekly worship services of PFM, which approximately 12 to 40 people attended. Approximately 30 to 40 people participated regularly in the activities or events that the Presleys hosted for PFM. In addition, Mr. Presley at times performed weddings and baptisms and distributed communion. He also met with young adults, taught classes, and conducted Bible studies three evenings each week.

Ms. Presley spent about four to five hours each week on certain activities and certain events relating to PFM. For example, she taught Bible studies and prepared meals for attendees of certain activities or certain events of PFM that the Presleys held at the petitioners' residence.

There was some very clever, perhaps too aggressive tax planning, and that is what ended up in Tax Court. We have here an illustration of **Reilly's Fourth Law of Tax Planning**—***"Execution isn't everything but it's a lot."***

The Problem

The deficiencies were for 2010 and 2012, which with penalties came to more than $100,000 related to charitable contributions. The 2010 donation was a little convoluted. Mr. Presley had started the blueberry farm on land leased from the ministry. In 2010, he claimed a deduction for a charitable contribution of a tractor used on the farm and improvements he made to the land. The 2012 donation was more straightforward but more eyebrow-raising. The Preselys donated their residence to the ministry, even though they would continue to reside there without paying any rent.

The court denied both those donations. Interestingly the grounds for denial were matters of execution rather than substance.

The 2010 Donation

A basic requirement of a more than negligible charitable deduction is contemporaneous acknowledgment. The ministry struggled with that.

Around the same time in late September 2010, when David Dryer prepared October 20, 2010, minutes at Mr. Presley's request, he also prepared at Mr. Presley's request and sent to him (or his designee) an undated and unsigned letter addressed to PFM Farms (Mr. Dryer's draft 2010 letter No. 1). The body of Mr. Dryer's draft 2010 letter No. 1 stated: "This is to acknowledge and thank you for your support of Presley Family Ministries during 2010. You donated the beautiful water ponds to the ministry enabling our youth and others to enjoy water sports, fishing, wildlife, and the beautiful setting. This provides a wonderful ministry setting and we thank you."

There were two subsequent drafts.

Judge Carolyn Chiechi expressed a good deal of skepticism about the transactions since there were inconsistencies in the narratives of the various players and the documents. In the end, though, she denied the deduction based on acknowledgment.

> Even if PFM Farms had paid the required land improvement expenses in 2010 and those expenses were directly connected with and solely attributable to the rendition of services to PFM by PFM Farms, we would find on the record before us that petitioners have failed to carry their burden of establishing that they satisfy the substantiation requirements in Section 170(f)(8)(A) and (C) and Section 1.170A-13(f)(1) and (3), Income Tax Regs. Those authorities, which apply to contributions of $250 or more, required petitioners to substantiate the claimed contribution relating to the required land improvement expenses with a contemporaneous written acknowledgment from PFM.

There was more, but that was enough.

The 2012 Donation

The IRS had three reasons not to like what the judge refers to as the purported donation of the residence. (By the way, pro tip: when reading Tax Court decisions, when any form of the word "purport" appears, things are not going to go well for the taxpayer.) The three reasons are:

> (1) petitioners retained dominion and control over petitioners' residence after they purportedly contributed it to PFM;[12]
>
> (2) when they made the purported contribution to PFM of petitioners' residence, petitioners expected to, and did, receive a substantial benefit in return because PFM allowed them to reside in that residence without paying any rent to it; and
>
> (3) petitioners failed to comply or substantially comply with certain charitable contribution deduction substantiation requirements that apply to the claimed charitable contribution of petitioners' residence.

The judge only considered the third argument, since this was a kind of one-strike-and-you're-out sort of deal. There were a couple of issues with the appraisal. It did not state that it was for income tax purposes. Rather, it stated that it was for financing. The appraisal was after the extended due date of the 2012 return. The appraiser's signature portion of Form 8283 was not complete.

Penalties

The judge also upheld the accuracy penalties. The taxpayers had advice from an attorney and relied on a preparer, but they did not check to see that the preparer followed through on the reporting requirements the attorney highlighted. **Reilly's Ninth Law of Tax Planning—"*Tell the preparer what the plan is.*"**

Too Bad

Setting up a church and then donating your house to the church while continuing to live there, with all the expenses run through the church and the benefit of living there excluded under Code Section 107(1), strikes me as a brilliant scheme[13]. You could also throw in a property tax exemption, depending on what state you're in and how hungry the local assessors are. I really would have liked to see how the plan would have flown, but the Tax Court never had to get to its merits because of poor execution. What a shame. Execution isn't everything, but it's a lot.

Reflections On the Ninth Law

The Ninth Law does not show up in case law that much. It does come up a lot in practice. One of its sources is a lack of respect for compliance work. You can have a great plan, but if the preparer doesn't understand it might get lost in translation. ◊

Footnotes

1. Kenneth Weissenberg, "Ken Weissenberg Talks Tax Reform and REITs on CNBC's 'Power Lunch,'" EisnerAmper, last modified December 26, 2017, https://www.eisneramper.com/weissenberg-tax-reform-reits-video-1217/.
2. Ellen E. Hoffman and Robert J. Firestone, In the Matter of GKK 2 Herald LLC (Albany: Tax Appeals Tribunal, 2016), https://www.nyc.gov/assets/taxappeals/downloads/pdf/1325DEC0716.pdf.
3. "Gramercy Capital Corp. and SL Green Realty Corp. Announce Acquisition of Fee Interest of 2 Herald Square," Gramercy Capital Corp., last modified April 19, 2007, https://www.sec.gov/Archives/edgar/data/1287701/000110465907029403/a07-11776_1ex99d2.htm.
4. "Gramercy Capital Corp. Changes Name to Gramercy Property Trust Inc.," Business Wire, last modified April 15, 2013, https://www.businesswire.com/news/home/20130415005289/en/Gramercy-Capital-Corp.-Gramercy-Property-Trust.
5. TRD Staff, "SL Green acquires three troubled properties," The Real Deal, last modified December 6, 2010, https://therealdeal.com/new-york/2010/12/06/sl-green-acquires-three-troubled-properties/.
6. Peter J. Reilly, "Ownership Through LLC Kills Local Charitable Property Tax Exemption," Forbes, last modified November 18, 2015, https://www.forbes.com/sites/peterjreilly/2015/11/18/ownership-through-llc-kills-local-charitable-property-tax-exemption/#4085d3153169.
7. "Dr. Presley & Associates," accessed May 27, 2023, https://www.drpresley.com/.
8. Presley Family Ministries Inc., "Form 990: Return of Organization Exempt From Income Tax," Guidestar, last modified August 15, 2006, https://pdf.guidestar.org/PDF_Images/2005/731/529/2005-731529269-02b46401-9.pdf.
9. "Universal Life Church," accessed May 27, 2023, https://www.ulc.org/.
10. Peter J. Reilly, "IRS Penalizes Plan Of Minister To Donate House To Ministry While Continuing To Live There," Forbes, last modified October 29, 2018, https://www.forbes.com/sites/peterjreilly/2018/10/29/irs-penalizes-plan-of-minister-to-donate-house-to-ministry-while-continuing-to-live-there/.
11. "World Christianship Ministries," accessed May 27, 2023, https://www.wcm.org/.

12. Reilly, "IRS Penalizes Plan of Minister."

13. Reilly, "IRS Penalizes Plan of Minister."

Once the Tax Is More Than You Can Pay, It Might Not Matter How Much More.

Many tax practitioners view themselves as helping clients become compliant and minimizing their tax liability. The assumption is that if the client takes an aggressive position and the IRS audits and ultimately prevails, the client will write a check. As it happens, though, there is another area of tax practice where the ultimate assessed tax is barely of academic interest. We are talking about collections where "reasonable collection potential" rules. Since the 90s, there is an appeals process about the IRS determination in that area and taxpayers (or maybe we could call them tax-not-payers) have the right to appeal determinations to the Tax Court. That is actually a pretty good part of the Tax Court's business.

Sometimes the advice that minimizes tax is not the best advice when it comes to collections.

This is a classic "I'm from the government, and I'm here to help you" story.

IRS Agent Causes Grief for Taxpayer's Spouse by Being Helpful

It probably would have been a bad idea for Maria Sanchez to file a joint return with her estranged spouse for 2006. She didn't do it and didn't have to file a return on her own. Her not-quite ex, Francisco A. Sanchez Rodriguez, did file. He claimed to be single. From there it got a bit strange, resulting in what is one of the oddest innocent spouse cases[1] I have ever seen. It seemed that the IRS nailed Ms. Sanchez with a catch-22, but at least one expert has some optimism that she might do better in the next round if there is one.

Some Background

Most tax practitioners will tell you that it is almost always a better deal to file jointly than married filing separately. I would downgrade that "almost always" to usually. That is because most tax practitioners assume too much, and that, in many cases, turns out to be unwarranted. That assumption is that if there is a balance due, the client will pay it. Here is the thing. There are two almost entirely distinct areas of tax practice. One is concerned with determining the correct tax and coming up with legitimate means to minimize that tax. That is the area in which filing a joint return is almost always the right answer.

The other area of tax practice is collections. That is when it is determined how much of the correct tax the client must pay. If the "correct tax" is significantly more than you can pay, it doesn't matter how much more it is. What becomes relevant, then, is your "reasonable collection potential" (RCP). RCP is how much blood they think they can get from the stone—the blood being money and you being the stone.

Let's say that married filing separately you owe $100,000. Assume that a joint return would produce a joint liability of $80,000. Should you file jointly? It all depends on whether there will be a check for $80,000 going in with that joint return. If all you can come up with is $20,000, then filing a joint return will probably hurt you because now the IRS will consider both your income and assets and your spouse's income and assets in determining RCP. I should mention that it is a different ball game if you live in a community property state, but don't get me started on community property, it gives me a headache.

The Helpful Auditor

Mr. Rodriguez's 2006 return ended up getting audited. The revenue agent who conducted the audit must have wanted to be a mensch. He realized that if Mr. Rodriguez had filed jointly the resulting deficiency would have been lower. So he prepared Form 4549, Income Tax Examination Changes (consent), as if Mr. Rodriguez and Ms. Sanchez had filed a joint return.

So of course, now to close the case, the signature of Ms. Sanchez is necessary, which she provided. The case does not indicate whether she asked anybody for advice on whether going from a larger tax for which she had no responsibility to a lower tax for which she was jointly and severally liable was good for her. It was good for her ex, and it was good for the IRS. For her not so much. It would only make sense for her to sign that form if a check from Mr. Rodriguez for the full amount was going to be forthcoming. It was not.

I suspect that is what the revenue agent expected. That division between tax determination and collection appears to be even stronger in the IRS. Once you consent to the assessment, the examining agent is through.

Innocent Spouse Relief

If joint and several liabilities are the dark side of joint returns, the light at the end of the tunnel is innocent spouse relief. It seems as if Ms. Sanchez would have a pretty good innocent spouse case. She didn't have a clue as to what went on the original return and she and Mr. Rodriguez were no longer married. Here is where the catch-22 came in. One of the requirements of innocent spouse relief is that you have filed a joint return. Of course, you only need innocent spouse relief if you have signed a joint return, except in this possible *sui generis* circumstance of a helpful examining agent. Ms.

Sanchez had not filed a joint return, so she was not eligible for innocent spouse relief.

Some Catch, That Catch-22

It doesn't seem fair, which requires me to invoke **Reilly's First Law of Tax Planning—"*It is what it is. Deal with it.*"** Lew Taishoff had a similar reaction to mine titling his post *I'm From the Government and I'm Here to Help*[3] and noting that "listening to an IRS RA can be hazardous to your tax health." ◊

It is amazing how stretched out tax payments can be if you have the right sort of constitution.

IRS Collection Action Can Be Delayed for a Long Time

I wrote[4] about a Tax Court decision[5] in the case of Bruce Hauptman. At issue were income taxes from the years 1992 through 1996. There is no dispute as to the amount of the taxes. In 2007, when the IRS started getting more serious about actually collecting, the tab was around $13 million.

What Is Reasonable?

The October 2014 Tax Court decision was about whether the IRS could levy on Mr. Hauptman's property. He was arguing that the IRS was being unreasonable in rejecting his offer of compromise. In July 2005, he made his third offer in compromise based on doubt as to collectability. He offered $500,000. An IRS collection specialist had pegged Mr. Hauptman's "reasonable collection potential" at more than $3 million and asserted that he was not in current compliance with income taxes for more recent years.

In 2007, the IRS issued a notice of intent to levy. Mr. Hauptman responded with Form 12153[6]—Request for a Collection Due Process or Equivalent Hearing. If you played the Magic the Gathering[7] card game, you would think of Form 12153 as a powerful counter-spell, but I may be the only reader of tax blogs who has played Magic. Regardless, IRS Appeals made quick work of determining that the levy was correct. Mr. Hauptman appealed to Tax Court. That was December 19, 2007. If his deficiencies were kids, the oldest would have been starting high school.

Time Marches On

Nearly seven years late, the Tax Court ruled that the IRS was correct in rejecting the offer in compromise. Mr. Hauptman appealed. The Eighth Circuit agreed with the Tax Court[8] in a decision released two decades, give or take, after the taxes were originally due.

One part of the appeal was procedural. Mr. Hauptman argued that the Tax Court had lost jurisdiction when the case went back to appeals. That argument went nowhere. He also tried to argue that the IRS had been unreasonable in rejecting his $500,000 offer.

Remember that the court rejected his offer nine years ago.

Is It a Good Idea?

A couple of thoughts on this. One is that you don't want to try this with a tax liability that you could pay without breaking yourself because you will get it to grow to that level. On the other hand, the IRS does agree that Mr. Hauptman couldn't pay the whole tab. Once the client crosses that threshold, the amount of the tax liability and accumulated interest and penalties is no longer important. So, what's the hurry?

I reached out to Russell Haynes, an attorney who practices in the collection area, for his thoughts on this case. He wrote me.

> I'm not surprised Hauptman lost, either on appeal or in the Tax Court. The service will always reject an offer when presented

with conflicting evidence of asset valuation or other indications that there are omissions or inaccuracies on the financial statement used to evaluate the offer. If they cannot establish what the taxpayer's actual ability to pay is, then there is no way they can reliably decide whether the taxpayer is able to pay the offered amount. The decision to reject an offer under such circumstances is appropriate, will probably be sustained by appeals, and will be nearly impossible to overturn on the "abuse of discretion" standard applied in the Tax Court.

But to your original point, a taxpayer can delay collection action in such cases by continuing to appeal, although it usually does more harm than good in the end. The statute of limitations on collection stops during the time the offer and any subsequent appeals are pending. Hauptman has been fighting this case for so long that the statute would have run twice if he hadn't filed at least four OICs, a Tax Court case, and appealed the Tax Court's decision.

I'm not sure what the moral is to this story is. If you keep appealing, you can go a long time before you have to pay anything. Whether that is a good idea or not, you be the judge. ◊

Every once in a while, a Tax Court decision[9] breaks the tax mold, for instance, the film star Wesley Snipes case.

Wesley Snipes Can Get Another Bite at the IRS Collection Apple and Another Trip to Tax Court If He Wants

A lot of the reports on the decision imply that it is game over as if Wesley Snipes is now going to just mail in a check. I don't think so. It may well be a long journey before the IRS gets any of the $23+ million in income tax that he owes for the years 1999 through 2006. Snipes concedes that $23+

million is the correct tax. Once you enter the world of collections, though, the correct tax can be merely of academic interest. **Reilly's Tenth Law of Tax Planning—"*Once the tax is more than you can pay, it might not matter how much more.*"**

The undisputed assessed tax is like the sticker price on a car, or perhaps more aptly, full tuition at a brand-name college with a generous financial aid program. That is what Wesley Snipes was arguing about with the IRS. How much could he afford? Reasonable collection potential (RCP). Why did he not take the seemingly generous offer the IRS made? And what further recourse does he have? Those are the questions I find interesting.

Wesley Snipes

Wesley Snipes refused to file and pay income tax based on something called the 861 argument[10]. It is a bad enough argument that it got him criminally prosecuted along with Eddie Ray Kahn[11] and Douglas P. Rosile[12], who, each in his way, promoted the scheme. Mr. Snipes was convicted of some charges and acquitted of others, earning a three-year sentence[13].

It is on completion of the sentence, that the more current drama starts. Mr. Snipes was free on April 2, 2013. Then, spring became the summer and on August 27, 2013, the IRS filed a Notice of Federal Tax Lien[14] (NFTL). Snipes and his team likely anticipated this, since they filed Form 12153 on September 4, just over a week later. (You have 30 days, but it is best not to cut it close). Mr. Snipes made an Offer in Compromise (OIC) of $842,061 on the basis of doubt as to collectability. That's less than four cents on the dollar.

The settlement officer started looking into Snipes' properties, some of which he claimed to have lost or transferred, although documentation on that was weak. The SO arrived at $17,482,152 as RCP. Snipes held firm at $842,061. SO issued a notice of determination rejecting the OIC on October 6, 2015. Then, Snipes filed the Tax Court petition on October 5, 2015, cutting it close this time. A year later, Judge Kerrigan kicked the case back to appeals. Mr. Snipes claimed that his financial adviser, W. Johnson, had diverted funds and, in effect, asked the IRS to chase Mr. Johnson. (It's called transferee liability.) The IRS and court viewed the documentation on that as being weak. Nonetheless, SO offered to cut the RCP by close to half, down to $9,581,027. Mr. Snipes did not budge from $842,061.

Finally, Judge Kerrigan ruled on November 1, 2018.

> Petitioner has failed to establish that the settlement officer did not properly determine that the requirements of any applicable law or administrative procedure had been met. We find that the settlement officer properly based her determination on the required factors. Accordingly, we conclude that the settlement officer did not abuse her discretion in determining that acceptance of the petitioner's OIC was not in the best interest of the United States.

And that is what all the coverage was about as if the matter ends there, but let's consider whether what Wesley Snipes is doing makes any sense.

Was This a Good Idea?

I spoke to a couple of practitioners who have substantial experience in collection work. Kathryn Morgan[15] is an enrolled agent and the United States Tax Court Practitioner who runs Puzzled by Taxes LLC. Frank Wolpe[16] is an attorney and professor emeritus in law, taxation, and financial planning at Bentley University. Both think that Wesley Snipes had bad advice. Ms. Morgan wrote me:

> Based on the info I have read, including the court case and other articles, I can see him (or his reps whom he needs to fire!!) trying to go through this circus all over again. They don't want to do that because if frivolous penalties start getting added, and then they could eventually start with more evasion charges, depending on how it goes, he could end up in even more trouble than he is in right now. Does he think that in a high-profile case like this that the IRS hasn't dotted every i and crossed every t?

Professor Wolpe, when I spoke with him, went on at some length on how he would handle the case, which is doing some serious negotiation with the IRS and working out a payment plan. He also believes that Snipes is ill-advised.

Not surprisingly, I had no luck in reaching out to the attorneys representing Mr. Snipes in Tax Court. I think Ms. Morgan and Professor Wolpe may be too quick in criticizing them. It is possible that Wesley Snipes is not following their advice and that they are following their clients' directions in a kind of scorched earth strategy, which brings us to what comes next.

Snipes' Next Bite at the Collection Apple

There was no mention of a levy in the litigation. Sometimes the IRS will issue both the NTFL and a levy and will combine the allowed CDP hearings. There is no indication that this happened. The decision only discusses an NFTL. So, assuming Wesley Snipes is not just writing a check, the next step is to levy. Take his stuff. Tell people that owe Wesley Snipes money that they should pay the IRS instead—or else.

Only they have to send Mr. Snipes a warning that they are going to levy, and with that, he gets the right to file Form 12153 **again** and have another CDP hearing. If he does not like the outcome of that hearing, he can appeal the result to Tax Court **again.**

So, if Wesley Snipes decides to be stubborn about it, there will be another long process. Maybe not another five years, but I have to think at least two. ◊

Joint returns are a major issue in collection cases and the most common situation where the right move for tax minimizing is the wrong move for collections.

Some People Should Just Not Be Filing Joint Returns

That is the lesson in a recent Tax Court Memorandum decision, TCM 2017-144. I will refer to the couple involved as Robin and Terry.

Going to Tax Court makes their identities public, but I figure they would just as soon as I did not spread their fame further. Robin is a physician specializing in family medicine, and Terry is a lawyer practicing in both probate law and bankruptcy.

It seems that Terry might have a certain affinity for one part of his client base. According to the decision, he has a "long history of failing to pay his debts when due." Robin became aware of this when, as is the common practice nowadays, they purchased a home before marrying in 2004. She did not know the specifics of Terry's financial past, but she was aware that he had a low credit score and outstanding student loans. As a result, Robin and Terry have separate credit cards, and the mortgage on the house is exclusively in Robin's name.

Filing Jointly

When it came to filing tax returns from 2004 to 2012, the way it worked was that Terry (i.e., the lawyer) gathered all the documents together and gave them to an accountant who prepared the return. When the return came back, Terry asked Robin to sign it, which she did. Robin was an employee with withholding, and Terry was self-employed. She thought that Terry was sending in the balance due. He was not.

In 2011, Robin learned about some of the balances due when her husband asked her to make a payment of $53,502 for 2007 and 2008. She thought that was it. She learned the details of the remaining liabilities in May 2014. She consulted with an accountant and has been filing separately beginning with the 2013 return. She and Terry are still married with four children.

The Decision

Robin was in Tax Court, pro se, on an innocent spouse claim for $55,859 for 2009 and 2012. She had no luck. She couldn't "streamline relief" because she and Terry were still married. That led to a "fact-specific inquiry" on whether it "is inequitable to hold an individual liable for all or part of any unpaid tax or deficiency arising from a joint return." There is a seven-factor test.

> The factors are the requesting spouse's (1) marital status; (2) economic hardship if relief is not granted; (3) knowledge or reason to know that the tax liability would not be paid; (4) legal obligation to pay the outstanding income tax liability; (5) receipt of a significant benefit from the unpaid income tax liability; (6) compliance with income tax laws; and (7) mental and physical health.

Although Judge Buch found that most of the factors were neutral or slightly favored relief, the overwhelming factor was the third "knowledge or reason to know that the tax liability would not be paid"

> Dr. _____ had reason to know that her husband was not paying the amount of tax owed each year and had actual knowledge of outstanding tax liabilities. The fact that she did not know the details of those outstanding liabilities is unfortunate, but for this inquiry, it is immaterial. Dr. ____ had reason to know the full extent of the liabilities; the fact that she lacked actual knowledge does not release her from the tax liabilities. ***(Name was included in the original)***

What Was the Husband Thinking?

The part of this story that I think is of most interest is not Robin's misfortune but trying to figure out what Terry was thinking. Terry is a bankruptcy attorney. He should have known better. By having Robin file jointly with him, he was putting more of the family's income in the hands of the IRS. Remember my law: Once the tax is more than you can pay, it might not matter how much more.

We don't know whether Terry's accountant knew whether or not he was paying the balance due on the return. If he or she did, then there was a failure to recognize that Robin was also a client, whose interest was not in alignment with Terry's. This is a pretty common failure of tax preparers who focus on minimizing the tax without considering collection issues. Even though it is usually not the right answer, filing separately should always be an option.

It is important to note that Robin and Terry did not live in a community property state, which would introduce another set of complications. Don't get me started.

Stop Calling It Tax Day

There is a lamentable tendency to refer to the individual tax due date as Tax Day. This creates the impression that filing on or near the last day is a good idea. Filing at the last minute is a terrible idea. Whenever an issue would crop up a year or two after filing a return, one of the first things we would do was look at the routing sheet. The closer the date was to the 15th, the lower would be our confidence in the quality of the work that went into the return.

Just Get an Extension

There are sensible CPAs who will just assume that anybody whose stuff comes in after April 1 (or possibly an earlier date) is going on an extension. The reasons to relax the assumption are not good reasons from the client's point of view.

Pretty common is that the client does not want to go on an extension. In a higher-end practice (but not possible for the highest), doing what the client wants (within the bounds of professional obligations) is practically a religion. Clients are a force of nature. Your whim is your CPA's command. If you insist to your CPA that you don't want to go on an extension, you won't. He's being smart. You're being an idiot.

There are two other reasons I've run into. One is that the CPA is trying to show up in the competition. If you come to her whining about the last guy putting you on extension, she'll tell you she'll make sure it won't happen. The other is one that I have inferred. When there is just a single bill being issued for the return, extensions are not good for the firm's cash flow. So, a managing partner may be pushing hard to get returns out to get the money in the door quicker.

Don’t Be Pressured into Signing a Joint Return

It is not unusual for a CPA to view one half of a couple as being “the client.” Back in the day, it was almost always the husband, but of course, times have changed. Now it will typically be either the one with a business as opposed to a job or the one from a wealthy family as opposed to the commoner who is marrying into the gentry. For purpose of discussion, let’s say that Robin is “**the** client” and you’re the tag-along partner Terry. Terry, this advice is for you.

The routine may be that on April 10, someone tells her, “Sign here,” and that is the extent of your involvement. Well, that is less than perfect but can be OK as long as you and Robin are getting along well. If things are not going so well or if you are, in effect, divorced but were married on December 31, don’t succumb to the pressure. Signing a joint return should no longer be routine.

Most tax CPAs lean toward compliance and planning. A joint return usually produces a lower tax, so it seems like a no-brainer even for a couple that is splitting. What such CPAs are neglecting is the area of collections. A joint return creates joint and several liabilities. The IRS can collect the whole balance due from either you or Robin.

It is not unusual to read Tax Court decisions where Terry signs a joint return that cuts Robin’s liability and Robin does not pay the reduced liability. Situations like that are the basis of this law: Once the tax is more than you can pay, it might not matter how much more. You cut Robin’s bill. Robin still can’t pay it, but now the authorities can collect it from you. If they tell you a story about “innocent spouse” relief, don’t buy it. It is a real thing, but not easy.

In the divorce scenario, you should only sign a joint return if you have legal counsel that assures you that you have protection from every angle. And Robin, even if it saves you a few bucks, you might not want to ask Terry to sign a joint return, as you might not want Terry involved if there is an audit.

If you do resist, be sure to file a separate return even if it is not technically necessary to avoid the contention that you consented to a joint return without signing.

And CPAs, remember that in preparing a joint return, you have two clients.

Reflections on the Tenth Law

The most important thing to remember is that regular compliance and collection may dictate different decisions. It may be that you have to explain it the client and let them decide. And remember that when you are preparing a joint return you have two clients, and it is not a certainty that their interests are aligned. ◊

TENTH LAW OF TAX PLANNING

Footnotes

1. Maria Sanchez v. Commissioner of Internal Revenue, United States Tax Court (No. 22622-12S), March 18, 2015, https://scholar.google.com/scholar_case?case=18271553048815400271&q=Sanchez+v.+Comm.,++T.C.+Summ.+2015-20&hl=en&as_sdt=6,39&as_vis=1.
2. Internal Revenue Service, Form 12153: Request for a Collection Due Process or Equivalent Hearing (Washington D.C.: Department of the Treasury, 2022), https://www.irs.gov/pub/irs-pdf/f12153.pdf.
3. ""I'm from The Government, and I'm Here to Help" – Part Deux," Taishoff Law, last modified March 19, 2015, https://taishofflaw.com/2015/03/19/im-from-the-government-and-im-here-to-help-part-deux/.
4. Peter J. Reilly, "IRS Collection Action Can Be Delayed For A Long Time," Forbes, last modified October 21, 2014, https://www.forbes.com/sites/peterjreilly/2014/10/21/irs-collection-action-can-be-delayed-for-a-long-time/#3c101b5fcea6.
5. Bruce A. Hauptman v. Commissioner of Internal Revenue, United States Court of Appeals (No. 15-1071), August 2, 2016, https://law.justia.com/cases/federal/appellate-courts/ca8/15-1073/15-1073-2016-08-02.html.
6. Internal Revenue Service, Form 4549: Income Tax Examination Changes Washington D.C.: Department of the Treasury, 2008), retrieved from https://www.hrblock.com/

tax-center/wp-content/uploads/2018/04/Form-4549.pdf.

7. "Magic – The Gathering," accessed May 27, 2023, https://magic.wizards.com/en.

8. Hauptman v. Commissioner of Internal Revenue.

9. W.T. Snipes v. Commissioner of Internal Revenue, United States Tax Court (No. 27902-15L), November 1, 2018, https://www.leagle.com/decision/intco20181101f75.

10. "Tax protester 861 argument," Wikipedia, last modified December 11, 2022, https://en.wikipedia.org/wiki/Tax_protester_861_argument.

11. "Eddie Ray Kahn," Wikipedia, last modified February 21, 2023, https://en.wikipedia.org/wiki/Eddie_Ray_Kahn.

12. Douglas P. Rosile Sr., Dirt Bags, Liars and Power Freaks: A Critical Look at the IRS, DOJ and Politicians (Bloomington: AuthorHouse, 2017).

13. Barbara Liston, "Wesley Snipes jailed for 3 years in tax case," Reuters, last modified April 25, 2008, https://www.reuters.com/article/us-snipes-sentence/wesley-snipes-jailed-for-3-years-in-tax-case-idUSN2419088420080425.

14. "Understanding a Federal Tax Lien," Internal Revenue Service, last modified May 17, 2023, https://www.irs.gov/businesses/small-businesses-self-employed/understanding-a-federal-tax-lien?sessionId=1542380795583&referrer=https%3A%2F%2Fwww.google.com%2F&lastReferrer=www.avalara.com.

15. "Kathryn Morgan," National Association of Tax Professionals, accessed May 27, 2023, https://www.natptax.com/EventsAndEducation/About/Pages/Kathryn-Morgan.aspx.

16. "Frank Wolpe," Bentley University, accessed May 27, 2023, https://faculty.bentley.edu/profile/fwolpe.

Pigs Get Fed. Hogs Get Slaughtered.

The Eleventh Law goes back to my earliest days at Joseph B Cohan and Associates. Not having much in the way of agricultural practice, we did not know what the analogy meant. We took the phrase to mean that you should be aggressive but not too aggressive.

Appraisals detached from economic reality are a great source of tax shenanigans.

Mann Case Sets Precedent for Building Material Reuse Tax Charitable Valuation

The Fourth Circuit sustained[1] a district court decision[2] that entirely denied any charitable deduction to Lawrence and Linda Mann for material from the tear-down of a Bethesda, Maryland, house that went to Second Chance, a not-for-profit organization. In January 2020, the Tax Court denied[3] any deduction to Chad and Dana Loube for the material donated to Second Chance from the tear-down of their Potomac, Maryland home.

Appraisal Standard

Both these decisions remind me a lot of what the IRS is doing with syndicated conservation easements. There are serious valuation problems, but the IRS ended up going after the deduction on technical grounds. The Manns had taken the position that they donated the whole house to Second Chance, which would have required a record of the transaction in the county land records. That theory supported a $675,000 appraisal. They had a fallback appraisal of $313,353 that was based on all the material making up the house regardless of whether they actually salvaged it.

According to the district court decision, the correct value was the resale value of the specific building materials that crossed the threshold of the Second Chance warehouse. Mike Gable of Build Reuse[4] has outlined some best practices in a piece[5] I published on *Your Tax Matters Partner.* The final step in his outline is a "complete inventory" that encompasses what the nonprofit takes possession of. That is what the basis for the appraisal should be.

Industry Reaction

The other thing that the material reuse industry has in common with the conservation easement is an idealistic element. Reuse takes the pressure off landfills, and it saves much of the energy embedded in the salvaged material. This leads to participation by earnest people who want to do things right and don't want bad actors to besmirch the purity of the industry.

They are similar in that regard to members of the Land Trust Alliance[6] who want to protect the charitable benefit of conservation easement deductions from being compromised by abuse. I heard from members of the National Organization of Reuse Appraisers[7] (NORA) who are pleased that the IRS is finally cracking down on abusive appraisals.

They note that the decision provides case law. Also, it was not a matter of lack of qualification but rather a violation of the Uniform Standards of Professional Appraisal Practice[8] (USPAP). They believe that the IRS should take action to disqualify appraisers who repeatedly violate USPAP by overvaluing deductions and creating tax underpayments.

They recommend avoiding large disallowances, and are making sure the appraiser will be valuing what goes to the not-for-profit and that the appraiser has the proper qualifications to perform the appraisal. The recipient not-for-profit is responsible for providing the final inventory, but it is good practice for donors to keep their records and photographs. If you are donating a "whole house," the house will move off your property. Otherwise, you are donating pieces of the house. Material destroyed in the deconstruction is not part of what you get credit for in valuing your deduction.

Practical Takeaway

Two court decisions are not enough to squash an attractive theory that purports a charitable deduction for much more than the charity receives. Taxpayers who take that sort of position, however, would be well-advised to make sure they have a solid inventory, including photographs, of what ended up going to the reuse charity to fall back on a reasonable deduction in the event of a challenge. That might have eased the pain the Manns are feeling now just a bit.

And those who want to do things right now have clear precedents to work from to support them. I doubt that the IRS is going to devote the sort of resources that have gone into fighting syndicated conservation easements in this area, but a bit more caution might be called for. Remember **Reilly's Eleventh Law of Tax Planning—*"Pigs get fed. Hogs get slaughtered."*** ◊

Here, I beat the problem of land building allocation to death.

IRS Leans on LA Tax Assessors for Land Building Allocation

One of the little puzzles that you have when dealing with rental real estate is the problem of allocation between depreciable and non-depreciable property—land and building. In the more advanced classes, we can get into the allocation among the depreciable items such as building and land improvements. There is a mini industry that does cost segregation studies to help you with that, but by my reckoning, you need a project in the $2 million and up neighborhood to make paying for a cost segregation study a worthwhile expenditure. A recent Tax Court summary decision (TCS 2017-31) sheds a little light on the basic land-building issue.

What Land?

The taxpayers, who probably don't need me to make them more famous, were disputing the IRS determination of the breakdown of land and building. The couple had paid $360,000 for one property in 2003 and $750,000 for another. In 2011, they purchased a third property for $520,000. On their 2012 return, they claimed $69,238 in depreciation on the three properties. That is more than the total of the three acquisition prices divided by 27.5, but the Tax Court did not go that deep into the math commenting:

> Petitioners claimed depreciation deductions concerning the rental properties as though the depreciable basis of each property included both the value of the improvements and the land.

Maybe there were some post-acquisition improvements.

What Does the Assessor Know?

The IRS looked at it differently and brought in some additional data. In 2012, the Los Angeles County Office of the Assessor valued the first property at $435,324 ($189,032 improvements, $236,292 land), the second at $795,000 ($305,800 improvements, $489,200 land), and the third at $532,807 ($163,940 improvements, $368,867 land). That gave improvement percentages on each of the three properties of 44.4 percent, 38 percent, and 31 percent, respectively cutting the depreciation deduction for the year by more than 50 percent for a deficiency of $5,297.

It could have been worse. If the IRS had pushed the adjustment through as an accounting method change, the excess depreciation deductions from prior years would have been an income pickup in 2012.

Being Too Aggressive

I suspected the couple might have fallen victim to **Reilly's Eleventh Law of Tax Planning—"*Pigs get fed. Hogs get slaughtered.*"** That was one of our sayings as we worked most tax season nights till 10:30 at Joseph B Cohan and Associates during the Reagan and first Bush administrations. At least we had indoor parking and did not have to scrape ice from our car windows before heading home. Many of the other sayings would not pass muster under the contributor guidelines. There was not much in the way of agriculture in our practice, so we had no idea what the phrase meant, but we interpreted it to mean that you should be aggressive, but not too aggressive.

The 10 Percent Club

Our rule of thumb on a rental building was 10 percent for land, which is pretty aggressive (note: The Tax Court would have called that 90 percent to improvements, which sounds even more aggressive), but not nearly as aggressive as the 0 percent adopted by the couple. Of course, there is nothing very scientific about the 10 percent, and its derivation is lost in the mists of time. My thinking at an emotional level is that if you are giving up 10 percent, you are giving up something. I was surprised when I looked into this; the method we tended to use back in the day is still floating around out there.

This is from the Bradford Tax Institute:[9]

> I own rental property and I just left my first IRS audit. The IRS auditor arrived at the audit with the county tax assessor's land and building values assigned to my property tax bill. That was a surprise to my new CPA. He said he had not previously seen the IRS arrive at an audit with the tax assessor's information in hand. Worse, the property tax bill shows the land as 37 percent of the value, meaning that I have only 63 percent that I can depreciate. My original accountant allocated 10 percent to land, so I am facing a sizable adjustment. I spoke with my old accountant who said he always used 10 percent and never had any trouble, but he offered no help for my

current mess.

I talked to somebody I know who is pretty old-school and asked him what he thought. He said he favored 10 percent until it got up to a million and then he would go with 20 percent. He admitted that he is playing the audit lottery, something that AICPA standards of tax practice forbid, but who am I to judge?

Looks Like the Real Estate Bill Might Be an Effective Safe Harbor

Tax Court Summary decisions cannot be cited as precedent, but that doesn't mean you can't bring them up in an audit. What this decision tells me is that you can feel pretty confident about using an assessor's breakdown, but if you don't like the assessor's breakdown, you better have some sort of narrative to support a different breakdown.

The practical problem that practitioners face when doing returns for people who own a couple of rental properties is that it is difficult to justify spending anything on an appraisal for rental properties in the sub-million dollar category. Moving $100,000 from land to residential real estate will give you a bit over $3,600 in additional depreciation, which might save you a thousand bucks unless as often happens, the passive activity loss rules suspend your losses. Somebody selling cost segregation studies will make a presentation showing the future value of depreciation deductions, but it can be an uphill battle with skinflint real estate operators.

Guidance

I thought it would make sense for me to look at what guidance/authority there is on the subject. Sadly, you will not find any authority for the 10 percent rule beloved by some practitioners. The governing regulation 1.167(a)-5[10] is no help.

> In the case of the acquisition on or after March 1, 1913, of a combination of depreciable and non-depreciable property for a lump sum, for example, buildings and land, the basis for depreciation cannot exceed an amount which bears the same proportion to the

> lump sum as the value of the depreciable property at the time of acquisition bears to the value of the entire property at that time.

The regulation tells you that you have to do something, but doesn't help you in how to do it.

IRS Publication 946—How to Depreciate Property has some amusing guidance.

> You bought a building and land for $120,000 and placed it in service on March 8. The sales contract showed that the building cost $100,000 and the land cost $20,000. It is nonresidential real property. The building's unadjusted basis is its original cost, $100,000.

I have been in the game for closer to 40 years than 30 and I have never seen a contract that broke down the price between land and building.

If you are playing in the bigger leagues, you should check out the *Cost Segregation Audit Techniques Guide.* Chapter Five, "Review and Examination of a Cost Segregation Study" stakes out a disturbing position:

> The fair market value of land should be based on the highest and best use of the land as though vacant, even if the land has improvements. The land value may equal the value of the total real estate even if the real estate has substantial improvements when such improvements do not contribute value to the property. **Whereas land has value, improvements contribute value.** The value of the total real estate, less the value of the land, results in the value of the improvements. Accordingly, it is inappropriate to estimate the value of the land by subtracting the estimated value of the improvements from the lump real estate price. Basis assigned to land in this residual fashion may result in understating the appropriate basis in the land and overstating the appropriate basis in the depreciable improvements. Examiners should also be wary if a cost segregation study relies solely on locally assessed values rather than appropriately determining fair market values. **(Emphasis added)**

Thus, if you bought a property in a place like Manhattan Beach in California or the actual Manhattan, the IRS might assert that the depreciable portion is negligible if the highest and best use is a tear-down.

The real estate bill allocation starts looking pretty good in a situation like that. ◊

Here is one about a cost segregation specialist wandering into hog country.

Cost Segregation Consultant Subjected to Severe IRS Penalties

One of my running jokes is that the Internal Revenue Code is a white-collar jobs program for college graduates who are not quite smart enough to become engineers.[11] But what happens when engineers realize that some types of tax work can be more lucrative than doing whatever it is that engineers do? That's how we get cost segregation specialists.

Blaise Dusenberry, a senior technical reviewer in the Office of Chief Counsel, IRS, refers to one such as a "tax consultant/engineer." The Chief Counsel Advice 201805001[12] designates the TCS as P. And P will be in a world of hurt if it follows STR Dusenberry's advice, but just for background, I will tell you a little about the cost segregation industry.

Why Cost Segregation?

When the taxpayer places a building in service in a trade or a business, they can recover its cost over a period. Typically, though, a building is not just a building. You also buy the land, the cost of which you don't recover until you sell the property. That sucks.

But there are all sorts of stuff inside the building and surrounding it. Some of that stuff the taxpayer gets to write off a lot faster than the basic structure of the building and its key components. Could be 39 years for the building and maybe 15 or even five years for the other stuff—or now thanks to the Tax Cuts and Jobs Act—instantly for the other stuff.

Figuring out the stuff in the building that isn't the building and how much you would need to spend to replace the parking lot and the outside lighting is not something you can expect an accountant to do. That's why you have the tax consultant/engineers.

They are usually paired with a really good sales team that goes around terrifying accountants with the threat that they will lose their clients[13] because they have been slow-pokes in writing off the assets. They do these great spreadsheets that illustrate the benefits of a faster write-off.

If someone missed cost segregation on the acquisition, there's an accounting method change that will create a whopping big deduction in the year it is put through.

The Magna Carta of the cost segregation industry is an excerpt from the *IRS Cost Segregation Audit Techniques Guide—Principal Elements of a Quality Cost Segregation Study and Report*. There are 13 elements of the quality study.

1. Preparation by an Individual with Expertise and Experience
2. Detailed Description of the Methodology
3. Use of Appropriate Documentation
4. Interviews Conducted with Appropriate Parties
5. Use of a Common Nomenclature
6. Use of a Standard Numbering System
7. Explanation of the Legal Analysis
8. Determination of Unit Costs and Engineering "Take-Offs"
9. Organization of Assets into Lists or Groups
10. Reconciliation of Total Allocated Costs to Total Actual Costs
11. Explanation of the Treatment of Indirect Costs
12. Identification and Listing of Section 1245 Property
13. Consideration of Related Aspects (e.g., I.R.C. Section 263A, Change in Accounting Method and Sampling Techniques)

A quality report has nine elements.

1. Summary Letter
2. Narrative Report
3. Schedule of Assets
4. Schedule of Direct and Indirect Costs
5. Schedule of Property Units and Costs
6. Engineering Procedures
7. Statement of Assumptions and Limiting Conditions
8. Certification
9. Exhibits

The salesmen imply that if you don't have the quality study and report, then you just must write the whole thing off over 39 years, but I don't think that is the case. The Cohan rule is, in my mind, clearly applicable here, but if you are dealing with big dollars, the study is probably worthwhile. My back of the envelope is that you want one on a project over $2 million or so, but somebody has told me that it might be as low as $500,000 on a medical building.

What Is Quality?

There are two types of quality. One is the technical quality, which will make the report stand up on audit. The other is how much the thing is saving you by pushing as much as conceivably possible into the five-year category. The second factor can create a race to the bottom in terms of the first factor. That is the tension poor P ran into and, at least in the eyes of the auditor, P got a little carried away.

Penalties

Code Section 6701 allows for the imposition of a penalty of $1,000 ($10,000 in the case of a corporation) on any person:

> who aids or assists in, procures, or advises with respect to, the

> preparation or presentation of any portion of a return, affidavit, claim, or other document, who knows (or has reason to believe) that such portion will be used in connection with any material matter arising under the internal revenue laws, and who knows that such portion (if so used) would result in an understatement of the liability for tax of another person.
>
> The CCA indicates that the penalty can apply to P.

Since a cost segregation study might cost $5,000 to $10,000, a thousand dollar penalty is kind of painful, but not the end of the world. Only it's worse. That report did not cause P's client to file one wrong tax return. There were five, since the deprecation deduction was wrong on each of the five returns. (It occurs to me that it should have been six and maybe that is what it will be. The five-year write-off spreads over six returns with a partial year in the first and sixth years.) And if the client was a corporation, it would be $10,000 times five (or maybe six). That is nasty.

What the advice does not address directly, although it alludes to it, is whether P is responsible for multiple individual returns in the case of partnerships. Think about it. If P's client was a partnership with 20 partners and P ends up penalized on each K-1—ouch!

Watch Out

The Tax Cuts and Jobs Act should increase the demand for cost segregation studies. The immediate write-off of a significant percentage of the acquisition cost will make for a significant benefit. This CCA is an indication that the IRS may have a project going on aggressive cost segregation consultants like what happened with appraisers who were overvaluing conservation easements. You may want to be a little cautious if the savings claims seem excessive. Remember **Reilly's Eleventh Law of Tax Planning—"*Pigs get fed. Hogs get slaughtered.*"**

Reflections On The Eleventh Law

How aggressive you should be is a question that is partly dependent on how much it will bother you if you ultimately lose and have to pay more. As an adviser, I always tried to give advice consistent with my client's attitude. Other practitioners will impose their own attitudes. Over time clients tend to end up with advisers who complement them. The important thing is to be aware of when you are being aggressive. ◊

ELEVENTH LAW OF TAX PLANNING

Footnotes

1. Lawrence P. Mann and Linda S. Mann v. United States of America, United States Court of Appeals (No. 8:17-cv-00200-TDC), January 6, 2021, https://www.taxnotes.com/research/federal/court-documents/court-opinions-and-orders/fourth-circuit-affirms-denial-of-deduction-for-house-donation/2dd6k.
2. Lawrence P. Mann and Linda S. Mann v. United States of America, United States District Court of Maryland (No. TDC-17-0200), January 31, 2019, https://casetext.com/case/mann-v-united-states-59.
3. Chad Loube and Dana M. Loube v. Commissioner of Internal Revenue, United States Tax Court (No. 5092-17), January 8, 2020, https://casetext.com/case/loube-v-commr.
4. "Build Reuse Board of Directors," Build Reuse, accessed May 27, 2023, https://www.buildreuse.org/board-and-governance.
5. "Build Reuse Chairman Mike Gable Responds To Mann Decision," Your Tax Matters Partner (blog), last modified February 4, 2021, https://yourtaxmatterspartner.com/build-reuse-chairman-responds-to-mann-decision/.
6. "Land Trust Alliance," accessed May 27, 2023, https://landtrustalliance.org/.
7. "NORA National Organization of Reuse Appraisers," LinkedIn, accessed May 27, 2023, https://www.linkedin.com/in/nora-national-organization-of-reuse-appraisers-1393291a3/.
8. "Uniform Standards of Professional Appraisal Practice," The Appraisal Foundation, accessed May 27, 2023, https://www.appraisalfoundation.org/imis/TAF/Standards/Appraisal_Standards/Uniform_Standards_of_Professional_Appraisal_Practice/TAF/

USPAP.aspx?hkey=62c73d17-9bcf-42b3-a6e4-d4b4b72c098f.

9. "IRS Arrives with Tax Assessor's Allocation to Land and Building," Bradford Tax Institute, accessed May 27, 2023, https://bradfordtaxinstitute.com/EMS_Base/EMS_Agent.aspx?Page=/Content/Avoid-IRS-Use-of-Tax-Assessor-against-Renta.aspx.

10. Internal Revenue Service, "§ 1.167(a)-5 Apportionment of basis," Code of Federal Regulations, last modified May 25, 2023, https://www.ecfr.gov/current/title-26/chapter-I/subchapter-A/part-1/subject-group-ECFRc4930337f38ecfd/section-1.167(a)-5.

11. Peter J. Reilly, "Cost Segregation Consultant Subjected To Severe IRS Penalties," Forbes, last modified February 19, 2018, https://www.forbes.com/sites/peterjreilly/2018/02/19/cost-segregation-consultant-subjected-to-severe-irs-penalties/.

12. Blaise G. Dusenberry, Memorandum No. 201805001 (Washington D.C.: Office of Chief Counsel Internal Revenue Service, 2018).

13. Reilly, "Cost Segregation Consultant."

TWELFTH LAW OF TAX PLANNING

Joint Filing Is An Election. It Is Not One Of Your Marital Vows.

There is a connection between this law and the **Tenth Law**. It used to be extremely rare for married filing separate returns to come to an aggregate tax lower than a joint return. Recently that has changed. It is unusual, but not rare. More to the point, this law is based on the dark side of joint filing: joint and several liabilitiy. The IRS can collect the whole tax from either spouse. Innocent spouse status can alleviate that, but innocent spouse status is extremely hard to establish.

This is a roundup of some of the most egregious cases of returns that should have been separate.

Watch That Last Minute Joint Return for Final Year of Marriage

This is for the people who year in and year out feel pressured into signing joint tax returns without really understanding them. Relax. I am not judging. There are things more important than taxes that I leave entirely in other people's hands. So, if your spouse has been tending to your tax compliance, that can be OK. Only now that you are getting divorced, it is not OK anymore. It is time to take charge and embrace **Reilly's Twelfth Law of Tax Planning—"*Joint filing is an election. It is not one of your marital vows.*"**

The Problem with Joint Filing

The pressure for joint filing comes from the assumption, generally accurate, that a joint return will close to inevitably result in a lower tax than two married filing separate returns. If you and your spouse have been living separately for the past six months of the year and you have one or more of the kiddies with you, you may qualify for the head of household rates, but let's put that possibility aside.

The big problem with joint filing is joint and several liability. Let's assume you are the spouse with a relatively modest W-2 with withholdings. It is relatively easy to figure out what your liability would be if married filing separately. If the only difference is the rate table, it should be no different from what it would be if you were single. Get that MFS (married filing separate) return prepared and be ready to file it. If your income is below the filing threshold, even zero, do that regardless. We will see why.

Joint and several liabilities mean that the IRS can collect the entire balance from either spouse. And here is where **Reilly's Tenth Law of Tax Planning—"*Once the tax is more than you can pay, it might not matter how much more*"** comes into play. If your ex would have a large liability from a separate return, helping them out by filing jointly is a losing proposition if your ex doesn't pay that lesser liability. If it is so large that it ends up with IRS Collection, you will not even have helped them out. What the IRS gets from people who do not send in the balance due with their return is their RCP (reasonable collection potential). By making it a joint return, you are increasing RCP, because now they can come after you also.

Assuming you are confident that there won't be an unpaid balance due, the other thing you need to consider is whether your ex has high audit potential. If you are a pokey W-2 person and they have high-flying complex business stuff going on, that is another good reason to avoid joint filing.

Innocent Spouse

There is potential relief from joint and several liabilities. It is called Innocent Spouse Relief, and you can read about it here[1]. I like to learn from experience—other people's experience. And I have learned a lot about innocent spouse status from other people's experience by reading Tax Court opinions. It can be hard to get innocent spouse status. And when I read those opinions, a very common takeaway is: why didn't that person file separately?

And here is why I want you to have that separate return ready. Even if you don't sign a joint return, you can deem to have consented to it. You can read that sad story in a recent Ninth Circuit opinion I covered in[2] 2022. Robin, as I named the prospective innocent spouse, always had somebody else take care of their filing, and for a brief time when they were on their own did not file at all. They would not have had much of a balance due on a separate return, but the liability for the joint return they did not sign was a doozy. And there was no innocent spouse relief.

I have thought that innocent spouse would be a great title for a mystery novel or a thriller. So, I checked to see if it exists. Turns out someone used the title in a memoir. *Innocent Spouse*[3] by Carol Ross Joynt is a memoir by a woman who found herself facing a huge liability from an audit of her husband's business after he died suddenly. Basically, if your spouse has a business that might be a little sketchy, you can love them and still file separately.

Your ex and their advisers may pressure you to sign a joint return and tell you that an innocent spouse can bail you out. Do not believe it. It is hard. Get some independent advice and make sure you make your adviser aware of your concern about getting stuck with an unexpected bill.

And for Tax Pros

We need to remember that when we are preparing a joint return we have two clients. Particularly when it comes to the final joint return, we need to recognize that their interests might not align. Make sure that both parties are aware of the implications of joint and several liabilities. And that joint filing is an election—not a marital vow. ◊

Note: I have not read Innocent Spouse yet. So many books, and so little time. Here is an excerpt[4], though, that gives you one of the more dramatic moments, and a Washington Post[5] review.

If Spouse Is Behind Bars, Think Before Filing Jointly

This fellow felt devoted enough to visit his spouse in jail to make sure they took care of the joint return. He did not realize that this would mean he would have to pay the tax on the money she embezzled.

Filing a joint return usually produces a lower tax than filing two separate returns. There is a disadvantage though: joint and several liabilities. Regardless of which half of the couple generated the income (or spent it), the IRS can collect any balance due, including one from an audit, from either spouse.

Joint Filing Is Elective

Here is something very important that does not sink in very well. Filing a joint return is an election, an irrevocable election. You do not have to do it. And there are times when you should not. A 2019 Seventh Circuit appeal of a Tax Court innocent spouse decision has me screaming "What were you thinking?" at the unsuccessful appellant.

Background

The real names of the couple are, of course, in the public record, and you can find them in the decision. But not wanting to add to their fame, I will call them Joe and Mary.

Mary, an accountant, took care of all the couple's finances. She worked for a blood bank where she processed payables and issued checks to vendors. Vague memories from the CPA exam make me think there might be a separation of duties problem there.

Joe worked as a machine operator for 14 12-hour shifts per month. In his spare time, he inspected homes for financial institutions and insurance companies. The machine operator's wages went into his bank account. The other income went into the joint account Mary tended.

I don't know whether it was that separation of duties thing, I noted, but in June 2011, the police arrested Mary, and they charged her with stealing $450,000 from her employer.

An Innocent Spouse

The court found Joe's claims that he knew nothing of the embezzlement quite credible.

> First, as discussed above, ——— was completely uninvolved with the couple's finances. Specifically, he never reviewed bank or credit card statements, nor did he look over their personal or business finances, which ——— managed. Nor would have to review their finances necessarily have alerted him to ——— embezzlement, given her practice of depositing the embezzled funds via check into the couple's joint account. These checks would have been difficult to distinguish from the checks for the home inspection business, which were also made out to ——— and tended to be for similar amounts.

That embezzlement income created a tax problem. There were deficiencies for 2009, 2010, and 2011 mostly but not entirely due to the embezzlement income. Joe claimed innocent spouse status for all three years.

2009 ended up being moot because, by the time the Tax Court got to it in 2018, bankruptcy had discharged the liability. For 2010, Joe got off as he checked off the required boxes for relief under Code Section 6015(b).

Not 100 Percent

Joe did not get relief for 2011, though. The reason is that when it came to doing that return in 2012, Mary was in prison, and Joe organized the information and brought it to the preparer. And he did not tell the preparer about the embezzlement.

It is possible to get innocent spouse relief under Code Section 6015(f) based on it being inequitable to hold the taxpayer liable. The knowledge of the embezzlement and the involvement in the preparation of the 2011 return was too much for Joe to overcome, though.

Joe argued he didn't know exactly how much his wife embezzled, but that did not get him anywhere.

> The Tax Court noted that by the time he filed the return in April, ——— was aware of a ——— arrest in June of 2011, her conviction in November 2011 of embezzling $485,681, and her January 2012 sentence to incarceration and restitution. ——— cites no authority, nor are we aware of any, suggesting that a finding of actual knowledge would be precluded by the fact that a petitioning spouse may not, as a result of his lack of investigation, be aware of the precise amount of embezzlement, particularly when he has not offered any explanation as to why he failed to access that information.

Some Sympathy

The appeal ended up not getting Joe anything other than a goodly amount of sympathy.

> We are sympathetic to the ——— situation, and recognize that the Tax Court could have easily decided on this record that ——— was entitled to equitable relief under Section 6015(f). Indeed, were we deciding the case in the first instance as opposed to on deferential review, we may have decided the case differently.

The fine points of the innocent spouse issue make this case worth studying, but that is not my main takeaway. I look back to April 2012 when Joe is arranging his tax filing. He was still married, and the couple did not become estranged until later, so it made sense for him to help arrange Mary's tax compliance.

Worst Joint Return Decision I Have Seen

But it is hard to see a compelling reason for him to file jointly with her. He knew she had embezzled, just not exactly how much. I have been noting these cases for a long time, and Joe takes the cake for the most egregious example of somebody who should not have filed jointly.

Looking back over the past decade, I have seen that I have written about this too many times to mention, so I will just refer you to this one piece[6], which sums it up pretty well. ◊

Probate judges will sometimes order joint returns. But—at least in Nebraska—not anymore.

Nebraska Supreme Court Rules State Court Cannot Order Joint Federal Return

Regarding divorcing couples filing joint returns, I have felt like a voice crying out in the wilderness. In practice, the default assumption seems to be that a couple will file jointly for the final year of the marriage. Given the hazard of joint and liabilities and the fact that filing jointly is an irrevocable election, I think the default assumption should be separate filing. I was rather shocked when a probate judge ordered a friend of mine, whose spouse probably had unreported income, to sign a joint return. I didn't think that such an order would stand up on appeal, but what did I know? State courts have been ordering divorcing spouses to file jointly with their soon-to-be exes. Well, thanks to the Nebraska Supreme Court decision in Bock v Dalbey[7], they won't be doing it anymore, at least in Nebraska.

The Nebraska Supreme Court overturned an appellate court decision[8] that an order to file a joint return was valid. Jennifer Lynn Dalbey, who was balking at signing a joint return, did not present any reason for not doing it other than that she preferred not to. I admire that.

The Nebraska Supreme Court gave four reasons why a state court cannot order someone to join in filing a joint return:

> First, the U.S. Tax Court is not bound by orders compelling the parties to sign a joint return. It will look to the husband and wife's intent, and if one of them signed only because a state court ordered him or her to do so, the return may or may not be treated as a joint return.

The second reason is on the "lawyerly" side, but the gist of it is to use a mandatory injunction sparingly and not when another remedy is available. The court has the authority to adjust the distribution of marital assets in a manner that is fair and equitable. If Ms. Dalbey's refusal to file a joint return is unreasonable and costly, the Court can make her bear the burden of the extra tax.

> Third, a resisting spouse's exposure to liability under the federal tax code is too difficult to predict if compelled to file a joint return.

This is what I constantly harp on. It comes from staying up late reading Tax Court decisions. Joint and several liabilities are the problem. If the taxpayer doesn't pay the balance due or there is a deficiency, the IRS can collect the entire balance from either party. The Court noted the existence of innocent spouse relief, but also noted that:

> Obtaining relief under the innocent spouse statute, however, is far from certain. The regulations are complicated and predicting liability would frequently require considerable tax expertise.

Planning Note

The appellate court decision said that Mr. Bock had made estimated tax payments. Although it may or may not have been a factor in this case, estimated tax payments are a complicating factor in the decision to file jointly or separately. If one spouse is a partner in a partnership or a Schedule

C proprietor and the other is a W-2 employee, the estimated payments will presumably relate to the non-employee spouse, but it is not a given that the non-employee spouse "owns" those payments if they are joint.

The W-2 employee does, however, own his or her withholdings. This is why I recommend that family offices, closely held businesses, and trustees that make estimated tax payments for beneficiaries and the like always make them out as individual estimated tax payments. There should be no harm if you file a joint return, but you will avoid trouble if choosing separate returns.

Reflections On the Twelfth Law

Often, relationships that we find problematic and wish to end were meeting some of our needs. We must recognize that and start figuring out another way to meet them. Tax compliance may be one of them. If your spouse was taking care of the tax compliance for both of you, the time to step up is on the final return of the marriage, which may be separate. ◊

TWELFTH LAW OF TAX PLANNING

Footnotes

1. "Innocent Spouse Relief," Internal Revenue Service, last modified December 8, 2022, https://www.irs.gov/individuals/innocent-spouse-relief.
2. "Innocent Spouse Loss Has Some Valuable Lessons," Your Tax Matters Partner (blog), last modified March 11, 2022, https://yourtaxmatterspartner.com/innocent-spouse-loss-has-some-valuable-lessons/.
3. Carol Ross Joynt, Innocent Spouse: A Memoir (Danvers: Crown, 2011).
4. Carol Ross Joynt, "Carol Ross Joynt: Excerpt From "Innocent Spouse"," Washingtonian, last modified June 2, 2011, https://www.washingtonian.com/2011/06/02/carol-ross-joynt-excerpt-from-innocent-spouse/.
5. Annie Groer, "Carol Ross Joynt's memoir "Innocent Spouse"," The Washington Post, last modified May 6, 2011, https://www.washingtonpost.com/entertainment/books/carol-ross-joynts-memoir-innocent-spouse/2011/05/02/AFHL1rAG_story.html.

6. Peter J. Reilly, "You Do Not Have To File A Joint Return And There Are Some Reasons Not To," Forbes, last modified February 1, 2016, https://www.forbes.com/sites/peterjreilly/2016/02/01/you-do-not-have-to-file-a-joint-return-and-there-are-some-reasons-not-to/#6cd455ea59f9.
7. Matthew John Bock v. Jennifer Lynn Dalbey, Court of Appeals of Nebraska (No. A-10-973), September 27, 2011, https://www.leagle.com/decision/inneco20110927337.xml.
8. *Bock v. Dalbey.*

THIRTEENTH LAW OF TAX PLANNING

When An Idea Makes You Think Of A Seinfeld Episode, It Is Not Going To End Well.

Sometimes you must dig a little to find the craziness in a tax scheme. I remember one from the 80s that involved investment credits on some sort of energy conservation system. The outsized lease payment that supported the outsized debt to acquire the property was based on energy savings. If you looked at what the equipment cost, it all fell apart. Reminds one a bit of the syndicated conservation easements.

Regardless, sometimes the silliness is right out there and plain to see, but it doesn't stop people from making arguments.

The funniest story in my tax blogging career came along early. And it's still on top. It is a plan that I would love to hear Kramer explaining to Jerry Seinfeld. A sperm bank that provides its product at no cost to women conceivably could qualify as a charity. But not if they only had one donor.

Free Fertility Foundation v. Com 135 TC 2 sounds like something you might read in The Onion, but it is a genuine tax court opinion. I noted its precursor ruling when I was not tax blogging.

Tax Court Crafts Ultimate Pickup Line

PLR 200736307 and related PLR 200737044 revoked the exempt status of a nameless organization whose charitable purpose was the provision of donated sperm to worthy women. The IRS (they don't say how) determined that 88 percent of said sperm, if you will excuse the expression, came from the same donor, who—along with his father—founded and ran the organization. The canned language of one of the rulings invites the organizers to apply to the Tax Court for declaratory judgment. They did.

So we can get details. Failure to obtain exempt status did not put the foundation under, but it appears to have gone inactive. You can still get details from the Wayback Machine. The donor catalog (which had one entry) has extensive information on the intellectual achievements of the donor, including for example:

> 4th grade: 3rd place in a school science fair with a science project entitled "Using Red Cabbage Juice to Determine Acidity."

I guess that is something that a prospective mom would want to know about.

At any rate, the Tax Court went along with the IRS on this one. It boils down to his exempt purpose not benefiting a broad enough class of people. The petitioner claimed it was a very broad class indeed namely all women in the world capable of bearing children. The tax court thought the class somewhat more limited, namely women who want to bear children fathered by him. In prefacing their decision, they did however make the following observation:

> The free provision of sperm may, under appropriate circumstances, be a charitable activity. ◊

Charity begins at home. When it ends at home, though, you don't have an exempt organization.

IRS Says Fixing Up Your Own House Is Not Charity

Got a run-down old house that needs some spiffing up? Here is an idea. Get it designated a historic landmark. Then you can form a not-for-profit and get grants to do some renovations. Since it is a historic landmark, you'll have to let people see it sometimes. Have them call you to make an appointment. When it is convenient. For you. After all, it is still your house. The proposition reminded me just a bit of the Seinfeld episode in which Kramer convinced NYU to provide him with an intern.

The Plan

And it did not end well for the organization (Let's call it This Really Old House [TROH]) that was the subject of Private Letter Ruling 201648020. The IRS redacts private letter rulings, so remember that the founder of TROH is B, and the actual property is C. And as we noted, B owns C.

> Once you establish your exempt status, you project all revenue to come in the form of donations and grants. You have not provided a detailed breakdown of your expenses, but they are all related to the restoration and maintenance of C and the property that surrounds it. C and the property surrounding it will continue to be owned by B. B will interview and select all workers that will perform the restoration of C as well as supervise all work. B's permission is needed for anyone to view the property and appointments to do so are encouraged. You wrote you may be interested in inviting school groups for educational field trips and plan to eventually provide an educational program on-site.

Why It Is Not Exempt

The owner didn't amend the articles of incorporation to include the required language. Presumably, she can fix that but other issues prevent the organization from being exempt. Let us count the ways:

You do not meet the provisions of Treas. Reg. Section 1.501(c)(3)-1(c)(1) because more than an insubstantial part of your activities is not in furtherance of an exempt purpose. You are operating to obtain grant funding to pay restoration costs of property owned by B, your incorporator and director. These facts show you were formed to further private purposes not public.

You are not described in Treas. Reg. Section 1.501(c)(3)-1(c)(2) because your net earnings inure to the benefit of B, who is your incorporator and director. This is illustrated by the fact you are funding the renovation of property owned by her, which she is supervising and overseeing. In addition, C can only be viewed with B's permission. Appointments are arranged with her.

You are not described in Treas. Reg. Section 1.501(c)(3)-1(d)(ii) because you are serving the private interests of B. You were formed to obtain grants to pay for the restoration of property in which B owns and resides. She is controlling all aspects of the restoration which also indicates her private interests are being served.

You are not similar to the organization described in Revenue Ruling 75-470. Unlike that organization, your primary purpose is to restore the property owned by your incorporator and director. This results in inurement. Any public benefit is secondary and incidental to your primary purpose of furthering the interests of B.

Love That 501(c)(3) Status

Reading between the lines, I'm thinking that TROH might not have been angling for 501(c)(3) status because of its tax issues, or even those of B, who, granted, could have started deducting the money that was going into renovating her house. The motivation to qualify for 501(c)(3) may have been to have a wider availability of grants.

For better or worse, 501(c) status has significance beyond federal income tax. It can be relevant for property tax and sales tax exemptions and be a requirement for an organization to serve liquor or run gambling operations in some jurisdictions. And then there is, in my view, an extra dose of credibility that 501(c) organizations have along with the ability to access certain types of grants.

All this means that it is not only people of good will seeking 501(c) status. There are more than a few scoundrels, or to be a little kinder to B and those that form non-profits to pay for their own kids' activities, people whose goals are a bit too self-centered to qualify as charitable.

And the gatekeeper sorting the wheat from the chaff is the IRS Tax Exempt and Government Entities Division, sometimes referred to as EO. There are also state agencies of greater or less ferocity, usually the Attorney General, rooting out phony charities, but mainly we seem to rely on the IRS EO to prevent the charitable sector from being overrun by the less-than-charitable. The reliance was probably never that reasonable, but the developments over the past few years have made things much worse. ◊

Bringing in a Ph.D. to testify that strip club fees should be exempt from sales tax did not win over the judges.

New York Strip Club Fights Tax Battle Using Scholars and Loses

Going to a strip club is not edifying, but contemplating tax litigation surrounding one can be. 677 New Loudon Corporation d/b/a Nite Moves[1] and its principals, Stephen Dick and Stuart Cadwell, were back before the State of New York Appeals Tribunal arguing about whether what their employees do on stage or in private rooms qualifies as "dramatic or musical arts performances", which would exempt their charges from sales tax under New York State Tax Law Section 1105(f)(1).[2]

The Anthropologist

The decision[3] is one of the most scholarly tax decisions I have ever read. There is a report cited by Judith Lynne Hanna Ph.D.[4]

> Dr. Hanna concluded that the shows at Nite Moves during the audit period were live, dramatic, musical, and choreographed performances in a theater, presenting shows composed entirely of dance routines.

Dr. Hanna fleshes the theory out a bit more in an article titled "Toxic Strip Clubs—The Intersection of Religion, Law, and Fantasy."

> Generally, there is a three-song performance in which the dancer appears on stage clothed for the first song, partially removes her clothes during the second, and as the climax of the dance strips to nudity at the end. In part two, for a fee a performer dances for individual patrons next to where they are seated (or in lap dancing a performer dances on, straddling, or between a patron's legs). The dancer acts out through body and facial movement, proximity, and touch, the fantasy of "I am interested in you; I understand you; you're special and important to me." Patrons are generally aware that their purchased "commodity" is a license to dream.

Interestingly, she puts a feminist spin on the whole thing.

> Consequently, exotic dance is perilous to the patriarchal social order: the "ungodly" exotic dance clubs destroy femininity and undermine men. "Passive," "modest" woman steps out of the domestic realm into the "demimonde" public arena where she shamelessly removes her clothing and moves her nude, or semi-nude, body for sexually enticing commercial purpose and economic independence. Moreover, single dancers compete in sexual appeal with married women and economically with men, in effect challenging their sense of masculinity.

This is in sharp contrast to the radical feminist critique of strip clubs and similar phenomena,[5] which it views as upholding patriarchy.

> Men increase their individual and collective power through all-male group bonding, which creates relationships and networks through which they pass along opportunities and knowledge. This power-sharing over misogyny is often contextual, such as business deals that take place in strip clubs or where business trips are organized

> around or include buying prostituted women, where the women performing are economically coerced and exploited, and where female associates are either not invited or do not feel comfortable so are unable or unwilling to participate and are denied opportunities that are in effect only available to men.

But dammit, Jim, I'm a tax blogger and a male one at that, so I'll just move on to the next scholar.

The Dance Expert

Then, there was Katherine Liepe-Levinson Ph.D., a highly skilled dancer who trained in ballet and worked as a choreographer. Her doctorate is in theater, and she is the author of *Strip Show: Performances of Gender and Desire*[6].

> Dr. Liepe-Levinson concluded that Nite Moves was a theater because it had a marquee with the name of the establishment, charged admission to the performance space, had a designated stage with lighting and props, few distractions for patrons, and a house protocol that encouraged the audience to focus on the performers. She believed that the exotic dances performed at Nite Moves were choreographed arrangements of steps or moves that included repetition and a clear beginning and end point, set to music. Routines used costumes and moves associated with the exotic dance genre as well as other genres, improvisation within set structures, and props like chairs and poles used to focus and limit movement. Dr. Liepe-Levinson noted how the larger dance community commonly incorporates elements of exotic dance into its productions, highlighting the artistic merit of the genre. She does not believe that the sexual "turn-on" aspect of the dance renders its choreography moot.

The Gymnast

Then there was Sabrina Madsen[7] who has coached gymnastics at the recreational and competitive levels. She is a certified personal trainer, and a bodybuilder, and holds a master's degree in sports medicine. She competes in pole dancing.

> Ms. Madsen opined that her experience with pole dancing competitions taught her that the sport has components of pole tricks and dance, both of which are part of the judging criteria. Ms. Madsen was shown the various stage videos from Nite Moves and the music video of Alize, a Nite Moves dancer. She described the pole moves and dance steps in great detail for each and concluded that both gymnastics and pole dancing have components of acrobatics skills and dance choreography.

Others

There was also testimony from someone who ran a dance studio, who, they did not say how, managed to observe what went on in the private spaces and opined that was also dancing.

Steve Barnes broke the gender barrier in the expert group. He is an entertainment critic from the *Albany Times Union.*

> Mr. Barnes observed the stage show and then paid for a lap dance. After his observations, Mr. Barnes concluded that "there's no question that the dancing at Nite Moves is art, which is most broadly defined as anything created with aesthetic intent."

Still, It Did Not Go Well

A lower court had a kind of split-the-baby ruling that the general admission charges were exempt but that the private dance fees were not. The latter is where the real money is. The appellate court agreed that the private dance fees were taxable.

> From these descriptions, it is clear that the rooms for the private performances do not constitute a theater, hall, or place of assembly, as such venues, by definition, require a public performance and the primary reason that Nite Moves customers pay extra for a private performance is privacy, i.e., the lack of additional people in the audience. Furthermore, the rooms for the private performances are physically too small for an audience, nor do the rooms have a stage

> or theatrical lighting, only a couch. Thus, the charges for the private performances, considered alone, do not qualify for the exception from taxation.

The appellate court disagreed with the notion that the general admission fees were exempt. The admission got you not only the show on the stage but also the right to pay for private dances.

Framing it that way, it doesn't matter whether what is going on up on the stage is art or not.

A Surprising Admission

The case is well worth reading with some interesting observations on the exotic dancing industry. You may feel shocked to learn this, but it turns out the club owners and the dancers are mainly interested in getting money from the patrons. Who knew?

> Mr. Dick stated that the ultimate goal at Nite Moves was and is to entice customers to purchase private dances, saying, "Ideally… I would like every customer to spend as much money as possible." This goal was repeated by one of the dancers, Taylor, who stated that her goal was to create a fantasy for customers during her stage dance so that they would buy a lap dance or private dance because her best opportunity to make the most money resided in the latter.

The more surprising admission concerned the personnel of the New York Department of taxation.

> The supervising auditor assigned to this audit, Mr. Haher, had significant prior personal experience with Nite Moves and its various offerings. He stated that he had purchased private dances at Nite Moves and that they entailed entering one of the small back rooms with the dancer, having her press a timer button, covering him with a protective cloth to prevent makeup or perspiration from soiling his clothes and then grinding and rubbing herself over his body. ◊

Giving a house you want to be razed to the local fire department to practice on is charitable, isn't it?

The Powder to Blow It Away

Theodore Rolfs purchased some lakefront property in 1996. For some time, he pondered exactly what he wanted to do with it. Then, his mother-in-law suggested that he build a residence on it to her specifications and exchange it for her residence. He decided that was a good idea and began planning accordingly. There was, however, already a residence on the property. Originally built in 1900, the existing structure was not and could not be mother-in-law worthy. Mr. Rolfe determined that it would cost him about $10,000 to have it torn down. Then, he came up with a better idea.

He wrote to Gary Wieczorek, who was chief of police and also of the volunteer fire department of the Village of Chenequa, where the house was located:

> As we have discussed, I would like to donate our house located at 5192 Oakland Road in the Village of Chenequa to the Fire and Police departments of the village for training and eventually demolition. This letter shall serve as an acknowledgment of that intention to donate the house for such purposes. The house is available immediately. If any further approvals are needed, please contact me.

Chief Wieczorek had a clear understanding that his department was not the recipient of a new recreational facility. He understood that the house was to be used exclusively for training purposes and that Mr. Rolfs expected that it would be burned down sometime in the first half of 1998. Matters developed with Mr. Rolf's expectations:

> Sometime shortly before February 18, 1998, the Chenequa Police Department used the lake house for a training exercise. On February 18, 1998, the VFD conducted an initial training exercise at the lake house. On February 21, 1998, 11 days after the petitioner's

> letter donating the lake house, the VFD conducted a second training exercise and burned the structure to the ground.
>
> The firefighter training exercises at the lake house allowed the VFD to satisfy monthly training requirements imposed under Wisconsin State law. Chief Wieczorek believed the firefighter training exercises conducted at the lake house were superior to the training exercises otherwise available to the VFD.

Mr. Rolf arranged for an appraisal of his property. The appraiser did a valuation of the property with and without the structure that after standing nearly a century went out in a blaze of glory to the edification of the Chenequa Volunteer Fire Department. The appraiser determined that the value of Mr. Rolf's property declined from $655,000 to $579,000. Accordingly, he claimed a charitable contribution of $76,000.

The IRS denied the charitable contribution and asserted a 20 percent accuracy-related penalty. Mr. Rolf filed a petition to Tax Court now claiming a deduction of $235,250, the appraiser's estimate of the reproduction cost of the house. The service responded by switching to a 40 percent gross valuation penalty.

The IRS got testimony from a professional "house mover," who indicated that it would have cost on the order of $100,000 to relocate the structure. Given its relatively modest nature and the high cost of land in the vicinity, there would not have been anyone willing to pay to relocate it. They also brought on someone from the state of Wisconsin responsible for knocking down houses to make roads who reiterated that this was not the type of house that could move somewhere else.

In the end, the tax court ruled that Mr. Rolfs couldn't have a deduction since he had received a "quid pro quo" in the form of the removal of the structure that could not meet mother-in-law standards.

All in all, the satisfaction of helping the fire department should have been enough for Mr. Rolfs, winning the deduction would have been icing on the cake.

Reflections On The Thirteenth Law

There is a tension between the **First Law** and the **Thirteenth Law.** There are some things that I find kind of preposterous, like family limited partnership valuation discounts that actually do work. Still it is worth taking a cold look at some ideas and asking yourself and others if it makes much sense outside of tax savings. If you are hesitant about that, proceed with great caution. ◊

THIRTEENTH LAW OF TAX PLANNING

Footnotes

1. "Nite Moves," accessed May 29, 2023, https://www.nitemovesny.com/.
2. FindLaw Staff, "New York Consolidated Laws, Tax Law - TAX § 1105. Imposition of sales tax," FindLaw, last modified January 1, 2021, https://codes.findlaw.com/ny/tax-law/tax-sect-1105.html.
3. Roberta Moseley Nero, James H. Tully, Jr., and Dierdre K. Scozzafava, Decision DTA Nos. 824333, 824334 and 824335 (Albany: Tax Appeals Tribunal, 2016), https://www.dta.ny.gov/pdf/decisions/824333.dec.pdf.
4. "Judith Lynne Hanna," accessed May 29, 2023, https://judithhanna.com/.
5. "radfem 101," A Radical Feminist Collective (blog), accessed May 29, 2023, https://radicalhubarchives.wordpress.com/radfem-101/.
6. Katherine Liepe-Levinson, Strip Show: Performances of Gender and Desire (London: Routledge, 2003).
7. "Sabrina Madsen," Twitter profile, accessed May 30, 2023, https://twitter.com/sabrina_madsen.

FOURTEENTH LAW OF TAX PLANNING

If Something Is A Listed Transaction, Just Don't Do It.

There is a lot to be said for following paths others have explored and not reinventing the wheel. But if the IRS has put you on notice that a certain sort of tax shenanigan is on their radar and requires special disclosure, maybe you should think twice before doing it.

I have lavished a good deal of coverage on conservation easements. As I write this, syndicated conservation easements are a major focus of IRS enforcement.

Tax Court Expects Better Tax Judgment from Submarine Skipper Than CPA/Lawyer

Another day, another penalty case[1] from the tax shelters of the turn of the millennium. This one has me a bit torn. I find the taxpayer very sympathetic. It was Corbin McNeill's role as a utility executive that sent him searching for tax shelter. Mr. McNeill became the chairman and CEO of Exelon when a merger formed it in 2000. Exercising stock options when he retired in 2002 had him facing potentially more than $66 million in taxable income.

What really impresses me about Mr. McNeill is his first career. He graduated from Annapolis in 1962[2] and served in the Navy until retirement at the rank of commander in 1981. His most notable assignment, to me anyway, was command of USS Tautog SSN-639[3]. I have this fascination with submarine skippers and devour their memoirs, a topic which I never expected to work into this chapter, but here it is. Tautog was a Sturgeon-class fast attack submarine. Command of a nuclear submarine and command of the Naval Nuclear Power School[4] convince me that Commander McNeill had an awful lot on the ball.

The DAD Deal

The particular shelter he chose was a DAD (distressed/asset debt). Rather than creating basis[5] out of thin air, like BOSS or Son of BOSS, DAD works by the taxpayer taking advantage of a foreigner's basis. BDO shuffled worthless receivables from one partnership to another. At the end of the chain, Mr. McNeill ended up with an interest in a partnership with more than $20 million in basis for $3 million (plus some hefty fees to BDO). Then he put in other assets to increase his basis in the partnership to take the loss. It strikes me that this is not entirely a free lunch. Basis in the contributed assets needs reduction. One uses things that are meant to be held indefinitely.

The Penalty

At this point, everybody is past arguing about whether DAD worked. What was before the Tax Court was whether Corbin and Dorice McNeill should pay a 40 percent penalty on the deficiency on their 2003 return. There were also procedural issues stemming from the case coming before the Tax Court as an appeal of a collection due process hearing. I will leave those for the lawyers.

The McNeills based their argument against the penalty on their reliance on EY[6] (one of the Big 4), which prepared their 2003 return and a letter from a law firm, De Castro, West, Chodorow, Glickfield & Nass,[7] recommended by BDO,[8] which designed and aggressively marketed DAD. BDO falls in the class of firms I call the not quite Big 4. BDO recommended

DeCastro and charged a fee based on the amount of expected losses from the DAD transaction.

Sadly, Mr. McNeill was witnessing the de-professionalization of law and accounting firms. One of the hard realities of professional practice is that to make money you need to either do some actual work or pay somebody some pretty good money to do the work. The tax shelter opinions were about the most extreme example of rebellion against the tyranny of the billable hour—value billing. The problem with value billing in this arena is that the consequent conflict of interest pretty well eliminates the value of the opinion, as the Tax Court noted in Canal Corporations and Subsidiaries in 2010.

EY (Ernst & Young)

EY was not the value biller in this scenario. EY was just preparing the McNeill tax return. You can't expect the preparer of an individual return to look through the individual's every deal. As it happens, EY did more than usual, but it was not enough for reliance. Most notably it did not include itself as a material adviser on the transaction.

I should mention here that this **Law of Tax Planning—*"If something is a listed transaction, just don't do it"*** I had not yet formulated.

De Castro

Value billing is what did in the De Castro opinion.

> While De Castro appeared to charge a flat fee for the tax opinions, there was a prearranged fee schedule with BDO. Instead of charging a fee based on the type or amount of work to be performed, De Castro charged DAD transaction investors a fee based on the amount of tax saved—0.5 percent of the expected recognized loss. Thus, De Castro had a financial stake in the transaction other than its normal billing; its fee was directly related to the size of the transaction and independent of actual work performed.
>
> The conflict of interest and lack of independence is also

> demonstrated by the direct correlation between referrals from BDO and the conclusion of De Castro's opinions. De Castro wrote these opinions with the understanding that BDO would refer more work to the law firm if the opinions were favorable to BDO's clients. This close relationship shows that De Castro had an inherent conflict of interest; De Castro had a financial incentive to give favorable opinions to BDO referrals.

According to the Tax Court, Mr. McNeill should have realized De Castro was not independent since it was "the promoter." What troubles me about the Tax Court opinion is that "the promoter" was not some guy that took up investment advising because he wasn't smart enough to get into Annapolis. The promoter was one of the top accounting firms in the country.

Tax Court Bottom Line

> If Mr. McNeill's business prowess did not allow him to make such a determination, then certainly the fact that the De Castro and BDO opinions were virtually identical in all material respects should have prompted inquiry from an independent adviser. Close inspection of the two opinions reveals that several sections were nearly verbatim. Mr. McNeill decided not to rely on the BDO opinion because he did not consider it to be an independent opinion. Because the substantive portions of the De Castro opinion and BDO's opinion were nearly verbatim, he should have known that if he could not rely on the BDO opinion, he also could not reasonably rely on the De Castro opinion. The Court concludes that after comparison of the BDO and De Castro opinions, any reliance which Mr. McNeill placed on the De Castro opinion was not reasonable.

So, it looks as if the McNeills will need to pay the penalty. Is that the end of the story?

District Court Saw It Differently

The McNeill's DAD transactions covered two years 2002 and 2003.

The Tax Court decision was about the 2003 penalty. When it came to 2002, the McNeill's paid the penalty and sued for refund. And the U.S. District Court for the District of Wyoming (McNeill v. United States, Case No: 14–CV–172–F) in 2017 found the penalty invalid.

> While perhaps sophisticated as a businessman in the direct sale of the debt, Mr. McNeill does not appear to have been sophisticated in terms of a contribution (not sale) of debt to a partnership by a foreign entity, and the acquisition of partnership interests (as opposed to the direct acquisition of debt). While unquestionably smart and accomplished in his own right, in the context of the complex DAD shelter before the Court which was specifically designed and implemented by others to exploit the Tax Code's partnership provisions, Mr. McNeill is not knowledgeable or sophisticated.

The Achilles' heel of many investors arguing against the penalty is that, as part of the process, they must make representations that are demonstrably false. The district court noted this problem, but

> [i]t is clear these representations were not true, and it is a narrow escape as to whether Mr. McNeill knew or should have known they were false. However, the Court finds the representations to be consistent with Mr. McNeill's reliance on Gramercy's track record of investing in distressed debt, along with his reasonable understanding that taxpayers may lawfully arrange their affairs to keep taxes as low as possible. The fact the tax strategy turned out to be an illegal DAD shelter and could not minimize taxes does not change the analysis as Mr. McNeill was told time and again that the scheme was legal. Mr. McNeill should not be penalized by way of inferring knowledge concerning sham transactions he did not know and reasonably should not have known, particularly when lawyer "code heads" and others apparently failed to discern or disclose the illegal and abusive nature of the transactions.

I'll have to leave it to the lawyers to sort out how much this apparent contradiction means.

Rooting for the Taxpayers

On net, I am rooting for the McNeills on this one. I took a look at the Corbin & Dorice S. McNeill Foundation[9] and noted the $25,000 donation to the USNA Foundation for support for the preservation on naval history along with other worthy causes, which makes me think they are pretty much all right people. If after hearing about DAD, they had been aware of **Reilly's Second Law of Tax Planning—*"Sometimes it's better to just pay the taxes"*—**they might have passed. But there was and still is an ideology that values tax minimization a bit more than it really deserves. Collusion by the most prestigious firms and weak enforcement led people like the McNeills astray.

I find this case coming on top of the Tax Court decision in the case of Keith Tucker[10] rather odd. The Tax Court found Keith Tucker's reliance on professionals in a Son of Boss deal reasonable. Tucker is a lawyer and a CPA and had been busy becoming a partner in KPMG and managing a national tax group while Commander McNeill was serving beneath the deep.

Reflection On The Fourteenth Law

If you have gotten this far, you probably realize that my "laws" are more in the nature of very strong recommendations. When it comes to listed transactions, what I am saying is that they should have a very strong benefit associated with them, and you should be willing to spend some money on professionals who are in no way promoting the transaction to make sure that you don't go astray. ◊

FOURTEENTH LAW OF TAX PLANNING

Footnotes

1. Corbin A. McNeill and Dorice S. McNeill, Petitioners v. United States of America, United States Court of Appeals (No. 15-8095), September 06, 2016, https://caselaw.findlaw.com/court/us-10th-circuit/1747653.html.

2. “Mr. Corbin Mcneill, Jr. ’62,” US Naval Academy Alumni Association and Foundation, accessed May 29, 2023, https://www.usna.com/document.doc?id=289.
3. “USS Tautog (SSN-639),” Wikipedia, last modified March 26, 2023, https://en.wikipedia.org/wiki/USS_Tautog_(SSN-639).
4. “Nuclear Power School,” Wikipedia, last modified May 26, 2023, https://en.wikipedia.org/wiki/Nuclear_Power_School.
5. “What Is Basis And Why It Is Important,” Your Tax Matters Partner (blog), accessed May 27, 2023, http://ytmp.blogspot.com/p/what-is-basis-and-why-it-is-important.html.
6. “EY,” accessed May 29, 2023, https://www.ey.com/en_uk.
7. 7. “De Castro, West, Chodorow, Mendler, & Glickfeld, Inc.,” accessed May 29, 2023, https://www.dwclaw.com/index.html.
8. “BDO,” accessed May 29, 2023, https://www.bdo.com/.
9. McNeill Family Foundation, “Form 990-PF: Return of Private Foundation,” Guidestar, last modified December 10, 2016, https://pdf.guidestar.org/PDF_Images/2015/364/475/2015-364475641-0d0ceacd-F.pdf.
10. Peter J. Reilly, “Keith Tucker Cashes KPMG Get Out Of Jail Free Card In Tax Court,” Forbes, last modified October 12, 2017, https://www.forbes.com/sites/peterjreilly/2017/10/12/keith-tucker-cashes-kpmg-get-out-of-jail-free-card-in-tax-court/#24f23f2a6016.

FIFTEENTH LAW OF TAX PLANNING

If Somebody Calls You Up To Talk About Your Unpaid Federal Taxes, Just Hang Up.

There are legitimate collection companies the IRS engages. And there are also a lot of scammers pretending to represent the IRS. As it happens, I cannot discern any good reason for engaging with the former. Engaging with the latter might be entertaining, but overall, just hanging up is probably the better course.

You Should Just Hang Up on IRS Collection Calls, Legitimate or Not

If somebody calls you up to talk about your unpaid federal taxes, just hang up. Period. Full Stop. That's it. I hold that view so firmly that I have decided to make it **Reilly's Fifteenth Law of Tax Planning.**

But the Call Might Be Legitimate

That's right. After years of warnings that anybody calling you out of the blue claiming to be from the IRS is running a scam of some sort, we now have a notice from the IRS—IR-2017-74[1] with the pithy title "Private

Collection of Some Overdue Federal Taxes Starts in April; Those Affected Will Hear First From IRS; IRS Will Still Handle Most Tax Debts."

The notice then explains to you how to separate the wheat from the chaff. Don't you need to know whether the person calling is a scammer or someone from CBE Group, Conserve, Performant, or Pioneer, the companies engaged by the IRS? Not really. Either way, you should just hang up.

Before you start getting legitimate calls, the IRS will contact you by mail and it will include Publication 4518[2], which explains the private collection program and even tells you what you can do to get out of it. Do you need to do that? You do not. As a matter of fact, there is good reason to think that being on the private collection naughty list is better for you, if you can put up with the occasional annoying phone call that you hang up on. To understand why, you need to know just a bit about IRS collections.

How It Works

For practical purposes, the IRS has four possible faces. At one extreme is a kind of black box. You send in timely returns with timely payments, or maybe you receive a refund. At the other extreme is IRS Criminal Investigation. You must get very extreme to get them interested in you. And you shouldn't be reading tax blogs; you should be finding a lawyer. The other two faces, which it is very important not to confuse are examination and collection.

You deal with examination if the IRS thinks that your return might be wrong. This can be extremely stressful and annoying. If there are significant dollars involved, the best advice is to hire somebody to deal with it; a CPA or an enrolled agent to deal with a revenue agent doing an audit, or a tax attorney if it goes beyond that. To maintain perspective, though, it is important to know that at the end of a process that might take years—audit, IRS appeals, Tax Court petition, back to IRS appeals, Tax Court decision, Appellate Court—all that happens is that you get a bill. It might be a big bill, but that is it. Once the final, final bill is issued after however much appealing you choose, examinations are over for you.

And maybe you just write a check, and that's it, and you will never deal with the part of the IRS that now has private companies making phone calls for it. That would be collections.

Collections

The job of the collections arm of the IRS is to, you know, collect. Once the matter is in their hands there should no longer be any question as to what the correct amount of the tax is. "Doubt as to liability" is an issue that you can raise with them, but generally if they have the account, there is no doubt. At the end of the day when you are dealing with collections, whose determinations you can appeal to Tax Court, you are arguing about "reasonable collection potential." Thanks to the RCP concept, if you are not interested in accumulating net worth and you are not a total chazer[3] about it, paying your income tax is somewhat optional.

Here is the funny thing about the people doing collections for the IRS. Congress forbids the IRS from evaluating them based on how much they collect. The private companies, on the other hand, will receive payment on a percentage basis. Go figure.

What You Need to Worry About

At any rate, if you end up with an unpaid tax (say you filed without paying, or there was an adjustment to your return, or you didn't file so the IRS filed for you) what IRS collections will do, if they do anything, is send you annoying mail telling you should pay, with subsequent letters getting progressively more ominous. Now if that mail really bothers you, you can get proactive. If the amounts are significant, you should probably hire somebody. That person will not be somebody who mostly does returns, nor should it be somebody who advertises on TV that you can settle your debt for penalties on the dollar. Collections are a specialty. I don't have a shortcut to tell you how to find somebody. Just make sure it is someone with one of the valid credentials CPA, enrolled agents, or attorneys, and that they focus on collection work to some extent. Check their references thoroughly and look up whether they have valid credentials.

The other thing you might do is nothing. I would suggest, however, that you read all those notices and save them. Also tell the IRS when you move. There is a form for that.[4] Because at some point you might get a notice that really matters. That is when you'd better do something.

> If the IRS pursues enforcement action, the taxpayer still has options. After the IRS files a Notice of Federal Tax Lien, and prior to the Service initiating levy action, a taxpayer is given the opportunity to request a hearing with the Office of Appeals. The taxpayer also has a right to appeal certain other collection actions. For example, if the taxpayer's request for an installment agreement is denied, the taxpayer has a right to appeal that determination. Each taxpayer subject to enforcement action receives Publication 1660,[5] Collection Appeal Rights. This publication explains a taxpayer's right to make an appeal and the procedures for requesting an appeal.
>
> At any time before or during collection action, a taxpayer who believes a pending collection action will create a significant hardship may apply for relief by submitting Form 911, Application for Taxpayer Assistance Order (ATAO). The Office of the Taxpayer Advocate will review the application, and if appropriate, take steps to resolve the taxpayer's problem with the IRS to relieve the hardship.

If you continue your passive-aggressive ways at that point, they can take your stuff or tell people who owe you money to pay them instead—or else.

Here is the funny thing, though. They might never get around to doing that because they don't have enough resources. And their evaluations are not on how much they collect, but rather on how well they do at answering the phone. And when they start threatening to take money from bank accounts, they start getting phone calls and filings and the like. So, they just sit on accounts. Lots of accounts, including maybe yours.

Light at the End of the Tunnel

It might seem that your passive-aggressive ways are dooming you to a life sentence of waiting for the other shoe to drop. But that is not the case. There is a statute of limitations on collections: 10 years. Now that may seem like a really long time, but if your account is one of the ones turned over to the private collectors, you might already be halfway there. And here is the beautiful part, from your viewpoint rather than that of good tax administration, the private collectors cannot do any of the nasty stuff that real IRS collection people can do. They can't do liens and levies, which can make your life miserable. All they can do is encourage you to pay in full either all at once or in installments.

Now when you get the really serious notices from the IRS and you file Form 12153[6] to request a collection due process hearing the result of which you can appeal to the Tax Court, the downside is that the 10-year clock stops ticking. And this is why having your account with the private collectors is such a beautiful thing. They can't do any of the nasty stuff, and the 10-year clock is still ticking. When they give up on you, they must hand you back to the IRS, which must start over. So maybe rather than hanging up on them, you should have long discussions, but that is only for the advanced passive-aggressive types.

Really You Should Pay

If you want to be a good citizen and a good person, you should pay the balance due if there is any way you can. If your account goes to these collections folks, you either have a different view of tax from me, or you really can't pay. In either case, the fact that your balance is growing because of interest likely does not matter, because people in your situation end up paying based on reasonable collection potential rather than the "correct tax," which is of academic interest. So, treat the callers from CBE Group or whichever of the gang of four happens to have your account the same way you treat the guys calling from Mumbai. But watch your mail and tell the IRS when you move.

Reflections On The Fifteenth Law

You may note that I find the whole topic of collections a little distasteful. I did not have a lot of experience with it during my career. I have learned about it from reading opinions and consulting with people who work in the field. I am of the mind that you should organize your life to live on your after-tax income, which given the progressive nature of the system, should generally not be that hard.

Still, as a professional, I don't impose my views on clients or readers and want to let you know how I see things actually working. And we are getting close to the point where paying taxes can be almost voluntary to people with the moxie to work the collection system. ◊

FIFTEENTH LAW OF TAX PLANNING

Footnotes

1. "Private Collection of Some Overdue Federal Taxes Starts in April; Those Affected Will Hear First From IRS; IRS Will Still Handle Most Tax Debts," Internal Revenue Service, last modified February 8, 2023, https://www.irs.gov/newsroom/private-collection-of-some-overdue-federal-taxes-starts-in-april-those-affected-will-hear-first-from-irs-irs-will-still-handle-most-tax-debts.
2. Internal Revenue Service, What You Can Expect When the IRS Assigns Your Account to a Private Collection Agency (Washington D.C.: Department of Treasury, 2019), https://www.irs.gov/pub/irs-pdf/p4518.pdf.
3. "chaser," Urban Dictionary, last modified February 24, 2005, https://www.urbandictionary.com/define.php?term=chazer.
4. Internal Revenue Service, Form 8822: Change of Address (Washington D.C.: Department of the Treasury, 2021), https://www.irs.gov/pub/irs-pdf/f8822.pdf.
5. Internal Revenue Service, Collection Appeal Rights (Internal Revenue Service, 2020), https://www.irs.gov/pub/irs-pdf/p1660.pdf.
6. Internal Revenue Service, Form 12153: Request for a Collection Due Process or Equivalent Hearing (Washington D.C.: Department of the Treasury, 2022), https://www.irs.gov/pub/irs-pdf/f12153.pdf.

SIXTEENTH LAW OF TAX PLANNING

Being Right Without Substantiation Can Be As Bad As Being Wrong.

Having a good substantiation is a boring and tedious process. You should do it anyway.

A Florida couple got a painful tax lesson following an even more painful lesson in how not to be a landlord.

Florida Couple Fails to Check References or Keep Receipts—Does Not End Well in Tax Court

The sad story is in Tax Court Summary Opinion 2017-79. Although they have made themselves public, they don't need me to make them more famous so, I will refer to them as Robin and Terry, my all-purpose generic couple. The case is about a theft loss on Robin and Terry's 2012 return.

The theft loss was the result of their foray into being a landlord. In August 2011, Robin and Terry entered into an agreement to rent a fully furnished 3,800-square-foot house to another couple. We'll call them the Tenants From Hell (TFH). There was a further agreement to sell some of the furniture and accouterments. A few days before move-in, TFH provided a check for initial rent and security deposit. The check bounced. Robin and Terry approached them about it, and the TFH promised another check.

Early November, Robin and Terry lost their patience and commenced an eviction action. When they got access to the house on November 15, they found all the furnishings gone—furniture, window coverings, draperies, and accouterments. There was also damage to the house and the need for a paint job.

Robin and Terry managed to track down TFH along with a sheriff's deputy and recovered some items. It was difficult sorting out what belonged to Robin and Terry and TFH, so the deputy said they should come back the next day. You might be shocked, *shocked* to learn that TFH disappeared the next day.

Deduction Pushed into Next Year

Robin and Terry did not give up right away and tried various ways and means to recover their property.

> During 2012, petitioners were in touch with attorneys and law enforcement officers to determine whether they would be able to recover their furnishings or seek monetary damages. **Petitioners discovered that the tenant and her husband had been involved in this type of activity before and had routinely made offers to purchase furniture and then disappeared without making payment.** During 2012, after petitioners were able to assess the tenant's financial situation, they determined that it would be a "waste of time" to pursue the tenant and her husband, either civilly or criminally. It was at this point in 2012 that petitioners became aware that they would not recover their furniture and other household items. **(Emphasis added)**

That sentence in bold is the business lesson in this sad tale. With a better reference check before renting to TFH, Robin and Terry might have found out about TFH's penchant for skipping out with recliners and armchairs and the like.

Tax deductions may have mitigated the pain of the tenant from hell somewhat. Robin and Terry were conservative in that they did not take a theft loss in 2011 when the theft occurred, but waited until 2012, when it was finally determined that there was no more point in chasing TFH. When it came to valuation, though they may have caught the Agent From Hell. AFH was willing to allow some loss, but nothing near the $29,979 they claimed. Also, AFH argued they should have taken the loss in 2011.

Documentation

Robin and Terry did a better job of documenting their loss, than most people would have.

> Petitioners were able to find and offered at trial photographs of the household furnishings taken shortly before the tenant and her husband moved in during September 2011. Based on the photographs and coupled with their recollection, petitioners made a schedule of the items that were the basis of their $29,979 theft loss deduction. To show fair market values of the items, petitioners found examples of the items for sale on websites such as eBay. They also researched the cost of fabrication of items such as drapery to arrive at values. They used the prices from their research and applied some discounts to arrive at their estimates of fair market values.

There was enough there for the court to refer to the famous Cohan rule. At Joseph B. Cohan and Associates, the young staff accountants thought the rule was for our managing partner Herb Cohan or his eponymous father, who still came in some days despite being older than 80. It is for George M. Cohan of Broadway fame, who was not big on documenting his expenses, but he still received something. Legislation has narrowed the scope of the Cohan rule and now requires specific documentation in some areas, but it remains.

So, Robin and Terry got somewhere with the Tax Court, but not that far. The Tax Court allowed $9,194. They were dismissive of an additional $5,467 in documented repairs since that was not part of the theft loss. Seems as if it should otherwise have been deductible. On the other hand, that would probably be a 2011 item. The Court also allowed the accuracy penalty, which I think is harsh.

It was their failure to prepare and maintain adequate records and documentation in support of their claimed $29,979 theft loss deduction that resulted in our reaching a $9,194 total value of the items lost....

Although petitioners sought advice about how to report a theft loss, they have not shown the specific source of the advice and whether it was reasonable for them to rely on the advice received. We accordingly hold that petitioners, on account of their negligence or disregard of rules or regulations, are liable for a Section 6662(a) accuracy-related penalty with respect to the underpayment.

You really can't tell from the decision whether Robin and Terry inflated their loss at all. If they did not, they got a raw deal with the accuracy penalty rubbing salt in the wound.

This is not exactly an instance of **Reilly's Sixteenth Law of Tax Planning—"*Being right without substantiation can be as bad as being wrong.*"** Robin and Terry probably had as much substantiation as you would expect assuming they rented out a house furnished with stuff they had accumulated over time and originally intended for personal use. ◊

The business lesson contained in the Tax Court decision in the case of Cecile Barker is probably a variation of an old joke—How do you make a small fortune creating a record label? Start with a large fortune.

Cecile Barker And Why You Need to Keep Records Longer Than You Thought

Cecile Barker has bad news from the Eleventh Circuit.[1] It upheld the Tax Court's disallowance of his multi-million-dollar net operating loss deduction (NOL) largely generated by SoBe Entertainment LLC. SoBe

Entertainment is a record label that has represented numerous artists included Brooke Hogan, daughter of Hulk Hogan[2]. The indirect Hulk Hogan connection[3] makes Mr. Barker a tangential figure in a fascinating story you can read about in *Conspiracy – Peter Thiel, Hulk Hogan, Gawker and the Anatomy of Intrigue*[4] by Ryan Holiday. For purposes of this article, we will stick to the tax story, which began with a Tax Court opinion[5] in 2018, which I covered previously.[6]

Background

Mr. Barker had been in the record business in the 60s and early 70s. He was also in aerospace engineering, where he made a fortune. It appears that he spent a good chunk of that fortune on SoBe, which he founded in 2002. According to SoBe partnership returns, he contributed more than $45 million to SoBe from 2002 to 2011. Coming into 2011, he had a net operating loss carryover of almost $17 million.

Identity theft complicated Mr. Barker's 2011 filing. The initial statutory notice of deficiency was based on missing income on a return somebody else filed. Mr. Barker filed a return, including that income and other income along with the NOL carryover and loss from SoBe. The IRS challenged the NOL on Section 183 grounds claiming that SoBe was, in fact, a hobby. Judge Pugh did not buy that, but the IRS had another arrow in its quiver.

The IRS argued that the NOL was unsubstantiated. There were two issues. One was that there was no substantiation for expenses provided beyond bank statements and general ledgers. The other was that he did not provide some of the earlier returns, leaving a question as to how much of the NOL was available for carryover. Judge Pugh bought those arguments. I usually think of the opinion as kind of the end of the story at least at the Tax Court, but it really isn't.

Tax Court Result

The Tax Court doesn't do the math. It has the IRS and the taxpayer sort out the implications of the decision with a 155 computation, a reference to the Tax Court rules.[7] This got very ugly, Mr. Barker had held off on filing his 2011 possibly because of the identify theft return. He had, however, been late in other years. At any rate, besides a late file penalty of more than $400,000, the lateness had other dire consequences.

The original notice of deficiency was for $1.2 million. Its starting point was the false identity theft return, which had, of course, omitted much income. Ultimately, Mr. Barker filed a complete 2011 return, which contained even more income, but also included more than $4.7 million in deductions besides the $19 million from SoBe, which included the NOL. Barker argued the SoBe loss in Tax Court, but the other deductions did not come up. When it came to the 155 computations, the IRS did not include them, although they did include the additional income that he reported on the actual return.

So, to review the bidding, Mr. Barker received a statutory notice of deficiency calling for an additional tax of $1,259,279 and an understatement penalty of $252,090 in September 2014. Rather than saying "Yeah, whatever" and sending in $1,511,369, he went to Tax Court largely relying on his massive NOL to clean things up. On March 11, 2019, Judge Pugh issued the final decision in which Mr. Barker owes $1,805,924 in tax and $451,481.13 in late file penalty. The trip to Tax Court cost Mr. Barker nearly $750,000 before we even consider interest.

The Appeal

The appeal did not go well. Among the problems the Tax Court cited was that Mr. Barker had not produced some of his tax returns from earlier years. That appears to be related to his having switched accountants. Thus, there could be no certainty that losses had not carried back. I spoke with David Garvin, the attorney who represented Mr. Barker, at the Eleventh Circuit. He focused significantly on Mr. Barker having elected to carry the loss forward and that there was still plenty of loss left over. The government pointed out that he filed returns with carry forward elections late. You can check out the oral arguments[8] if you have a taste for that sort of thing.

The Appellate Court confirmed the Tax Court decision entirely in an opinion written by Senior Circuit Judge Frank Hull.[9]

Reflection

It is a little difficult for an accountant like me to wrap my head around what happened here. Clearly, Mr. Barker got a raw deal. This is the sort of court decision that, while very lawyerly (i.e., tied up in court procedural issues) has important lessons for preparers and taxpayers.

The first is that you should not let the fact (or belief) that you don't owe anything make you blasé about timely filing your return. As they say in Washington—meaning something else—elections have consequences. And many elections need to be timely. It is not just that, though. If the IRS had started with the return that Mr. Barker filed and audited it, the revenue agent would have asked for substantiation and possibly disallowed some deductions. And, ultimately, that would have been fought about in court.

But Mr. Barker would not have to be introducing evidence for every single deduction on his return. It would have been just about the ones the IRS challenged. Having the return go in after the original notice of deficiency meant that Barker had to prove everything to the Tax Court, not just the specific items the IRS challenged.

The other lesson that is very hard to absorb is the principle that every year stands on its own, and the client must substantiate every number. When you are working on a 2011 return you probably think of the 2002 return as old and cold. But for someone like Mr. Barker, it is not. That huge NOL deduction is subject to substantiation. There is a sense that the 2002 return will end up staying open for almost 20 years. It is rare that this comes up in practice, but it is something to bear in mind, particularly when there is a switch in accountants.

Remember **Reilly's Sixteenth Law of Tax Planning—"*Being right without substantiation can be as bad as being wrong.*"** ◊

After a long hiatus, the Tax Court broke the ice with a substantiation decision.

Big Dollars for a Summary Decision

Towards the end of 2018 the Tax Court stopped issuing opinions as it adopted new software. It was a trying time for me to have not Tax Court opinions to read. The long dark night finally ended with T.C. Summary Opinion 2019-1.[10]

The name of the petitioner is, of course, public record and you can easily find it, but it is one of those cases where I figure the taxpayer does not need me to help him be more infamous so I will call him Joe.

Joe had deficiencies for 2009 and 2010. With penalties, the tab was close to $70,000. With those kinds of stakes it starts getting worth hiring a lawyer, but Joe was on his own. He also prepared his own return using the expensive and unreliable software that Robert Flach[11] condemns when he does not have his sights on the "idiots in Congress" and reality TV.

There were 11 issues, including the penalties. It was almost like every number on the return was wrong—except maybe Joe's house number and SSN.[12]

Not A Rollover

The biggest issue was a $43,503 IRA distribution, which Joe reported he rolled over. He hadn't. Joe tried to beat the 10 percent penalty by arguing that he had a disability, or alternatively, spent the money on medical expenses. The former argument failed because he was driving many miles a day on his job selling medical supplies, so while he may not have been doing so well, he clearly did not have a disability. And he did not substantiate the medical expenses.

Substantiation

The other big adjustment was Schedule A employee business expenses, mostly mileage on his car. The Tax Court kind of believed him, but the documentation was very weak. He said that he had a copy of his employer's policy that showed that he would not receive reimbursement but did not bring the policy with him. And when it came to his logs, which are necessary, don't get them started:

> The monthly mileage logs for the years at issue list four weeks per month from Monday to Friday without any corresponding dates and list the names of medical facilities or hospitals with a corresponding figure representing an alleged mileage calculation. The mileage logs fail to identify a business purpose for the miles recorded, including whether sales were made for his employer or the medical sales company or both at each location. According to the mileage logs, petitioner drove a total of 28,752 business miles and 11,849 business miles in 2009 and 2010, respectively, for his business, less than the figures reported on the Forms 2106-EZ for both years.

There were similar substantiation issues with charitable deductions and a repair deduction on a rental property. Receipts, carefully placed in an envelope, substantiated the repair deductions. That envelope is probably in the same place as the notebook with information about the charitable contributions and that employer reimbursement policy statement. It's not just having substantiation. It's also bringing it with you.

All in the main theme of the case is **Reilly's Sixteenth Law of Tax Planning—"*Being right without substantiation can be as bad as being wrong.*"**

The case is a good lesson for do-it-yourselfers. After you finish the return, look at each number and create a little schedule with the numbers that make up that number and something that supports each of those numbers. The education requirement of an IRS revenue agent is a bachelor's degree with 30 credit hours in accounting. Accountants respond well to those ticked and tied schedules.

Reflection On The Sixteenth Law

A common question fielded by tax pros is how long it is necessary to keep things. I remember a handy chart we used to give out with different periods for different sorts of records. The real answer is "as long as you need to". ◊

SIXTEENTH LAW OF TAX PLANNING

Footnotes

1. Cecile Barker v. Commissioner of Internal Revenue, United States Court of Appeal (No. 19-11994), April 27, 2021, https://law.justia.com/cases/federal/appellate-courts/ca11/19-11994/19-11994-2021-04-27-0.html.
2. "Hulk Hogan," Wikipedia, last modified May 26, 2023, https://en.wikipedia.org/wiki/Hulk_Hogan.
3. Martenzie Johnson, "Is it too soon for Hulk Hogan to return to WWE?," Andscape, last modified July 16, 2018, https://andscape.com/features/is-it-too-soon-for-hulk-hogan-to-return-to-wwe/.
4. Ryan Holiday, Conspiracy – Peter Thiel, Hulk Hogan, Gawker and the Anatomy of Intrigue (Harefield: Portfolio, 2018).
5. "Docket Number: 21067-14," Welcome to DAWSON, accessed May 29, 2023, https://dawson.ustaxcourt.gov/case-detail/21067-14.
6. "IRS Does Not Get Hip-Hop And Hold Onto That NOL Substantiation," Your Tax Matters Partner (blog), last modified July 2, 2018, https://yourtaxmatterspartner.com/irs-does-not-get-hip-hop-and-hold-onto-that-nol-substantiation/.
7. "26 USC App Rule 155: Computation by Parties for Entry of Decision," United States Code, last modified January 23, 2000, https://uscode.house.gov/view.xhtml?req=granuleid:USC-1999-title26a-titleXV.-rule155&num=0&edition=1999.
8. "Oral Argument Recordings," United States Court of Appeals for the Eleventh Circuit, accessed May 29, 2023, https://www.ca11.uscourts.gov/oral-argument-recordings?title=&field_oar_case_name_value=barker&field_oral_argument_date_value%5Bvalue%5D%5Byear%5D=&field_oral_argument_date_value%5Bvalue%5D%5Bmonth%5D=.

9. "Hon. Frank M. Hull," United States Court of Appeals for the Eleventh Circuit, accessed May 29, 2023, https://www.ca11.uscourts.gov/judges/hon-frank-m-hull.

10. Christopher John Totten v. Commissioner of Internal Revenue, United States Tax Court (No. 10691-14S), January 29, 2019, https://www.casemine.com/judgement/us/5c529de7342cca279550d0ed.

11. The Wandering Tax Pro (blog), accessed May 29, 2023, http://wanderingtaxpro.blogspot.com/.

12. Peter J. Reilly, "Here is the first post on a 2019 tax court decision," Forbes, last modified January 29, 2019, https://www.forbes.com/sites/peterjreilly/2019/01/29/here-is-the-first-post-on-a-2019-tax-court-decision/.

SEVENTEENTH LAW OF TAX PLANNING

Don't Cut Your Deadlines Close And Use The U.S. Mail With Proof Of Mailing.

My mother had a number of expressions. One of her favorites was advising me to not be a "Last Minute Louie." Tax Court rules are particularly hard on Last Minute Louies, but the misnamed mail-box rule offers some relief.

A Day Late Forecloses Tax Court Hearing Regardless of Misleading IRS Notice

When you miss deadlines in tax matters, the consequences vary. Sometimes it is "no harm, no foul," sometimes there is a mild financial penalty, and sometimes there is a severe financial penalty. And then there is the Tax Court. If you miss the initial Tax Court deadline for filing a petition, that is it. No Tax Court for you.[1] One sad tale in that regard is the appeal of Phillip Duggan to the Ninth Circuit.[2] There is an important lesson in this case, but I'll give you the story first.

What the Opinion Is About?

To get his day in Tax Court, Mr. Duggan had to file his petition within 30 days of January 7, 2015. Mr. Duggan figured that January 8, 2015, was day zero. So, he mailed his petition on February 7, 2015, which was Day 31 as they count the days in Tax Court. From there, it gets lawyerly.

The question is whether the deadline is "jurisdictional." In the Tax Court decision,[3] you will see the sentence "This Court is a court of limited jurisdiction." A sentence like that is almost inevitable in decisions of this sort. The Ninth Circuit leads with "The Tax Court is an Article I court of "limited jurisdiction." Nobody gets hauled before the Tax Court[4]. It is optional and to exercise the option you need to follow the procedure. If you don't, there is nothing they can do for you.

Help From Harvard Not Enough

A lot of pro se litigants miss the deadlines. In this case, that led to an amicus brief by Linda Jean Matuszak. Ms. Matuszak was tripped up similarly.[5] Carlton Smith and Professor T. Keith Fogg, Director Harvard Federal Tax Clinic[6], filed the brief, which gives students at Harvard Law School the opportunity to do some tax litigation for the other 95 percent. They are making a push on the deadline issue. This is from their website:

> In addition to representing local clients, the Clinic looks to comment on proposed rules and regulations impacting low-income taxpayers, and it looks to litigate broadly on issues impacting this community. The Clinic is currently litigating whether the Tax Court has the ability to equitably toll the time frame for filing a Tax Court petition. It represents clients in the 2nd, 3rd, 4th and 10th Circuits that the Tax Court dismissed as untimely despite the fact that the taxpayers filed late based upon oral and written statements made by the IRS regarding the last day to file.

The amicus brief[7] makes the argument that the IRS notice of determination misled Mr. Duggan as to the due date of the petition. The notice of determination the IRS issued read:

> If you want to dispute this determination in court, you must file a petition with the United States Tax Court within a 30-day period beginning the day after the date of this letter.

That is different from the statutory language and adds to the confusion about day counting.

The legal principle is that if the deadline is "jurisdictional," it does not matter whether the IRS told Mr. Duggan he had a year instead of 30 days, because the statute says that the Tax Court is not involved. If the deadline is not "jurisdictional," then the concept of "equitable tolling" comes into play, and the Tax Court can cut the taxpayer a break on the deadline because of misleading info.

The Ninth Circuit was not buying it.

> Accordingly, we hold that because the text of Section 6630(d)(1) conditions the Tax Court's jurisdiction on the timely filing of a petition for review, the thirty-day deadline in Section 6330(d)(1) is jurisdictional. Duggan's failure to meet this deadline divested the Tax Court of the power to hear his case and foreclosed any argument for equitable tolling.

There's More

Professor Fogg sent me a copy of a Fourth Circuit decision. Semyya Lanise Cunningham had pretty much the same fact pattern as Phillip Duggan, filing a day late from following what she thought were the IRS instructions. The Fourth Circuit didn't touch the jurisdictional question. It decided the appeal on the basis that there was nothing misleading about the IRS notice and certainly nothing to suggest the IRS acted with negligence. The Harvard team was all over this case also.

The Lesson

If people would pay attention to **Reilly's Seventeenth Law of Tax Planning—*"Don't cut your deadlines close and use the U.S. Mail with proof of mailing,"*** you wouldn't have cases like this. When it says, "within thirty days," tell yourself that it is 20 days and precisely how you count the days stops mattering. You could even have transposed the digits on the letter you received thinking that January 12 was January 21, and you will still be timely. I ran that notion by Professor Fogg and here is his response:

> I totally agree with your Seventeenth Law. I do not know why people think filing at the very last second is a clever idea, but it seems hardwired in many people—lots of lawyers included.

Other Coverage

Carlton Smith had something in Procedurally Taxing[8] noting that Mr. Duggan was one of at least eight taxpayers the IRS notice misled.

I've modified my seeming judgmental attitude of why people let things go to the wire a bit in the case of Ms. Cunningham. I listened to the oral arguments,[9] when the speaker mentioned that because of certified mail, it was already day 20 when Ms. Cunningham received the notice. ◊

It's nice to see people inside the IRS rooting for the little guy who has gotten a raw deal. That is one of the reasons I am covering CCA 201822027[10] even though I can't construct the story behind the story as well as I would like. There is also an important lesson in there.

IRS Identity Theft Victim May Have Asked for Money Back Too Late

CCA stands for Chief Counsel Advice and the IRS Office of Chief Counsel is where the knotty problems end up. The advice is short so I will reproduce most of it.

> Hi _______. Thanks for your patience. I've closely studied this case, as well as discussed, the facts with several of my Counsel

colleagues who have extensive experience with ID theft cases. Unfortunately, we agree with SBSE Counsel that the taxpayers are not entitled to a refund. Because they had no filing requirement, the "3 years from the time the return was filed" timeframe in Section 6511(a)" isn't applicable. Consequently, their claim must have been filed within 2 years from the date the tax was paid. In this case, the tax was paid on——-, when the IRS offset their ——— refund to the ——— balance due. So, any claim for refund would have had to be filed by ————-.

Two points of clarification: (1) The last paragraph in the SB/SE Counsel opinion is perhaps a little confusing, as it assumes that the return filed by the thief was really the taxpayers' return and applies the Section 6511 analysis accordingly. Yet it is my understanding that these taxpayers did not have a filing requirement. In addition, SB/SE Counsel doesn't explain that the taxpayers get the longer of the 3-year/2-year timeframe in Section 6511(a). (2) Before you close out this case, be sure you have explored with the taxpayers whether there is anything that could be a timely informal claim for refund. Did the taxpayers contact the IRS between the date of the offset and —————, to indicate they wanted a refund of the amount offset and ———, to indicate they wanted a refund of the amount offset? There needs to be something in writing; the writing requirement can be satisfied in certain circumstances by IRS records (e.g., suppose the taxpayers called the IRS and any case history documented by the IRS reflects the taxpayers wanted the offset amount back—that could be sufficient—I would want to see the documentation).

I'm sorry this isn't the result for which you were hoping, but Section 6511 bars relief for these taxpayers unless you can advocate that they filed a timely informal claim for refund by ————-.

Please let me know if you have any questions.

So, what happened here is the victim had some money due from the IRS, but no requirement to file a tax return. I'm having trouble coming up with a plausible scenario that accounts for that. Maybe they applied a refund to the subsequent year, which turned out to be an awful year.

Regardless, an identity thief managed to grab that money and apply it to their own tax or have it refunded.

Of course, the victim has the right to get the money back from the IRS as long as they request it in time, but that is where the glitch is. The statute of limitations on amending a return is three years, but the statute on requesting refunds generally is two years.[11] For example, you file your return, and the IRS has three years to adjust it (which it might extend in various ways). If you decide to pay rather than appeal to the Tax Court, you have two years from then to file for a refund. Since they had no required return, the victim fell under the two-year rule rather than the three-year rule.

The larger lesson there is a variation on **Reilly's Seventeenth Law of Tax Planning—"*Don't cut your deadlines close and use the U.S. Mail with proof of mailing.*"** Of course, there is not enough information here to figure out the drama that created this situation.

What I really like is the way they are endeavoring to find something that will let them do the right thing by the victim—"suppose the taxpayers called the IRS and any case history documented by the IRS reflects the taxpayers wanted the offset amount back—that could be sufficient..." I wonder if that is a subtle hint to look really, really carefully through your desk drawer for a phone message or something. Maybe not. That would be above and beyond.

Reflections On The Seventeenth Law

There has been litigation since the cases I discussed here that have produced more taxpayer friendly results, but those opinions do not make me rethink the law. The taxpayers still had to engage in additional litigation to get their case heard that would have been avoided by not cutting the deadline close. ◊

Footnotes

1. Peter J. Reilly, "A day late forecloses tax court hearing regardless of misleading IRS notice," Forbes, last modified January 25, 2018, https://www.forbes.com/sites/peterjreilly/2018/01/25/a-day-late-forecloses-tax-court-hearing-regardless-of-misleading-irs-notice/.
2. Philip A. Duggan v. Commissioner Of Internal Revenue, United States Court of Appeals (No. 15-73819), January 12, 2018, https://cdn.ca9.uscourts.gov/datastore/opinions/2018/01/12/15-73819.pdf.
3. "Docket Number: 14610-13L," Welcome to DAWSON, accessed May 29, 2023, https://dawson.ustaxcourt.gov/case-detail/14610-13.
4. Reilly, "A day late forecloses tax court."
5. Linda Jean Matuszak v. Commissioner of Internal Revenue, United States Court of Appeals (No. 16-3034), July 05, 2017, https://caselaw.findlaw.com/court/us-2nd-circuit/1867041.html.
6. "Tax Litigation Clinic," Harvard Law School, accessed May 29, 2023, https://hls.harvard.edu/clinics/in-house-clinics/tax-litigation-clinic/.
7. Keith T. Fogg and Carlton M. Smith, Brief of AMICUS CURIAE Linda Jean Matuszak in support of petitioner-appelant (Counsel for Amicus, 2016), https://drive.google.com/file/d/1N5FYPVrG3IiaT3wOxI6vHmHajTLxCUbp/view.
8. Carlton Smith, "Ninth Circuit Holds Period to File Tax Court Collection Due Process Petition Jurisdictional Under Current Supreme Court Case Law Usually Treating Filing Deadlines as Nonjurisdictional," Procedurally Taxing (blog), last modified January 12, 2018, https://procedurallytaxing.com/ninth-circuit-holds-period-to-file-tax-court-collection-due-process-petition-jurisdictional-under-current-supreme-court-case-law-usually-treating-filing-deadlines-as-nonjurisdictional/.
9. "Semyya Lanise Cunningham v. Commissioner of Internal Rev," Court Listener, last modified December 5, 2017, https://www.courtlistener.com/audio/33394/semyya-lanise-cunningham-v-commissioner-of-internal-rev/.
10. Internal Revenue Service, "Refund Claim Would Be Denied for Identity Theft Victim," TaxNotes, last modified June 1, 2018, https://www.taxnotes.com/research/federal/irs-private-rulings/e-mail-chief-counsel-advice/refund-claim-would-be-denied-for-identity-theft-victim/283fp.

11. Peter J. Reilly, "IRS identity theft victim may have asked for money back too late," Forbes, last modified June 6, 2018, https://www.forbes.com/sites/peterjreilly/2018/06/06/irs-identity-theft-victim-may-have-asked-for-money-back-too-late/.

EIGHTEENTH LAW OF TAX PLANNING

Honest Objective Trumps Realistic Possibility.

My laws have tended to lean a little on the conservative side, as tax planners understand the word conservative. I first became interested in hobby losses because they tend to be such entertaining stories. Over time, though, I have come to conclude from studying the case law that practitioners tend not to be as aggressive in this area as they might be. And there are some serious misunderstandings about how the statute works.

The birth of a tax planning law.

Hobby Loss Roundup and a New Law of Tax Planning Announced

There has been a bit of hobby loss action since the Tax Court decision in the case of James and Elaine Donoghue on June 11, 2019, which I covered here.[1] None of the decisions struck me as quite interesting enough to merit a post, but I have resolved to be your go-to guy when it comes to hobby loss, so I thought I would combine them. And hold your excitement, my hobby loss work has inspired this latest of **Reilly's Laws of Tax Planning.**

Know When to Fold Them

We'll start with the gamblers. Here are the latest.

The Fourth Circuit affirmed,[2] without comment, the Tax Court 2017 decision in the case of James Boneparte. Boneparte worked full-time for the Port Authority of New York and New Jersey at the Lincoln Tunnel but spent a lot of time in Atlantic City at racetracks and casinos. He did not keep detailed records and did not get a lot of credit for reading books and watching videos about winning at slots and baccarat. It is interesting to note that the Tax Court found that his $82,000 from the Port Authority was substantial income in 2013.

Next up is Jun Wu, a Tax Court Summary Opinion.[3] Summary opinions are not precedent, but I still find them instructive, and if I like the result, I will not hesitate to use it with a revenue agent. This is not such a decision. Jun Wu lived and worked in San Francisco, and his gambling was in Vegas. Among the multitude of things that have stayed in Vegas are Jun Wu's gambling losses.

Wu's pro se status comes through loud and clear:

> Petitioner intended to win when he gambled, and he developed his winning strategies by reading a book he could not remember the name of, talking to people and casino employees at the various casinos, taking a class that lasted "a couple hours," and "just by playing."

It strikes me that his trial prep left a bit to be desired. At any rate, only the first of the regulatory factors (business-like manner) is part of a lengthy discussion. However the recreational aspect was enough to sink his claim.

> Other than the win/loss statements provided by the casinos, petitioner did not maintain any records for the activity, and he did not develop or follow any form of business plan.

Finally, for the gamblers, there is Theodore Zalesiak, another summary opinion. Zalesiak's game was poker, and he was actually positive in some years. Still, the Tax Court dealt him aces over eights[4] without much in the way of illuminating discussion.

And a Horse of Course

The horse is RS Noble Heir starring in the Tax Court memorandum decision in the case of Sheldon Sapoznik and Melissa McCrossen. RS Noble Heir had that great job that certain horses get as their final career. Unfortunately, he died before performing. A gelding who was for sale succeeded him. Major Sugarfixxx sold at a breakeven.

The Tax Court found that there was not a business going on there.

> Petitioners did not create written business plans for their horse-related activities, nor did they maintain complete books or records.

You will search hard to find a taxpayer who wins when the analysis starts out that way.

And My Newest Law

It was not an upbeat month or two for IRC Section 183 (Activities not engaged in for profit) victims, but my fundamental view on 183 has not changed. If your client really is trying to make money, they should claim the losses, even if the chance of profits is remote. Hence, we now have **Reilly's 18th Law of Tax Planning—"*Honest objective trumps realistic possibility.*"**

It is rooted in one of the earliest and most significant 183 decisions, the first time an appellate court discussed 183. It concerned Maurice Dreicer[5], a trustafarian who spent years (and hundreds of thousands of dollars) searching for the perfect steak. The Second Circuit ruled that the Tax Court had used the wrong standard in denying Dreicer's losses.

> We hold that a taxpayer engages in an activity for profit, within the meaning of Section 183 and the implementing regulations, when profit is actually and honestly his objective though the prospect of achieving it may seem dim. Because the Tax Court applied a different standard, we reverse and remand for redetermination of Dreicer's deduction claims.

Even on that standard, Dreicer still lost, but that is irrelevant. If you want the juicy details, keep reading... ◊

A particularly important decision. And a very funny story.

Searching for the Perfect Steak with an Imperfect Tax Plan

Travel the world going from one fine restaurant to the next searching for the perfect steak. It just doesn't get any better than that, or so it seems. But one thing that could make it better is doing it with tax-deductible dollars. That was what Maurice Dreicer did. And it worked for many years.

Finally, the IRS challenged his deductions asserting that his never finished book with the title *My 27 Year Search for the Perfect Steak—Still Looking* was an "activity not engaged in for profit." The IRS was looking for about $30,000 in additional tax from Mr. Dreicer for 1972 and 1973. That would be more than $150,000 in today's dollars.

Most Colorful Hobby Loss Litigant

The Tax Court decision[6] and the subsequent appeal to the Second Circuit[7], remain important precedents, but the case grabbed my attention because Mr. Dreicer was so colorful. Colorful is a common attribute of Section 183 (so-called "hobby loss") litigants, but as I have been combing through the cases in preparation for my seminar for the Boston Tax Institute,[8] I have yet to find someone more colorful than Maurice Dreicer, Founder of the Order of the Golden Dozen (world's leading chefs) and The Order of the Great Dining Establishments of the World, Special Gourmet Adviser to the Dinkier Hotel Chain, President of Cigar Smokers United, and the Ale League of the World.

Background

According to his obituary in the *New York Times*,[9] Dreicer was born in New York in 1910 and graduated from Deerfield Academy and Rollins

College. He attended law schools (Harvard, Pennsylvania, and Virginia), but there is no indication he ever practiced law.

Dreicer did quite a bit in the radio industry in the 30s and 40s including a show called What's It Worth, which was the inspiration for the TV show The Price Is Right.

He recorded Here's How to Mix Them,[10] about the proper mixing of drinks. In the footnotes is a link to a sample[11]. He sounds great.

He did manage to get one book published, *The Diner's Companion.*[12]

> Dining out is a fine art. To get the most enjoyment for your time and money, you need to know not only how to plan and where to go for fine food and drink in general, as well as for unusual specialties, but you must also know how to command attention, service, comfort, complete satisfaction.

I suspect I have been doing it wrong all this time, but I am probably too old to change.

And His Day Job

I recently caught some flak from *Going Concern*[13] for reflecting that tax accounting is actually a pretty soft job. As a matter of fact, I have trouble thinking of anything where the money is anywhere near as good that is not harder. There is one exception, that I forget to mention—trust fund beneficiary.

That was Dreicer's main job in terms of income. That hurt him on the eighth factor in the standard Section 183 test (financial status of the taxpayer), but frankly, that one is often a gimme to the IRS since you wouldn't be there if you did not have other income sheltered by the activity in question.

And the Romance

In describing Dreicer's efforts, Tax Court Judge Charles Simpson gets into the role of Brigitte Kimmich who, to use the language of another era, was something of a Girl Friday to the enterprise.

The decision came down in 1979, so I thought it was a nice touch to learn that Dreicer married Ms. Kimmich in 1984. He died in 1989 at the age of 78. I'm wondering if the plan was to have her be a trust beneficiary after he died.

How the Case Went

There are nine factors to consider,[14] but the more cases I read, the more I am convinced that the first factor, "manner in which the taxpayer carries on the activity," is what makes or breaks you. The judges often seem to fudge the other factors to make them fit the overall narrative they have selected.

There are three subfactors to the first factor. One is keeping good records. Then comes behaving like other people who make money in the chosen field. And the third is modifying your plan based on experience. Rather than making the same mistakes over and over, it is better to keep making new mistakes.[15]

Judge Simpson did not do a full drill on the factors but wrote more holistically. Basically, he thought that Dreicer was having a good time traveling around the world and had no realistic expectation of ever making serious money doing what he was doing.

> Although the petitioner spent a fair amount of time traveling around the world in his endeavors, we are not convinced that such activity is anything more than his lifestyle, a lifestyle to be envied by those who do not have independent income to sustain it.

The Appeal

The Second Circuit did have an issue with Judge Simpson's opinion, which is what makes this case an important precedent. It is a subtle point.

> We hold that a taxpayer engages in an activity for profit, within the meaning of Section 183 and the implementing regulations, when profit is actually and honestly his objective, though the prospect of

achieving it may seem dim.[16]

Section 183 was new at this point, a provision of the Tax Reform Act of 1969. The Second Circuit dug into the legislative history and found that Congress required that you have an "honest objective" of making a profit rather than a "reasonable expectation."

The decision sent the case back to Judge Simpson[17]. It was no help to Dreicer, who still lost even under the more generous standard.

A Practical Takeaway

I have not taken my study of 183 case law far enough to compile reliable statistics. Superficially, taxpayers lose these cases more often than they win. Of course, actual Tax Court decisions are a bad sample of outcomes, since the IRS might give up based on hazards of litigation and settle cases that are more marginal, only fighting the ones where people are being stubborn.

Putting the sampling problem aside, are the losers actually losers? At some point, they decided that something that they wanted to do could qualify as a business. Eventually, the IRS came in and said, "No. That's not a business, we are disallowing losses for the last two or three years," and the Tax Court agreed. If that disallowance happens after 20, 10 or even five years of allowed losses, the taxpayer has still come out ahead on the decision to treat the activity as a business.

So, if your client tells you about some preposterous scheme, but you think they are sincere, if deluded, don't be so quick to tell them not to claim the losses. Coach them to keep good books and document their fantasies and keep revising their plans. If and when the audit comes, bring a nice ticked and tied set of schedules along with regularly revised business plans. Go ahead and agree with the revenue agent, one accountant to another, that maybe the scheme is a little crazy but insist that does not matter.

Reflection On The Eighteenth Law

In studying over 300 opinions on concerning Section 183, there is a clear trend towards behaving in a businesslike manner being the determinative factor, despite all the protestations that no one factor is determinative. That is the factor that accountants can really help their clients with the most. ◊

EIGHTEENTH LAW OF TAX PLANNING

Footnotes

1. Peter J. Reilly, "Horse Breeders V IRS: Even The Losers Win," Forbes, last modified June 14, 2019, https://www.forbes.com/sites/peterjreilly/2019/06/14/horse-breeders-v-irs-even-the-losers-win/#606caf03550e.
2. James Boneparte, Jr. v. Commissioner of Internal Revenue, United States Court of Appeals (No. 19-1017), June 24, 2019, https://law.justia.com/cases/federal/appellate-courts/ca4/19-1017/19-1017-2019-06-24.html.
3. Jun Wu v. Commissioner of Internal Revenue, United States Tax Court (No. 8009-16S), July 25, 2019, https://casetext.com/case/wu-v-commr.
4. "Dead man's hand," Wikipedia, last modified May 17, 2023, https://en.wikipedia.org/wiki/Dead_man%27s_hand.
5. Peter J. Reilly, "Searching For The Perfect Steak With An Imperfect Tax Plan," Forbes, last modified April 11, 2019, https://www.forbes.com/sites/peterjreilly/2019/04/11/searching-for-the-perfect-steak-with-an-imperfect-tax-plan/#5fad5f036e69.
6. Maurice C. Dreicer v. Commissioner of Internal Revenue, United States Tax Court (No. 5407-76), September 24, 1979, https://scholar.google.com/scholar_case?case=8222411590969865643&q=kurdziel+tax&hl=en&as_sdt=6,43.
7. Maurice C. Dreicer v. Commissioner of Internal Revenue, United States Court of Appeals (No. 5407-76), September 24, 1981, https://casetext.com/case/dreicer-v-c-i-r.
8. "Video Conference Descriptions," Boston Tax Institute, accessed May 29, 2023, https://bostontaxinstitute.com/video-conferences/seminars/.
9. "Maurice C. Dreicer, 78; Was Radio Entertainer," The New York Times, last modified August 29, 1989, https://www.nytimes.com/1989/08/29/obituaries/maurice-c-dreicer-78-was-radio-entertainer.html.
10. Listener Mindwrecker, "Here's How / To Mix Them," WFMU's Beware of the Blog (blog), last modified August 22, 2009, https://blog.wfmu.org/freeform/2009/08/heres-how-to-mix-them.html.

11. Maurice Dreicer, "The Martini Family," WFMU Blog, audio recording, accessed May 30, 2023, http://blogfiles.wfmu.org/MW/1_Maurice_Dreicer_-_The_Martini_Family.mp3.

12. "The Diner's Companion by Maurice Dreicer /Signed /1st," eCrater, last modified February 16, 2013, https://www.ecrater.com/p/12213942/the-diners-companion-by-maurice.

13. Adrienne Gonzalez, "This Forbes Columnist Thinks You're All a Bunch of Whiny B*tches," Going Concern, last modified April 5, 2019, https://www.goingconcern.com/this-forbes-columnist-thinks-youre-all-a-bunch-of-whiny-btchcs/.

14. Robert Gard, "Business or hobby? The nine factors," Journal of Accountancy, last modified October 1, 2013, https://www.journalofaccountancy.com/issues/2013/oct/20138370.html.

15. Reilly, "Searching for the Perfect Steak."

16. Reilly, "Searching for the Perfect Steak."

17. Maurice C. Dreicer v. Commissioner of Internal Revenue, United States Tax Court (No. 5407-76), April 19, 1982, https://casetext.com/case/dreicer-v-commr-of-internal-revenue.

Conclusion

I don't know how much it comes through in my writing about taxes, but I was not, like some people I know, *born* to be an accountant. I had literary leanings that may have been dashed by a professor who thought I was an idiot because I considered *Moby Dick* a story about a bunch of guys who worked in the whaling industry. I switched to history, where I did much better, and after a year in VISTA took a run at graduate work in history. Shifting gears into accounting without running up more debt meant that I was 27 when I got my first, and arguably only, job in public accounting in 1979.

I was the last person to become a partner in the large local that hired me, and the only person to be an equity partner as it grew into a regional firm. The regional sold itself to a not quite Big 4 firm, which made me a managing director rather than a partner because of my advanced age. They fired me in 2013 and I never went back to working full time, giving me more time for the writing that I had started in 2009.

During all those years I kept reading history, including even a bit about the history of the profession. Among the most useful forms of historical reading are biographies and memoirs. From these readings, and from paying attention, I came up with an observation that has made me unpopular sometimes. Public accounting generally gives you a life that is free from any real hardship other than those inherent in the human condition. You work long hours and encounter a plethora of first world problems. The worst stress I believe is the result of envy—not necessarily your envy, but possibly those further up in the organization.

Whenever I thought things were tough, I would think about the homeless guy that picked our dumpster. He had never learned to read because he was dyslexic. I used to buy him lunch sometimes. I would also think about what it must have been like to be a company commander in Afghanistan. I remember being stressed about feeling responsible for the careers of ten or so people on my affordable housing team. Being responsible for the lives of over a hundred seems incredibly daunting.

At any rate, more has gone into creating Reilly's Laws than just tax litigation, even though that is the major source. Some of them have broader implications:

The First Law—"*It is what it is. Deal with it*" teaches us to accept the things we cannot change. This includes the attitudes, beliefs and limitations of the people—management, clients, staff—that you have to work with. In a far more serious matter, there is a quote attributed to Donald Rumsfeld, "You go to war with the army you have, not the army you might want or wish to have at a later time." People who were good at getting work out and being technically astute would sometimes lament that *the ability to bring in business* was treasured beyond all others. Well, it was what it was. Learn to appreciate it. It is a lot more fun to do tax research well than it is to play golf poorly, even though the latter might bring a higher paycheck.

The **Third Law,** admonishing that there could be a tax rule that made your clever idea not work, might help you realize that is not the only thing that might frustrate your plans.

The **Fourth, Sixth and Seventh Laws** are really about being thorough and not cutting too many corners—certainly not the wrong ones. The **Eighteenth Law** is different from the rest, because it encourages you to try to achieve great things even if the chance of success is small.

When I look back, I think the things that I admire most in others, and feel good about having done myself, are those things that come out of kindness and compassion. Strive to treat everyone that you encounter as a fellow being whose wellbeing you would like to enhance—even if, actually especially if, they seem to be acting like an asshole.

So among my greatest professional achievements, I count the outcome of my "work" for the homeless guy who was picking our dumpster. He actually had a pretty systematic business riding around on a bicycle picking up cans and bringing them to the recycling center. Beyond buying him lunch occasionally and getting him some warm clothes for the upcoming winter, I found him some yard work for a client who owned a couple of buildings. Then I talked to some of my affordable housing friends about how to get him more services. We didn't keep in touch but when I ran into him again a few years later he was living in subsidized housing and seemed to be doing OK. ◊

That thing in the Boy Scout Oath – to help other people at all times – try to remember it even if you are an underachiever who barely makes first class and never gets a merit badge.

Want More of the Wisdom of Peter Reilly?

Subscribe to Think Outside The Tax Box

The Premiere Tax Reduction Source! ***TOTTB.tax***

What is Think Outside the Tax Box?

Think Outside the Tax Box (TOTTB) is the premiere online publication for tax reduction information. We have hundreds of articles featuring in-depth, easy to understand, exhaustively cited, essays on the topic of tax reduction for our subscribers. And, every two weeks, we add more articles, and more features like our live webinar events, and downloadable "Client Alerts". We'd love for you to be a part of it!

What's in a Think Outside The Tax Box subscription?

- **The Newsletter** – *Two Times Per Month!*

On the first and fifteenth of each month we post a newsletter to our website featuring a variety of new, exclusive articles. Our articles are written by some of the most recognized and reliable tax professionals in the industry who bring decades of knowledge and experience to their craft. In addition, every single article is overseen by Editor-In-Chief, Dominique Molina, the visionary mastermind responsible for eight best-selling tax books and the driving force behind the American Institute of Certified Tax Planners!

- **Around the Tax World** – *Two Times Per Month!*

Twice per month, along with a sneak peek of the next newsletter, we send out our "Around the Tax World" email feature. This curated, concisely written feature acts as your own personal aggregator of all the news happening in and around the world of tax. Your days of endless scrolling and combing the internet for the tax stories of the day end now because we're doing that work for you!

- **Private Facebook Group** – *Join the Community!*

Our free private Facebook Group serves as a community for subscribers to engage with one another, ask tax planning questions, and engage with your favorite authors!

- **Live Webinars** – *Every Quarter!*

Every few months, we bring our subscribers a free, live webinar to help educate and inspire them on all things tax! These webinars feature a wide variety of excellent speakers and topics, are 100% exclusive, and include continuing education credits for those who qualify! *(And, if you become an Annual subscriber – make sure to check out the "Exclusive Bonus" section of the site to see recordings of our past webinars!)*

- **Client Alerts** – *Twice Per Month!*

As a tax professional, are you looking for ways to educate and engage with your clients on a regular basis? We've done the work for you! Look for the downloadable "Client Alert" attached to at least one article per newsletter. These "Client Alerts" are yours to openly share with your clients and associates!

- **Infographics**

Sometimes, a picture is worth a thousand words! Our crack graphic design team is constantly on the lookout for ways to improve articles by including helpful informational graphics and, best of all, the infographics are always downloadable and shareable!

Get PAID What You're WORTH!

Using Tax Planning to Get Paid For Your Expertise

✓ Tired of getting paid low fees?

✓ Chasing clients for payment?

✓ Looking to earn more while enjoying more free time?

Most tax professionals simply trade their time for money. The problem with this is, like it or not, tax preparation is a commodity business. Clients can always find someone faster, cheaper, or more convenient. This makes it difficult to charge premium fees. You can master the art of getting paid for your expertise by shifting your focus to tax planning. Pricing your services and changing your tax practice to highlight your expertise gives you the extra value you need to get paid what you're worth, dramatically increasing your income and providing the freedom that owning a business is supposed to bring you.

Learn how to use tax planning as a lead for attracting new clients paying premium fees, breathe new life into your existing book of business, and create loyalty by reinforcing your value.

By following the advice in this book, you'll be able to:

- Increase your net worth with clients
- Spotlight your expertise with tax planning
- Learn the secret formula for selling planning engagements at premium fees
- Identify opportunities for tax planning and use this information to sell your engagement
- Learn how to value price your planning services
- Recognize pitfalls when converting hourly billing to value pricing
- Eliminate the primary cause for low profits and long hours

The solution to growing a healthy practice lies with mastering the art of getting paid for your expertise. This book will allow you to focus on high value tax planning concepts and strategies.

Available on Amazon.com

Dominique Molina, CPA, MST, CTS

Dominique Molina, a CPA since 2000, has devoted her career to enhancing the expertise of accounting professionals while helping small businesses minimize their tax burden. She emphasizes proactive tax planning strategies, enabling small companies to leverage tax laws in the same way large corporations do. Molina founded the American Institute of Certified Tax Planners (AICTP) in 2009 to share her approach with other accounting professionals.

As an early adopter and proponent of value pricing, Molina challenges the century-old hourly billing model still used by 86% of firms. Her thought leadership encourages a focus on service value and cost predictability for clients. Molina also cautions the industry about potential pitfalls of DIY planning software, emphasizing the irreplaceable expertise of professional tax planners.

Ms. Molina is an accomplished key note speaker, teacher, best-selling author and mentor to tax professionals across the United States. She remains a champion for modernizing and elevating the accounting industry, highlighting the value CPAs offer in guiding clients toward better business outcomes.